SO-AAZ-622

SAN RAFAEL PUBLIC LIBRARY
1100 E STREET
SAN RAFAEL, CA 94901
415-485-3323
srpubliclibrary.org

Margreet de Heer

LOVE

A DISCOVERY
IN COMICS

nbm GRAPHIC NOVELS

Nantier · Beall · Minoustchine
NEW YORK

Copyright @ 2017 Uitgeverij Meinema, Zoetermeer, The Netherlands
English translation © 2017 Margreet de Heer

Original title: Liefde in Beeld
Published originally in Dutch by Uitgeverij Meinema, 2017

Publication in the U.S.: NBM Publishing, first printing 2019
Printed in India

ISBN 9781681122106
Library of Congress Control Number: 2019935045

Text & drawings: Margreet de Heer
Colors: Margreet de Heer & Yiri T. Kohl
Translation proofreader: Dan J. Schiff

DEDICATED
TO OUR
PARENTS

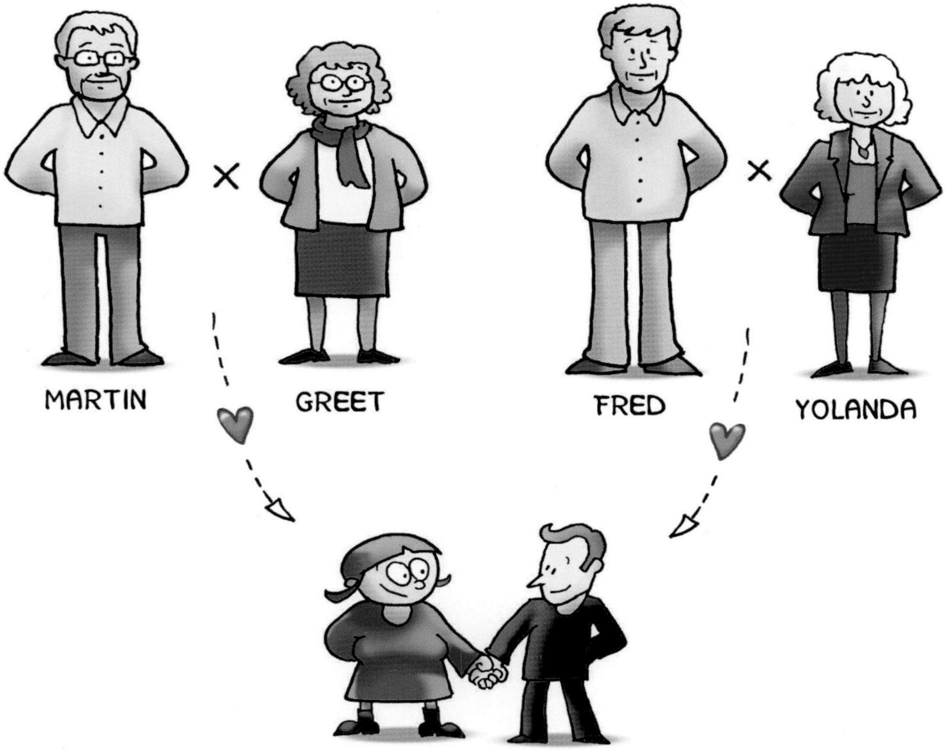
MARTIN
GREET
FRED
YOLANDA

DISCLAIMER

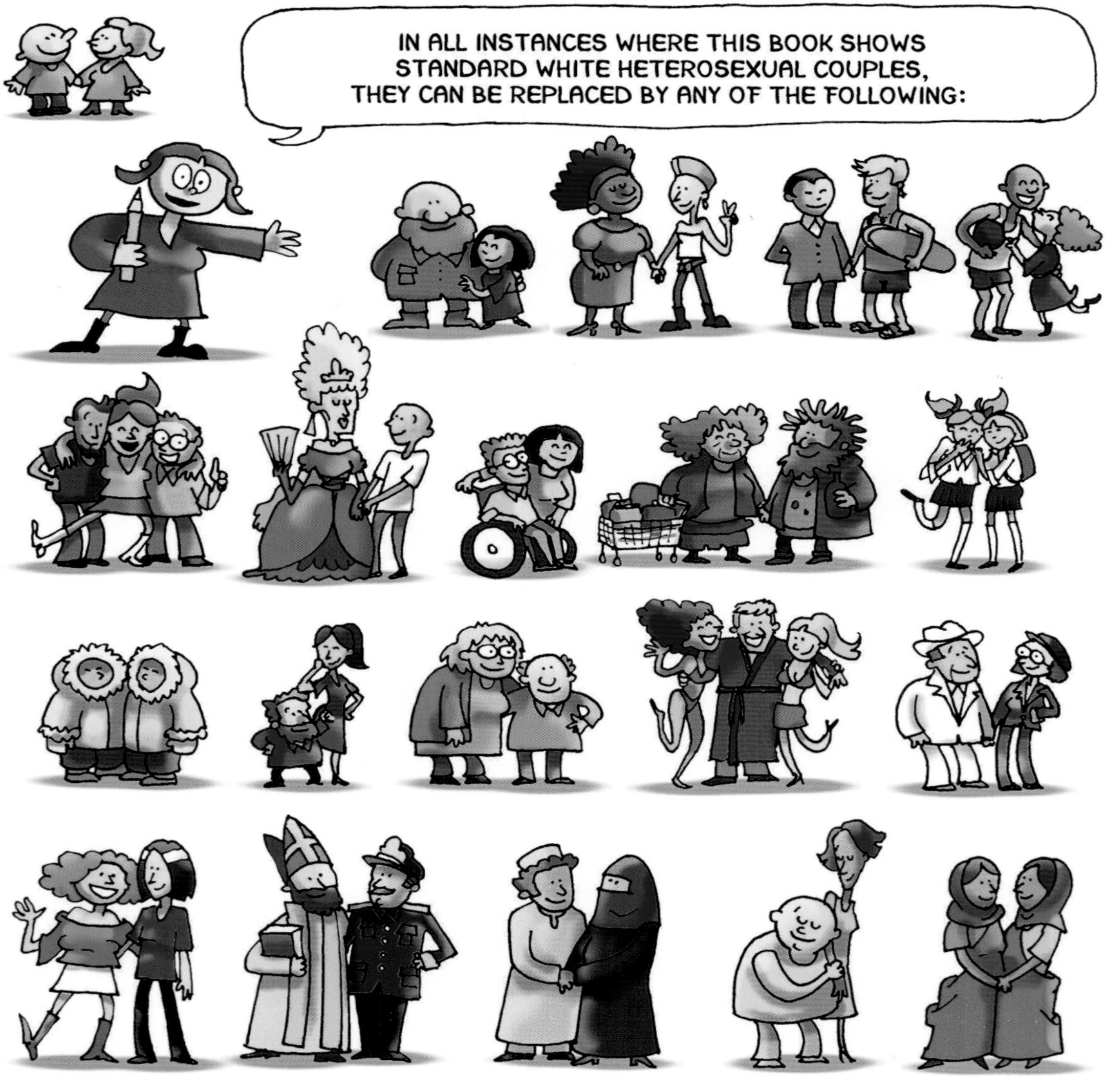
IN ALL INSTANCES WHERE THIS BOOK SHOWS STANDARD WHITE HETEROSEXUAL COUPLES, THEY CAN BE REPLACED BY ANY OF THE FOLLOWING:

CONTENTS

4   DISCLAIMER
5   CONTENTS
7   PROLOGUE
9   SEVEN KINDS OF LOVE

18   MY LOVE LIFE
23   THE SEVEN YEAR ITCH
26   MY IMAGINARY BOYFRIEND

29   SEX
30   ADVICE TO MY 17-YEAR OLD SELF
35   THE KAMA SUTRA
38   TANTRIC SEX
40   SONG OF SONGS

44   THE ONE
46   DOES THE ONE EXIST?
48   THREE TRUE LOVES
49   HOW TO RECOGNIZE THE ONE?

50   THE PERFECT MOMENT

57   THE TRAGEDY OF ROMANCE
58   ROMANCE NOVELS
62   THE FAIRY TALE
64   THE DANGERS OF LIVING TOGETHER
66   THE DANGER OF CHILDREN
69   HOW DO YOU KEEP THINGS GOOD?

73   MARRIAGE
78   KINDS OF MARRIAGES
80   SHORT HISTORY OF (WESTERN) MARRIAGE
82   DIVORCE

85   FALLING IN LOVE
86   WHAT HAPPENS WHEN YOU FALL IN LOVE?
90   THE DATING GAME

93   THE DARK SIDE OF LOVE
98   TEN TIPS FOR A BROKEN HEART
100 LOVE ADDICTION
102 PITFALLS

105 THE SEVEN YEAR ITCH: RECONCILIATION

109 EPILOGUE

113 EXTRAS

121 NOTES

125 INDEX

128 BY THE SAME AUTHOR

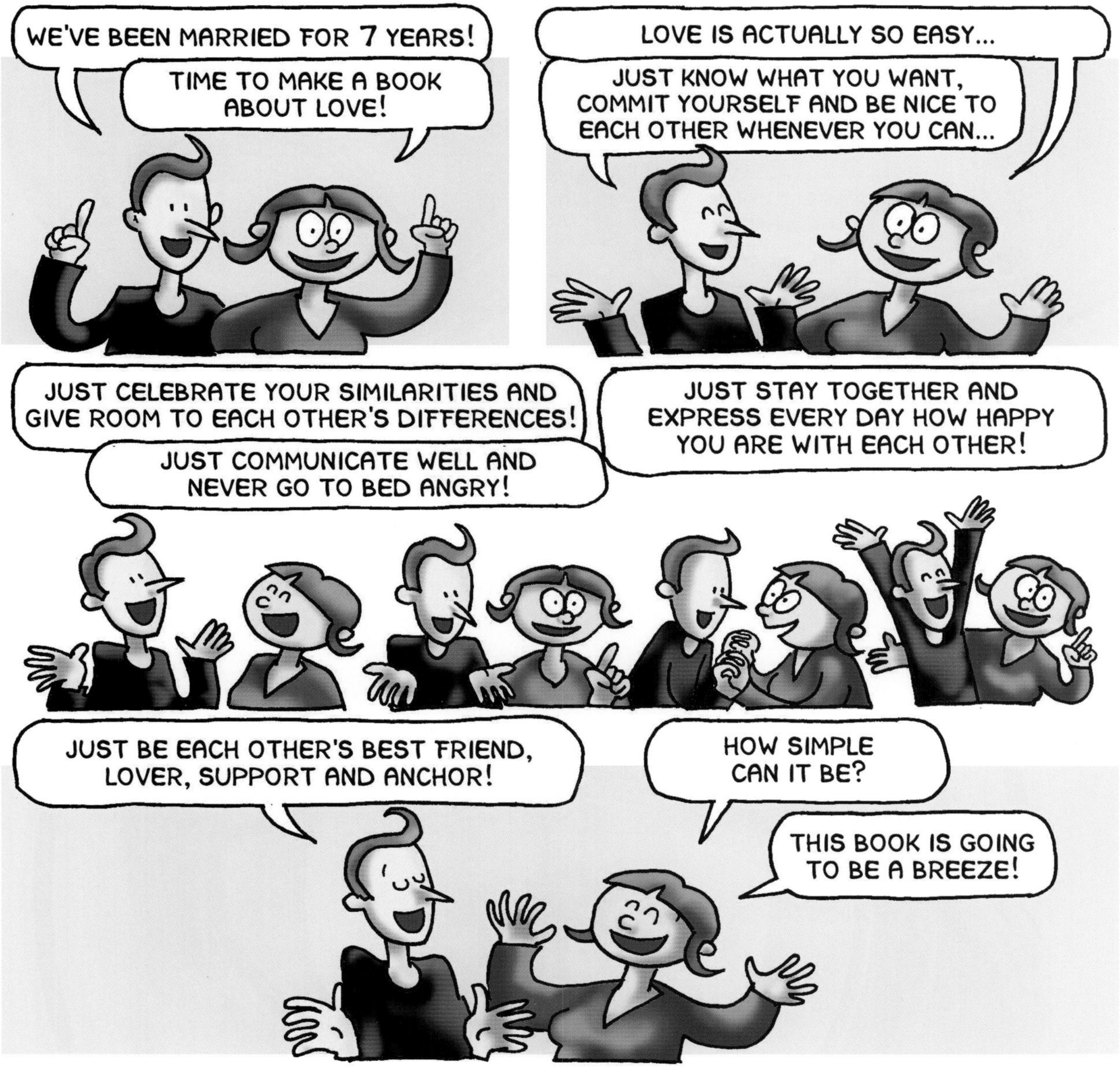
WE'VE BEEN MARRIED FOR 7 YEARS!
TIME TO MAKE A BOOK ABOUT LOVE!
LOVE IS ACTUALLY SO EASY...
JUST KNOW WHAT YOU WANT, COMMIT YOURSELF AND BE NICE TO EACH OTHER WHENEVER YOU CAN...
JUST CELEBRATE YOUR SIMILARITIES AND GIVE ROOM TO EACH OTHER'S DIFFERENCES!
JUST COMMUNICATE WELL AND NEVER GO TO BED ANGRY!
JUST STAY TOGETHER AND EXPRESS EVERY DAY HOW HAPPY YOU ARE WITH EACH OTHER!
JUST BE EACH OTHER'S BEST FRIEND, LOVER, SUPPORT AND ANCHOR!
HOW SIMPLE CAN IT BE?
THIS BOOK IS GOING TO BE A BREEZE!

WHAT IS LOVE?

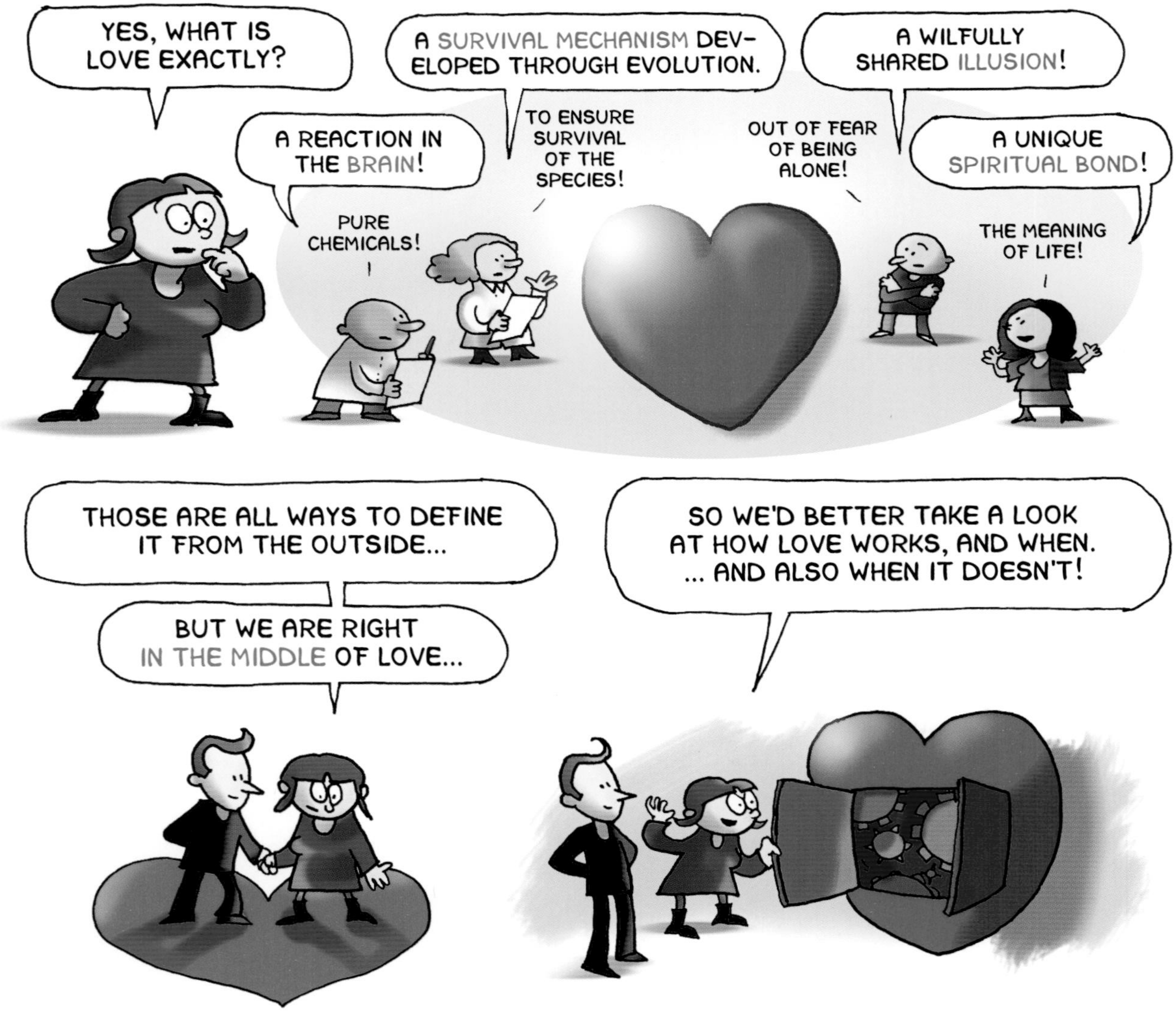
YES, WHAT IS LOVE EXACTLY?
A SURVIVAL MECHANISM DEVELOPED THROUGH EVOLUTION.
A WILFULLY SHARED ILLUSION!
A REACTION IN THE BRAIN!
TO ENSURE SURVIVAL OF THE SPECIES!
OUT OF FEAR OF BEING ALONE!
A UNIQUE SPIRITUAL BOND!
PURE CHEMICALS!
THE MEANING OF LIFE!
THOSE ARE ALL WAYS TO DEFINE IT FROM THE OUTSIDE...
BUT WE ARE RIGHT IN THE MIDDLE OF LOVE...
SO WE'D BETTER TAKE A LOOK AT HOW LOVE WORKS, AND WHEN.
... AND ALSO WHEN IT DOESN'T!

SEVEN
KINDS OF
LOVE

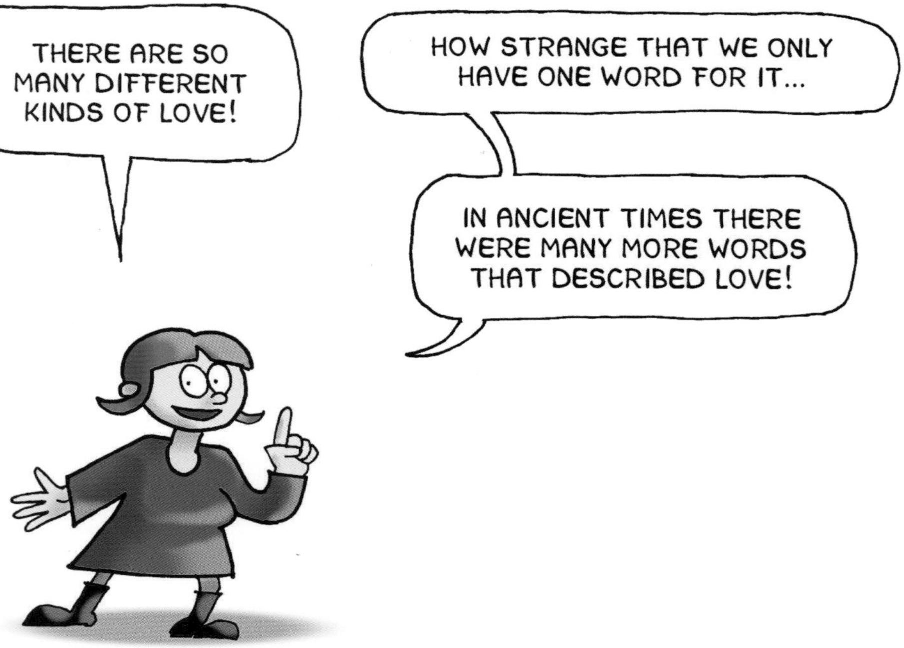
THERE ARE SO MANY DIFFERENT KINDS OF LOVE!
HOW STRANGE THAT WE ONLY HAVE ONE WORD FOR IT...
IN ANCIENT TIMES THERE WERE MANY MORE WORDS THAT DESCRIBED LOVE!

AGAPÈ

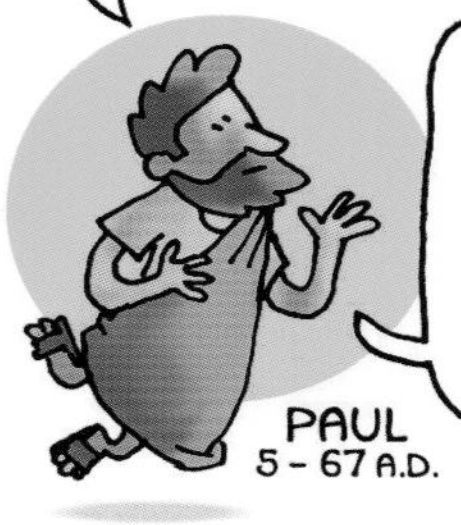
THE HIGHEST FORM OF LOVE: UNCONDITIONAL, UNSELFISH, ALL-ENCOMPASSING...
THIS NOTION OF LOVE IS MAINLY FOUND IN THE BIBLE: IT IS USED TO DENOTE THE LOVE OF GOD FOR PEOPLE AND THE OTHER WAY AROUND, AND ALSO FOR PEOPLE AMONG EACH OTHER, AS CHARITY OR BROTHERLY LOVE.
PAUL
5 - 67 A.D.

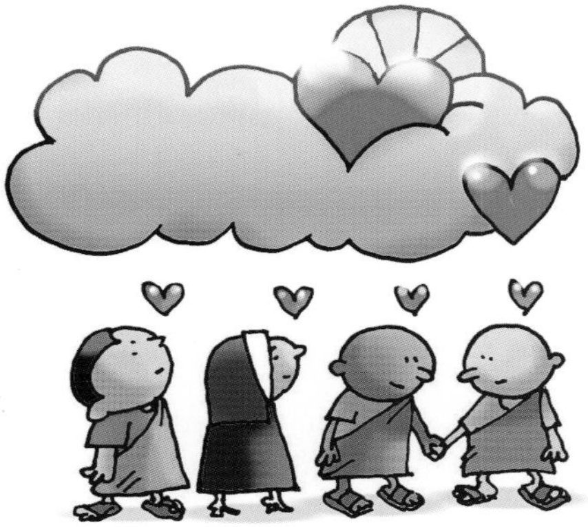

AGAPÈ IS THE WORD FOR LOVE WHICH IS USED IN THIS FAMOUS TEXT, THAT IS OFTEN READ AT WEDDING CEREMONIES:

If I speak in the tongues of men or of angels, but do not have love,
I am only a resounding gong or a clanging cymbal.
If I have the gift of prophecy and can fathom all mysteries and all knowledge, and if I have a faith that can move mountains, but do not have love,
I am nothing.
If I give all I possess to the poor and give over my body to hardship that I may boast,
but do not have love, I gain nothing.
Love is patient, love is kind.
It does not envy, it does not boast, it is not proud.
It does not dishonor others, it is not self-seeking, it is not easily angered, it keeps no record of wrongs.
Love does not delight in evil but rejoices with the truth.
It always protects, always trusts, always hopes, always perseveres.
Love never fails.
But where there are prophecies, they will cease; where there are tongues,
they will be stilled; where there is knowledge, it will pass away.
For we know in part and we prophesy in part, but when completeness comes, what is in part disappears.
When I was a child, I talked like a child, I thought like a child, I reasoned like a child.
When I became a man, I put the ways of childhood behind me.
For now we see only a reflection as in a mirror; then we shall see face to face.
Now I know in part; then I shall know fully, even as I am fully known.
And now these three remain: faith, hope and love.
But the greatest
of these is love.

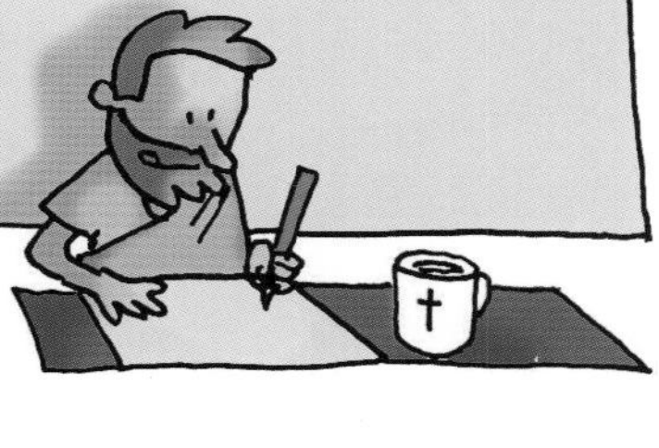

1 COR. 13

FROM THE FIRST LETTER TO THE CORINTHIANS
WRITTEN BY THE APOSTLE PAUL IN THE FIRST CENTURY A.D.

EROS

STANDS FOR LUST, PASSION AND ROMANTIC LOVE. THE GOD EROS IS REPRESENTED AS A YOUTH WITH BOW AND ARROWS – WHOMEVER HE HITS, FALLS IN LOVE

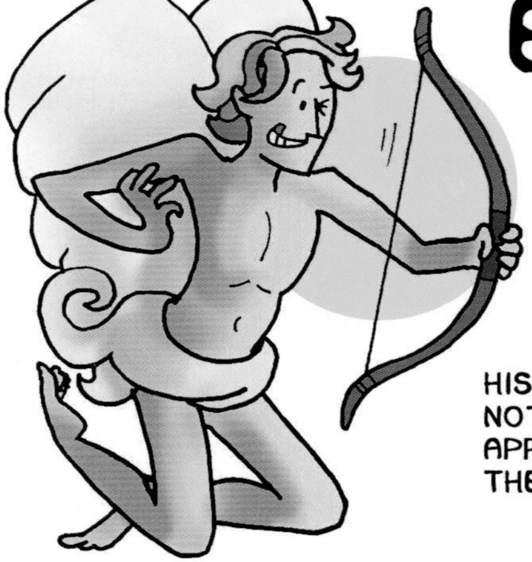

HIS PRANKS WERE NOT ALWAYS APPRECIATED BY THE OTHER GODS.

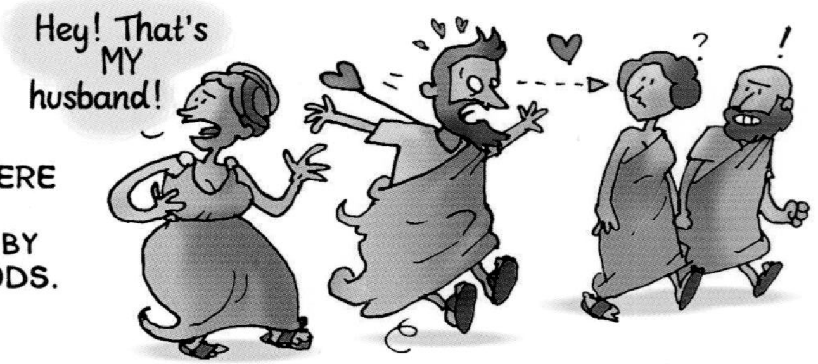
Hey! That's MY husband!
?
!

HE WAS ONE OF THE EROTES, A GROUP OF WINGED GODS AROUND APHRODITE, GODDESS OF LOVE. IT IS ALSO SAID THAT THE EROTES REPRESENT DIFFERENT ASPECTS OF EROS:

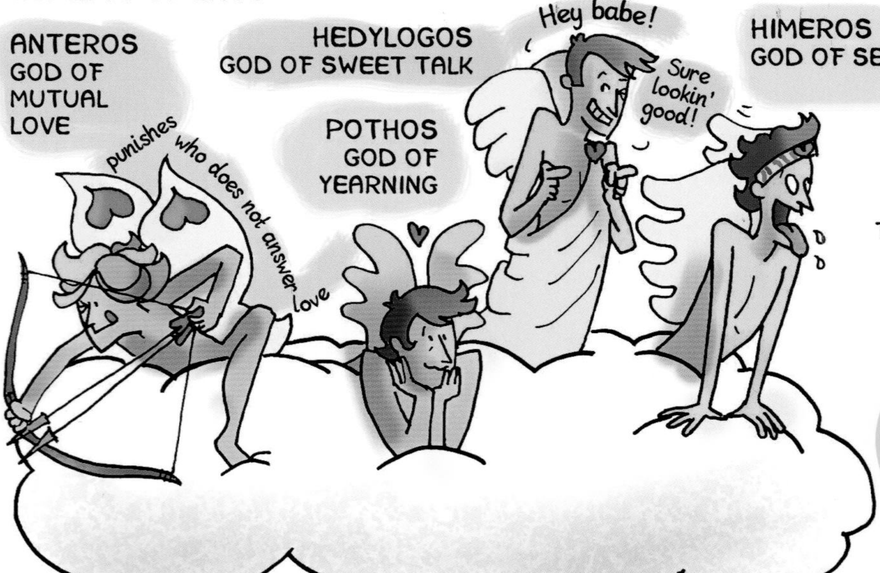
ANTEROS
GOD OF MUTUAL LOVE
punishes who does not answer love
HEDYLOGOS
GOD OF SWEET TALK
POTHOS
GOD OF YEARNING
Hey babe!
Sure lookin' good!
HIMEROS
GOD OF SEXUAL DESIRE

THE ROMAN NAME FOR EROS IS **CUPID.**
THROUGHOUT THE AGES HE HAS EVOLVED INTO THE DEPICTION OF AN ANGELIC BABY...

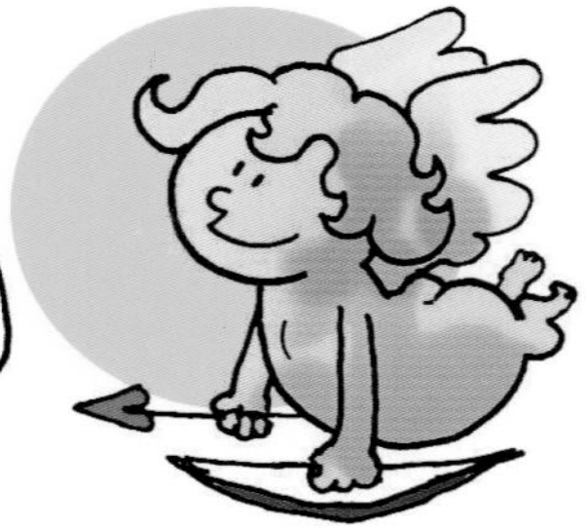

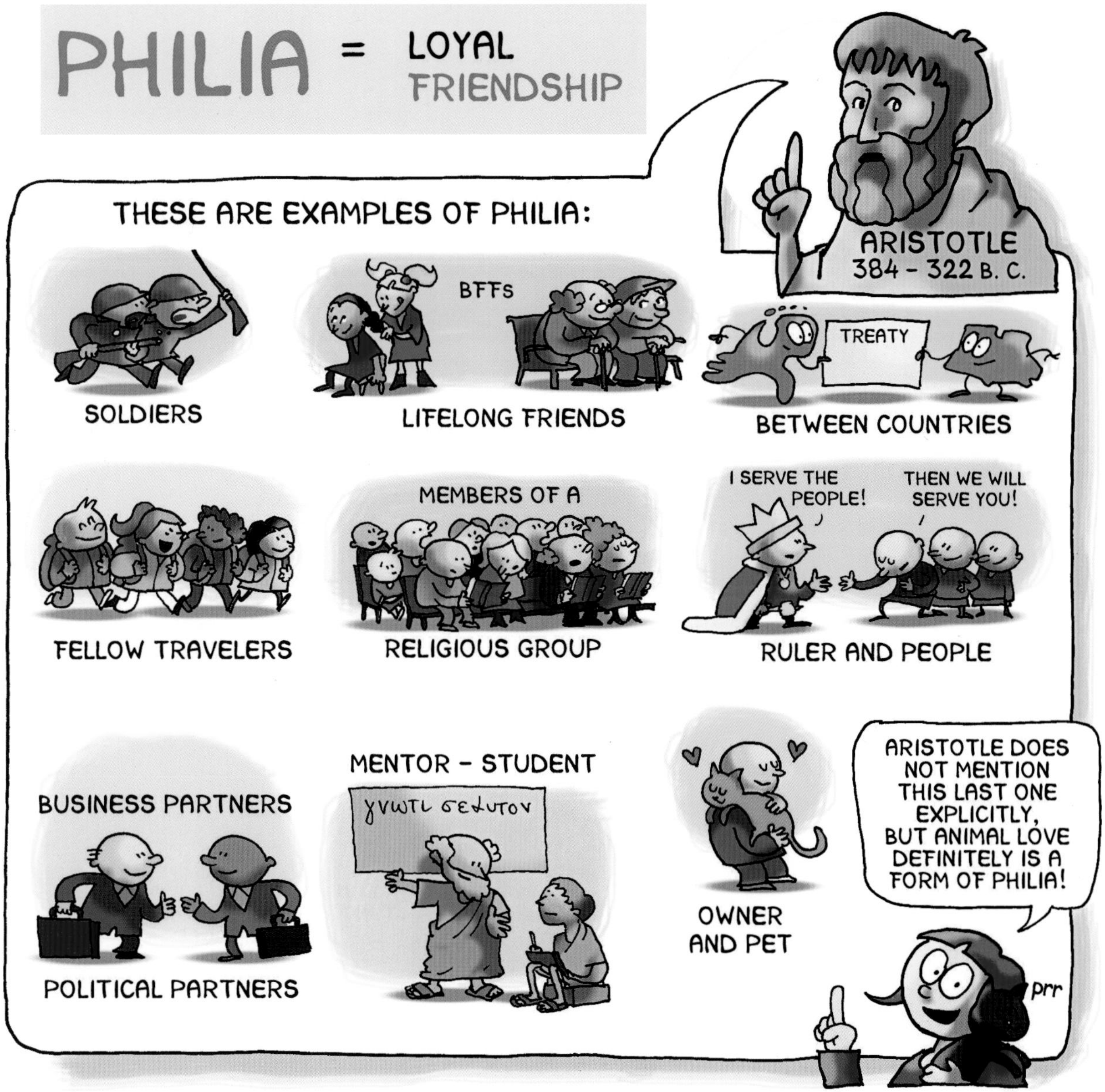
PHILIA = LOYAL FRIENDSHIP
THESE ARE EXAMPLES OF PHILIA:
ARISTOTLE
384 - 322 B. C.
SOLDIERS
BFFs
LIFELONG FRIENDS
TREATY
BETWEEN COUNTRIES
FELLOW TRAVELERS
MEMBERS OF A
RELIGIOUS GROUP
I SERVE THE PEOPLE!
THEN WE WILL SERVE YOU!
RULER AND PEOPLE
BUSINESS PARTNERS
POLITICAL PARTNERS
MENTOR - STUDENT
OWNER AND PET
ARISTOTLE DOES NOT MENTION THIS LAST ONE EXPLICITLY, BUT ANIMAL LOVE DEFINITELY IS A FORM OF PHILIA!
prr

STORGE
FAMILY LOVE

THIS IS THE LOVE BETWEEN FAMILY MEMBERS – A NATURAL BOND WHICH IS OFTEN UNCONDITIONAL, EVEN WHEN THERE ARE GREAT DIFFERENCES.

HE'S STILL MY BABY BOY!

CAN'T BE HELPED!

GOOD! GET THAT JERK!

YEAH!

NOBODY INSULTS MY BROTHER!

BRO SIS

BETWEEN LOVERS, STORGE IS THE KIND OF LOVE THAT COMES AFTER EROS: INVESTING IN A FUTURE TOGETHER, WITH OR WITHOUT CHILDREN, SOMETIMES FORMALIZED IN AN OFFICIAL MARRIAGE.

NOURISHING

DEVOTED

LOYAL

LONG TERM

IT DOESN'T REPLACE EROS AND/OR PHILIA, BUT BUILDS ON IT:

THIS IS A DEEP, INVOLVED AFFECTION THAT PERSISTS SOMETIMES EVEN AFTER A DIVORCE, BETWEEN PEOPLE WHO HAVE BUILT A CLOSE FAMILY TOGETHER.

STORGE

PHILIA EROS

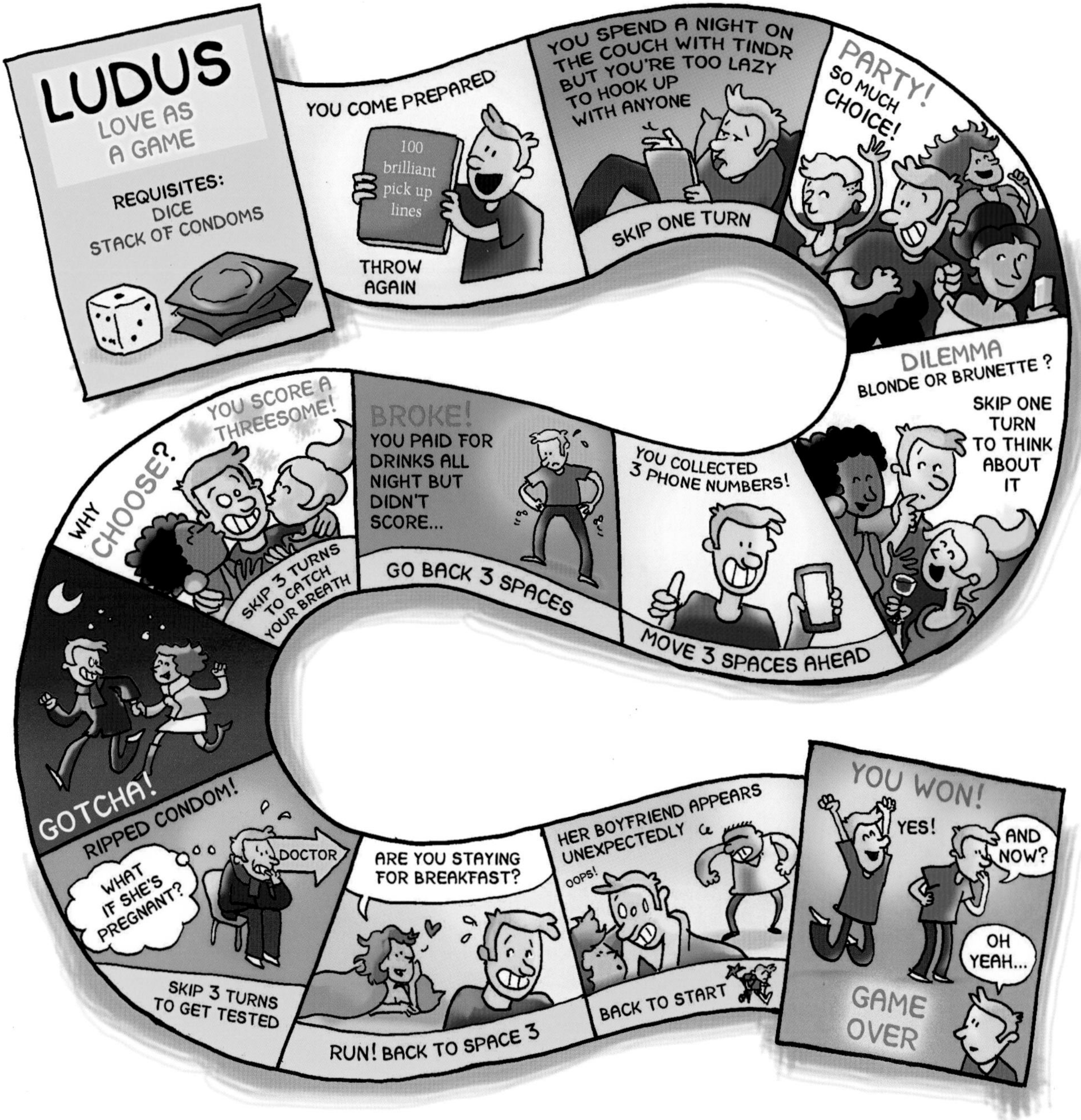
LUDUS
LOVE AS A GAME
REQUISITES:
DICE
STACK OF CONDOMS
YOU COME PREPARED
100 brilliant pick up lines
THROW AGAIN
YOU SPEND A NIGHT ON THE COUCH WITH TINDR BUT YOU'RE TOO LAZY TO HOOK UP WITH ANYONE
SKIP ONE TURN
PARTY!
SO MUCH CHOICE!
DILEMMA
BLONDE OR BRUNETTE ?
SKIP ONE TURN TO THINK ABOUT IT
YOU COLLECTED 3 PHONE NUMBERS!
MOVE 3 SPACES AHEAD
BROKE!
YOU PAID FOR DRINKS ALL NIGHT BUT DIDN'T SCORE...
GO BACK 3 SPACES
YOU SCORE A THREESOME!
WHY CHOOSE?
SKIP 3 TURNS TO CATCH YOUR BREATH
GOTCHA!
RIPPED CONDOM!
WHAT IF SHE'S PREGNANT?
DOCTOR
SKIP 3 TURNS TO GET TESTED
ARE YOU STAYING FOR BREAKFAST?
RUN! BACK TO SPACE 3
HER BOYFRIEND APPEARS UNEXPECTEDLY
OOPS!
BACK TO START
YOU WON!
YES!
AND NOW?
OH YEAH...
GAME OVER

PRAGMA

THIS IS A RATIONAL, PRAGMATIC FORM OF LOVE, THAT CAREFULLY WEIGHS ALL PROS AND CONS AND FOCUSES ON THE LONG TERM.

PRAGMA EMPHASIZES SHARED BACKGROUNDS, VALUES AND GOALS.

MANY ARRANGED MARRIAGES PRODUCE THIS KIND OF LOVE.

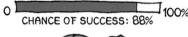

0 ████████████████ 100%

CHANCE OF SUCCESS: 88%

A GOOD EXAMPLE OF PRAGMA IS CHARLES DARWIN, WHO WROTE THIS LIST IN JULY 1838 (WHEN HE WAS 29 YEARS OLD), SUMMARIZING THE PROS AND CONS OF MARRIAGE:

Marry	Not Marry
Children — (if it Please God) — Constant companion, (& friend in old age) who will feel interested in one, — object to be beloved & played with. — better than a dog anyhow. — Home, & someone to take care of house — Charms of music & female chit-chat. — These things good for one's health. — but terrible loss of time. — My God, it is intolerable to think of spending one's whole life, like a neuter bee, working, working, & nothing after all. — No, no won't do. — Imagine living all one's day solitarily in smoky dirty London House. — Only picture to yourself a nice soft wife on a sofa with good fire, & books & music perhaps — Compare this vision with the dingy reality of Grt. Marlbro' St.	Freedom to go where one liked — choice of Society & little of it. — Conversation of clever men at clubs — Not forced to visit relatives, & to bend in every trifle. — to have the expense & anxiety of children — perhaps quarelling — Loss of time. — cannot read in the Evenings — fatness & idleness — Anxiety & responsibility — less money for books &c — if many children forced to gain one's bread. — (But then it is very bad for one's health to work too much.) Perhaps my wife won't like London; then the sentence is banishment & degradation into indolent, idle fool —

Marry — Marry — Marry   Q.E.D.

HE MARRIED HIS COUSIN EMMA WEDGWOOD IN JANUARY 1839. THEY HAD TEN CHILDREN AND A HAPPY MARRIAGE UNTIL DARWIN'S DEATH IN 1882.

PHILAUTIA - LOVE OF YOURSELF

NEGATIVE:
EGOCENTRISM, NARCISSISM

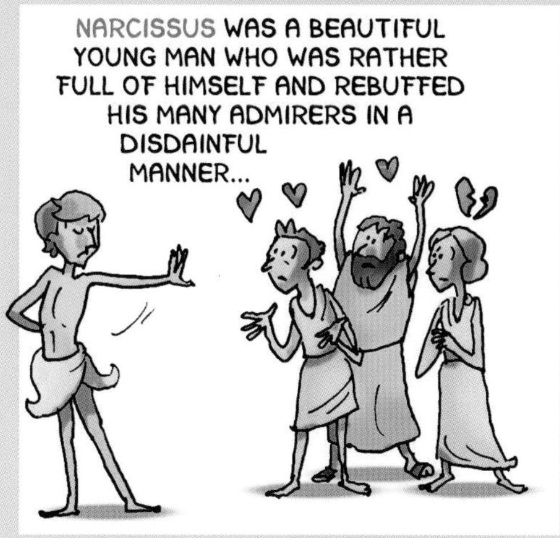
NARCISSUS WAS A BEAUTIFUL YOUNG MAN WHO WAS RATHER FULL OF HIMSELF AND REBUFFED HIS MANY ADMIRERS IN A DISDAINFUL MANNER...

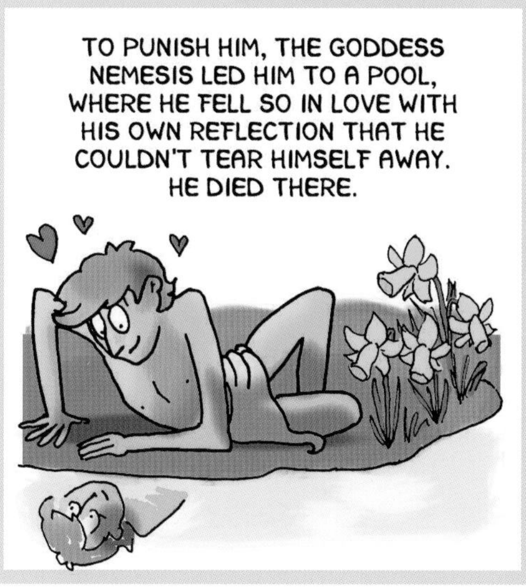
TO PUNISH HIM, THE GODDESS NEMESIS LED HIM TO A POOL, WHERE HE FELL SO IN LOVE WITH HIS OWN REFLECTION THAT HE COULDN'T TEAR HIMSELF AWAY. HE DIED THERE.

POSITIVE:
CONFIDENCE, SELF RESPECT

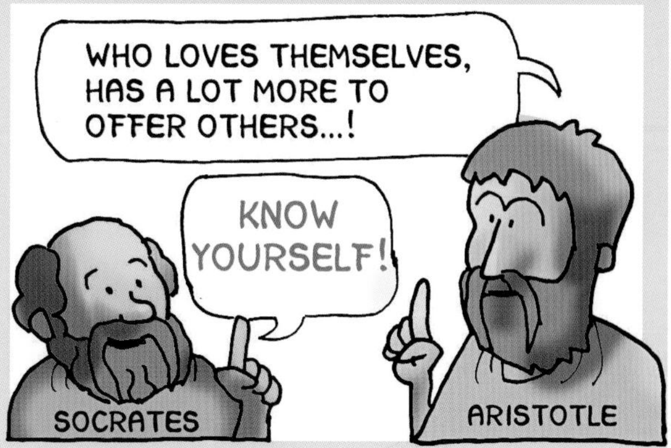
WHO LOVES THEMSELVES, HAS A LOT MORE TO OFFER OTHERS...!
KNOW YOURSELF!
SOCRATES
ARISTOTLE

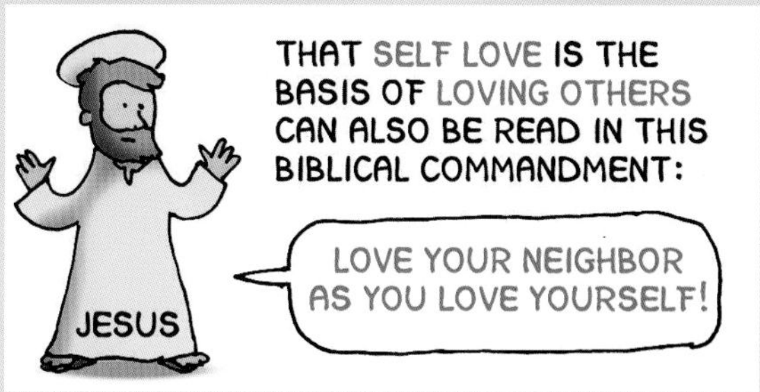
THAT SELF LOVE IS THE BASIS OF LOVING OTHERS CAN ALSO BE READ IN THIS BIBLICAL COMMANDMENT:
LOVE YOUR NEIGHBOR AS YOU LOVE YOURSELF!
JESUS

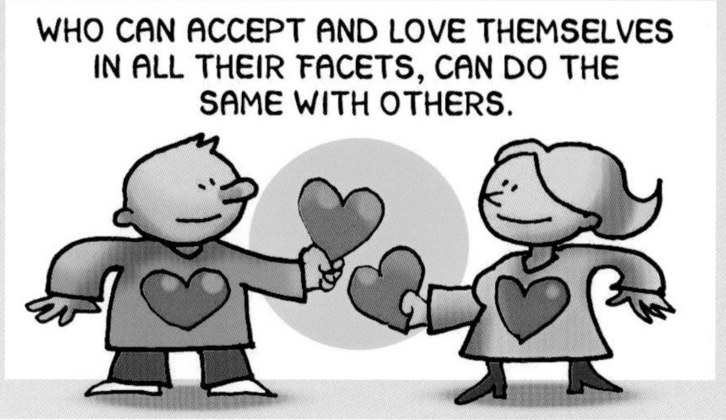
WHO CAN ACCEPT AND LOVE THEMSELVES IN ALL THEIR FACETS, CAN DO THE SAME WITH OTHERS.

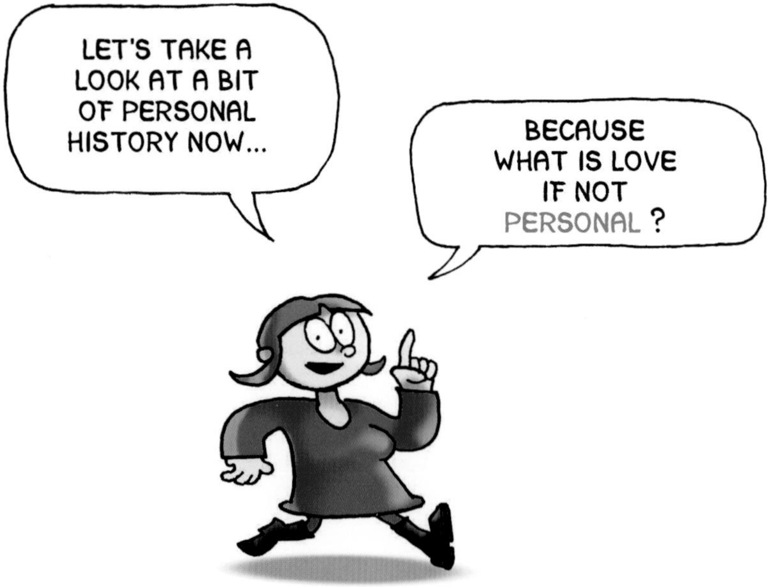
LET'S TAKE A LOOK AT A BIT OF PERSONAL HISTORY NOW...
BECAUSE WHAT IS LOVE IF NOT PERSONAL ?

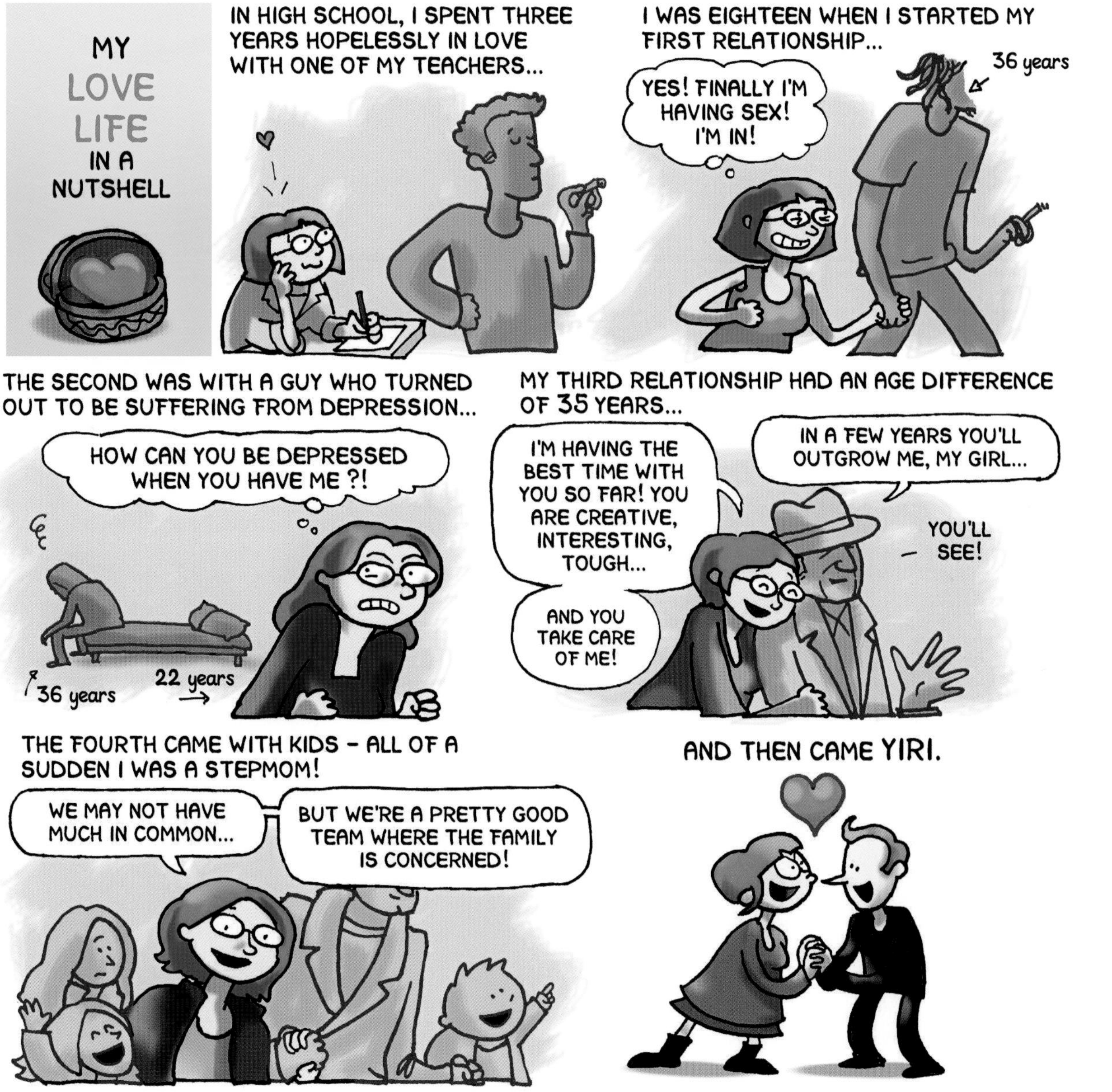
MY LOVE LIFE IN A NUTSHELL
IN HIGH SCHOOL, I SPENT THREE YEARS HOPELESSLY IN LOVE WITH ONE OF MY TEACHERS...
I WAS EIGHTEEN WHEN I STARTED MY FIRST RELATIONSHIP...
YES! FINALLY I'M HAVING SEX! I'M IN!
36 years
THE SECOND WAS WITH A GUY WHO TURNED OUT TO BE SUFFERING FROM DEPRESSION...
HOW CAN YOU BE DEPRESSED WHEN YOU HAVE ME ?!
36 years
22 years
MY THIRD RELATIONSHIP HAD AN AGE DIFFERENCE OF 35 YEARS...
I'M HAVING THE BEST TIME WITH YOU SO FAR! YOU ARE CREATIVE, INTERESTING, TOUGH...
AND YOU TAKE CARE OF ME!
IN A FEW YEARS YOU'LL OUTGROW ME, MY GIRL...
YOU'LL SEE!
THE FOURTH CAME WITH KIDS - ALL OF A SUDDEN I WAS A STEPMOM!
WE MAY NOT HAVE MUCH IN COMMON...
BUT WE'RE A PRETTY GOOD TEAM WHERE THE FAMILY IS CONCERNED!
AND THEN CAME YIRI.

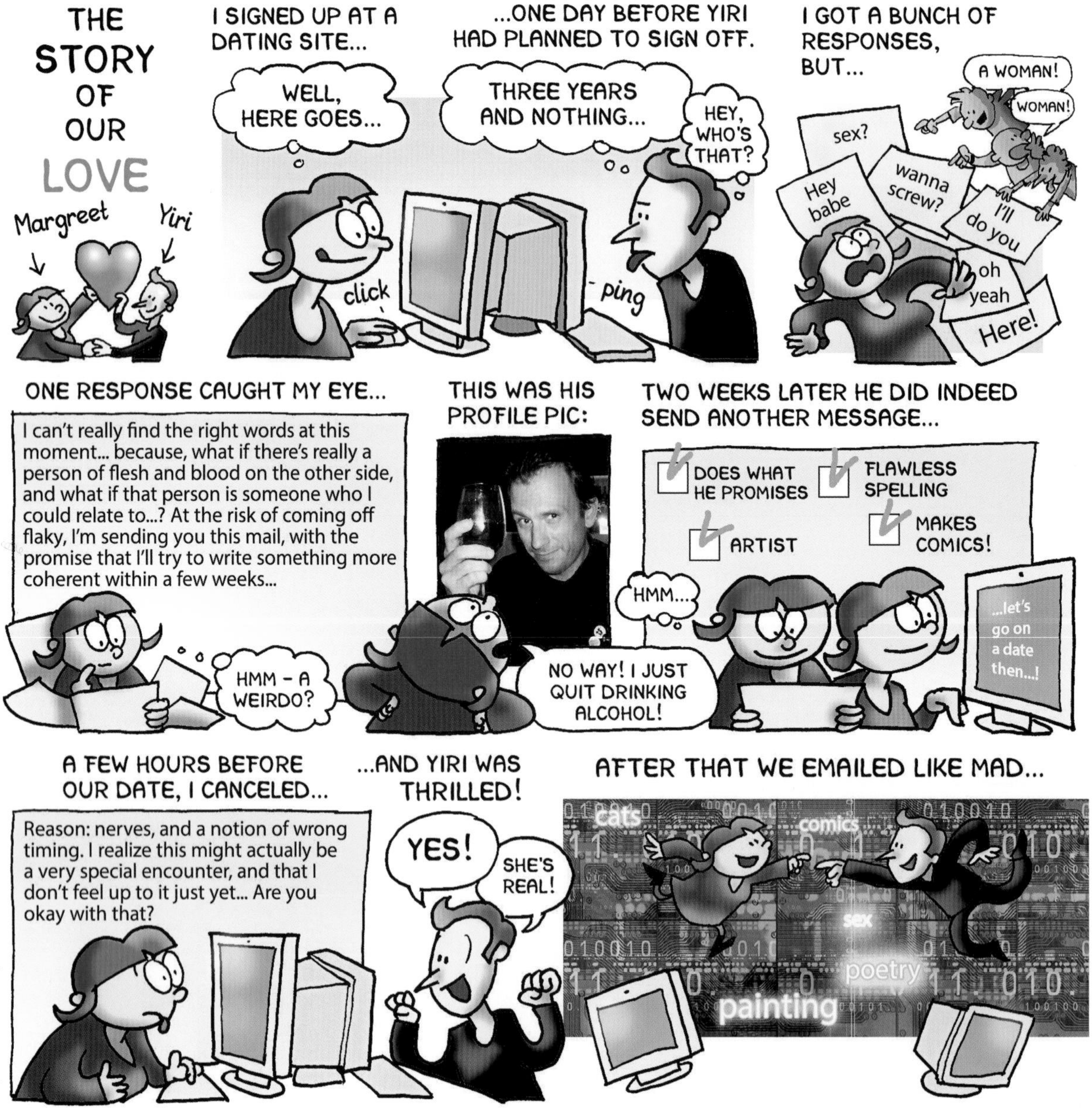
THE STORY OF OUR LOVE
Margreet
Yiri
I SIGNED UP AT A DATING SITE...
WELL, HERE GOES...
click
...ONE DAY BEFORE YIRI HAD PLANNED TO SIGN OFF.
THREE YEARS AND NOTHING...
ping
HEY, WHO'S THAT?
I GOT A BUNCH OF RESPONSES, BUT...
A WOMAN!
WOMAN!
sex?
Hey babe
wanna screw?
I'll do you
oh yeah
Here!
ONE RESPONSE CAUGHT MY EYE...
I can't really find the right words at this moment... because, what if there's really a person of flesh and blood on the other side, and what if that person is someone who I could relate to...? At the risk of coming off flaky, I'm sending you this mail, with the promise that I'll try to write something more coherent within a few weeks...
HMM – A WEIRDO?
THIS WAS HIS PROFILE PIC:
NO WAY! I JUST QUIT DRINKING ALCOHOL!
TWO WEEKS LATER HE DID INDEED SEND ANOTHER MESSAGE...
DOES WHAT HE PROMISES
FLAWLESS SPELLING
ARTIST
MAKES COMICS!
HMM....
...let's go on a date then...!
A FEW HOURS BEFORE OUR DATE, I CANCELED...
Reason: nerves, and a notion of wrong timing. I realize this might actually be a very special encounter, and that I don't feel up to it just yet... Are you okay with that?
...AND YIRI WAS THRILLED!
YES!
SHE'S REAL!
AFTER THAT WE EMAILED LIKE MAD...
cats
comics
sex
poetry
painting

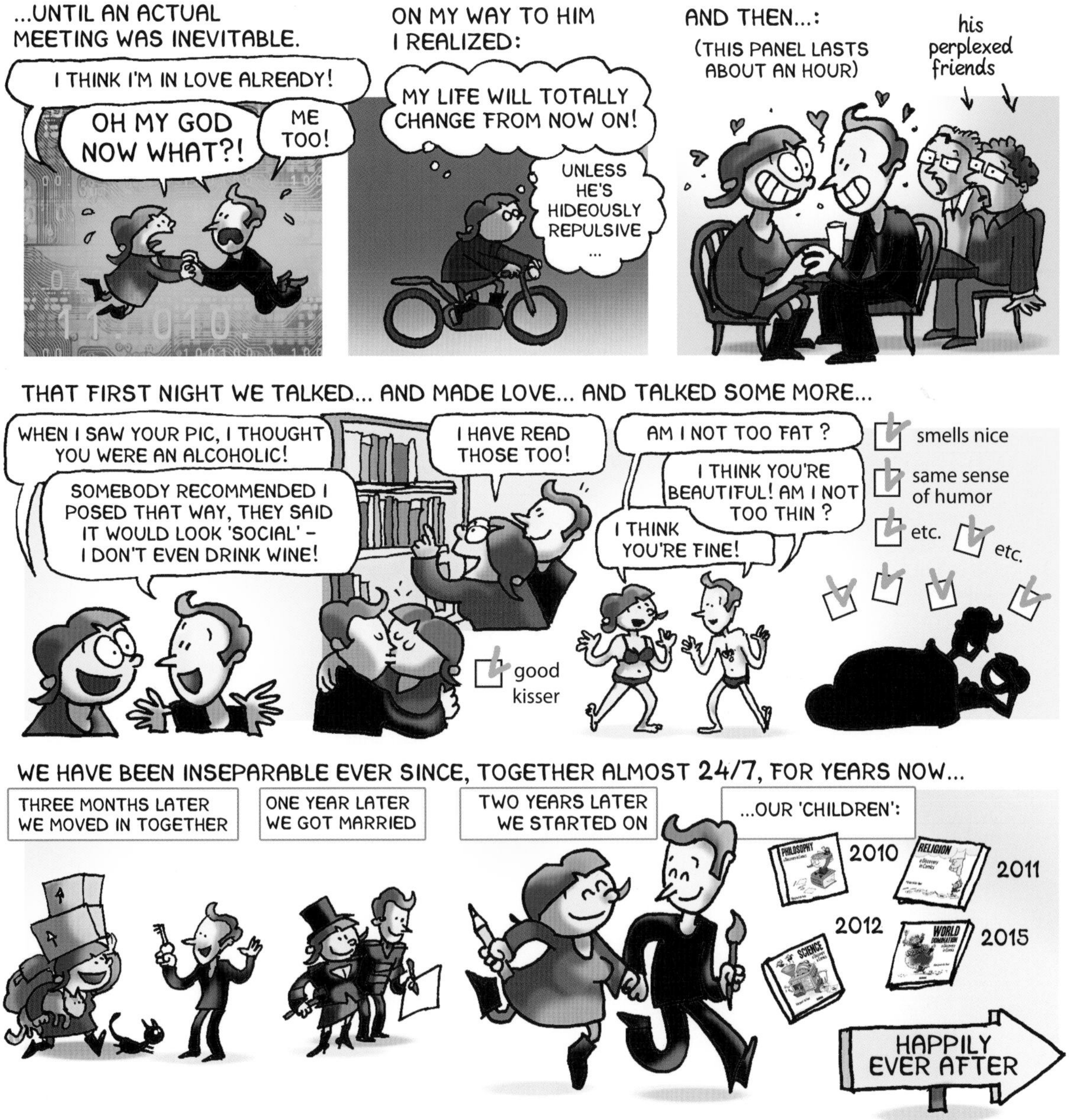
...UNTIL AN ACTUAL MEETING WAS INEVITABLE.
I THINK I'M IN LOVE ALREADY!
OH MY GOD NOW WHAT?!
ME TOO!
ON MY WAY TO HIM I REALIZED:
MY LIFE WILL TOTALLY CHANGE FROM NOW ON!
UNLESS HE'S HIDEOUSLY REPULSIVE ...
AND THEN...:
(THIS PANEL LASTS ABOUT AN HOUR)
his perplexed friends
THAT FIRST NIGHT WE TALKED... AND MADE LOVE... AND TALKED SOME MORE...
WHEN I SAW YOUR PIC, I THOUGHT YOU WERE AN ALCOHOLIC!
SOMEBODY RECOMMENDED I POSED THAT WAY, THEY SAID IT WOULD LOOK 'SOCIAL' – I DON'T EVEN DRINK WINE!
I HAVE READ THOSE TOO!
good kisser
AM I NOT TOO FAT ?
I THINK YOU'RE BEAUTIFUL! AM I NOT TOO THIN ?
I THINK YOU'RE FINE!
smells nice
same sense of humor
etc.
etc.
WE HAVE BEEN INSEPARABLE EVER SINCE, TOGETHER ALMOST 24/7, FOR YEARS NOW...
THREE MONTHS LATER WE MOVED IN TOGETHER
ONE YEAR LATER WE GOT MARRIED
TWO YEARS LATER WE STARTED ON
...OUR 'CHILDREN':
PHILOSOPHY
2010
RELIGION
2011
SCIENCE
2012
WORLD DOMINATION
2015
HAPPILY EVER AFTER

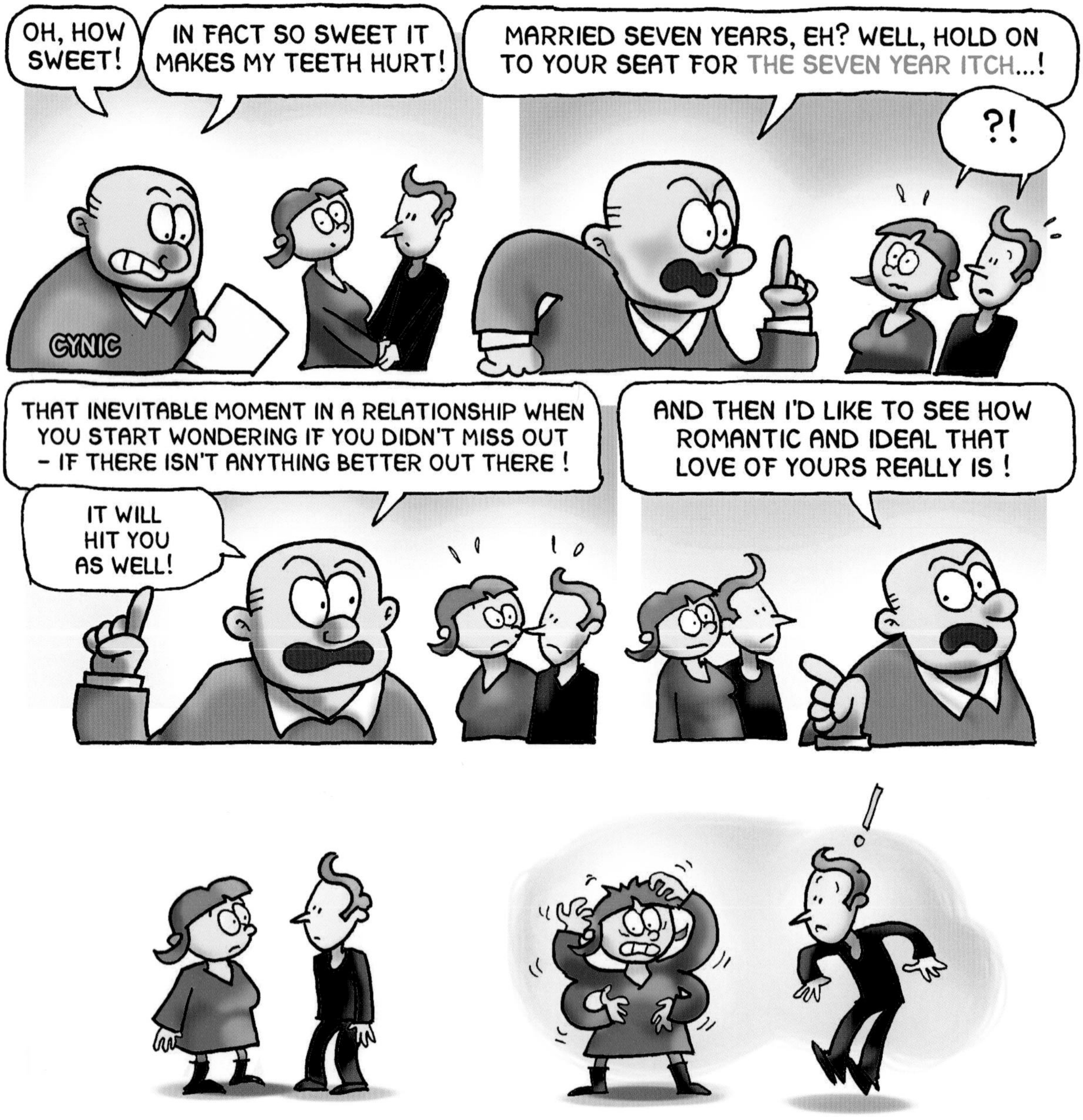
OH, HOW SWEET!
IN FACT SO SWEET IT MAKES MY TEETH HURT!
CYNIC
MARRIED SEVEN YEARS, EH? WELL, HOLD ON TO YOUR SEAT FOR THE SEVEN YEAR ITCH...!
?!
THAT INEVITABLE MOMENT IN A RELATIONSHIP WHEN YOU START WONDERING IF YOU DIDN'T MISS OUT - IF THERE ISN'T ANYTHING BETTER OUT THERE !
IT WILL HIT YOU AS WELL!
AND THEN I'D LIKE TO SEE HOW ROMANTIC AND IDEAL THAT LOVE OF YOURS REALLY IS !

dr. Rita Lin
therapist
& matchmaker

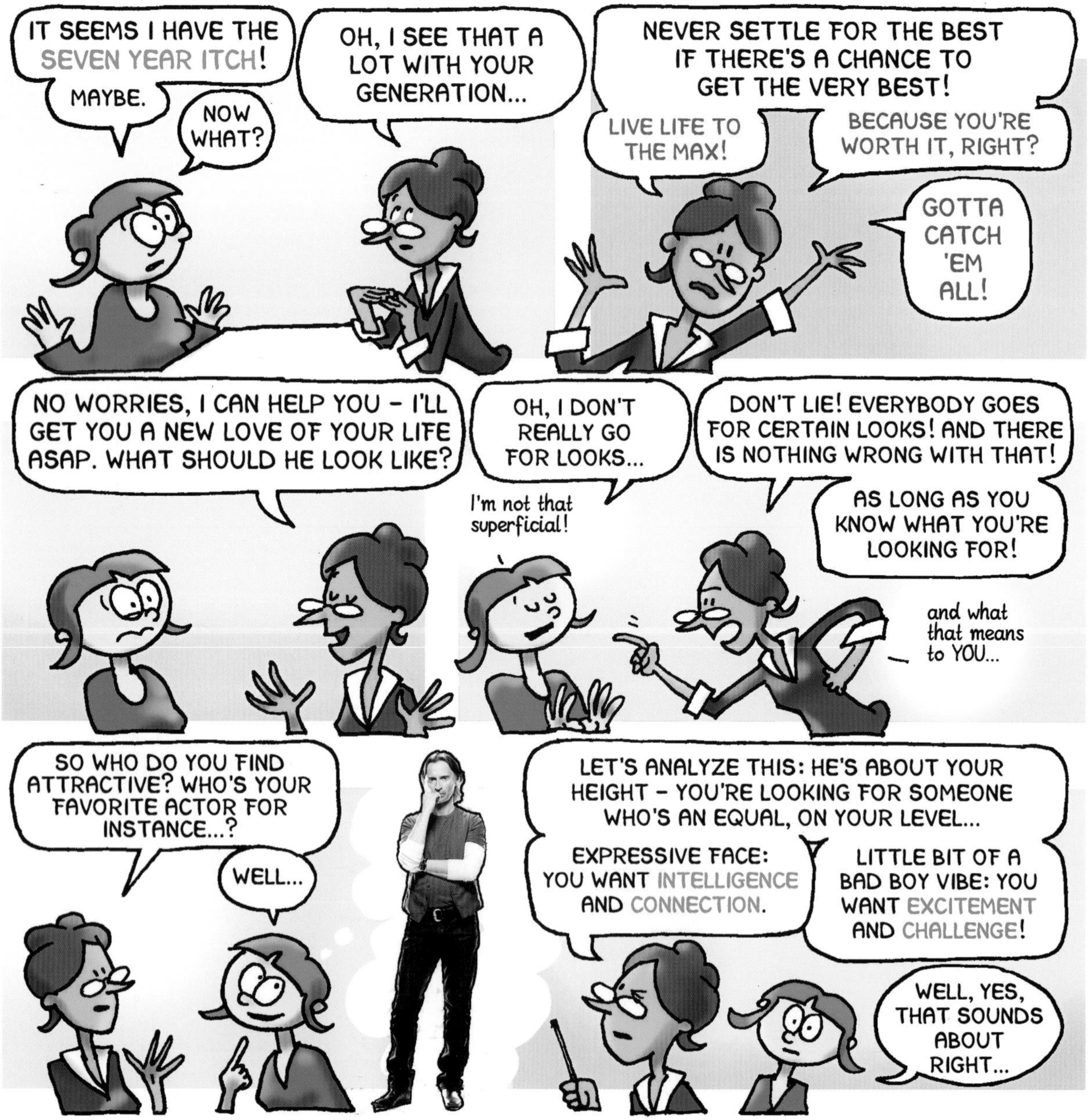
IT SEEMS I HAVE THE SEVEN YEAR ITCH!
MAYBE.
NOW WHAT?
OH, I SEE THAT A LOT WITH YOUR GENERATION...
NEVER SETTLE FOR THE BEST IF THERE'S A CHANCE TO GET THE VERY BEST!
LIVE LIFE TO THE MAX!
BECAUSE YOU'RE WORTH IT, RIGHT?
GOTTA CATCH 'EM ALL!
NO WORRIES, I CAN HELP YOU - I'LL GET YOU A NEW LOVE OF YOUR LIFE ASAP. WHAT SHOULD HE LOOK LIKE?
OH, I DON'T REALLY GO FOR LOOKS...
I'm not that superficial!
DON'T LIE! EVERYBODY GOES FOR CERTAIN LOOKS! AND THERE IS NOTHING WRONG WITH THAT!
AS LONG AS YOU KNOW WHAT YOU'RE LOOKING FOR!
and what that means to YOU...
SO WHO DO YOU FIND ATTRACTIVE? WHO'S YOUR FAVORITE ACTOR FOR INSTANCE...?
WELL...
LET'S ANALYZE THIS: HE'S ABOUT YOUR HEIGHT - YOU'RE LOOKING FOR SOMEONE WHO'S AN EQUAL, ON YOUR LEVEL...
EXPRESSIVE FACE: YOU WANT INTELLIGENCE AND CONNECTION.
LITTLE BIT OF A BAD BOY VIBE: YOU WANT EXCITEMENT AND CHALLENGE!
WELL, YES, THAT SOUNDS ABOUT RIGHT...

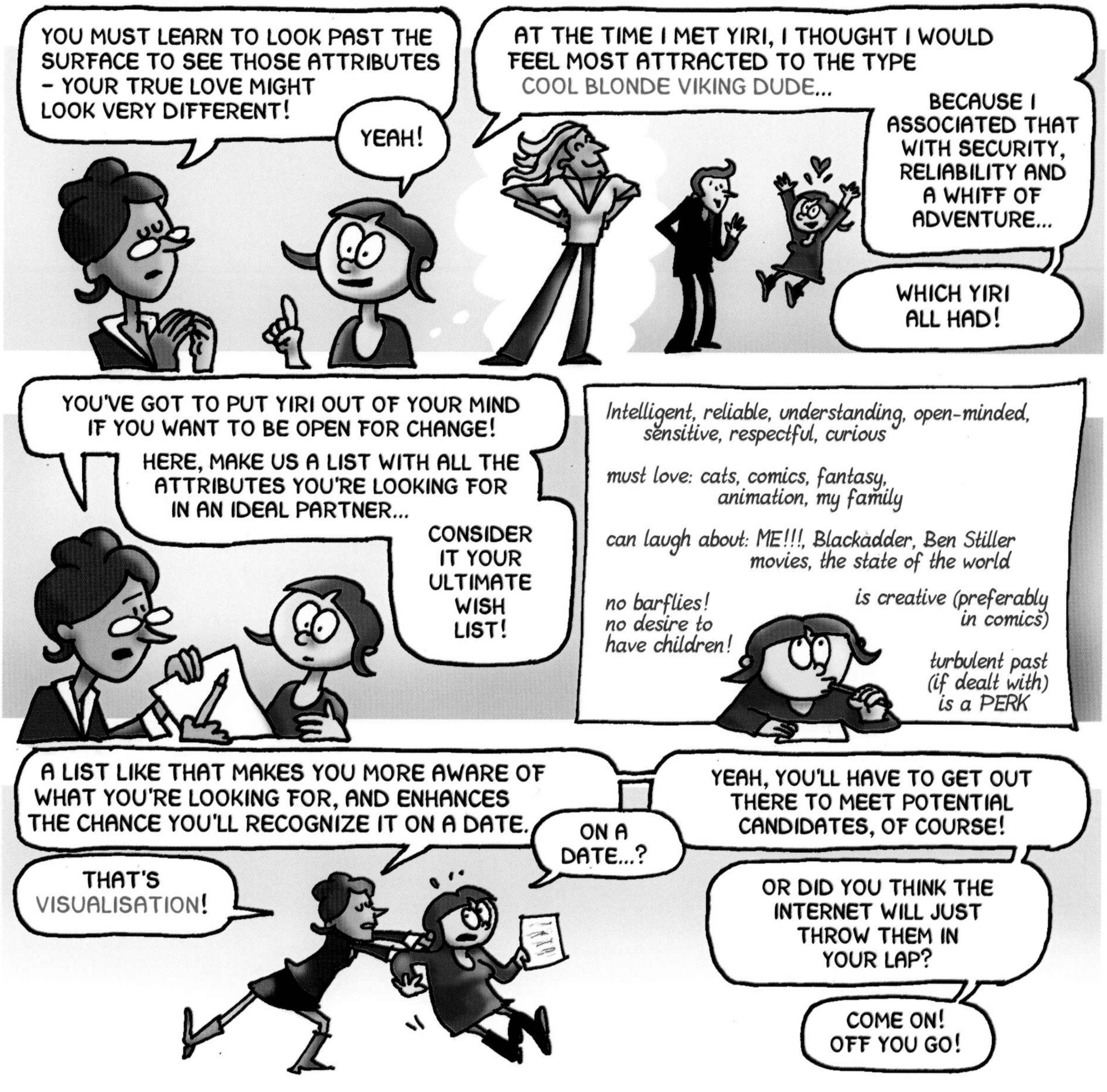

YOU MUST LEARN TO LOOK PAST THE SURFACE TO SEE THOSE ATTRIBUTES - YOUR TRUE LOVE MIGHT LOOK VERY DIFFERENT!
YEAH!
AT THE TIME I MET YIRI, I THOUGHT I WOULD FEEL MOST ATTRACTED TO THE TYPE COOL BLONDE VIKING DUDE...
BECAUSE I ASSOCIATED THAT WITH SECURITY, RELIABILITY AND A WHIFF OF ADVENTURE...
WHICH YIRI ALL HAD!
YOU'VE GOT TO PUT YIRI OUT OF YOUR MIND IF YOU WANT TO BE OPEN FOR CHANGE!
HERE, MAKE US A LIST WITH ALL THE ATTRIBUTES YOU'RE LOOKING FOR IN AN IDEAL PARTNER...
CONSIDER IT YOUR ULTIMATE WISH LIST!
Intelligent, reliable, understanding, open-minded, sensitive, respectful, curious
must love: cats, comics, fantasy, animation, my family
can laugh about: ME!!!, Blackadder, Ben Stiller movies, the state of the world
no barflies! no desire to have children!
is creative (preferably in comics)
turbulent past (if dealt with) is a PERK
A LIST LIKE THAT MAKES YOU MORE AWARE OF WHAT YOU'RE LOOKING FOR, AND ENHANCES THE CHANCE YOU'LL RECOGNIZE IT ON A DATE.
THAT'S VISUALISATION!
ON A DATE...?
YEAH, YOU'LL HAVE TO GET OUT THERE TO MEET POTENTIAL CANDIDATES, OF COURSE!
OR DID YOU THINK THE INTERNET WILL JUST THROW THEM IN YOUR LAP?
COME ON! OFF YOU GO!

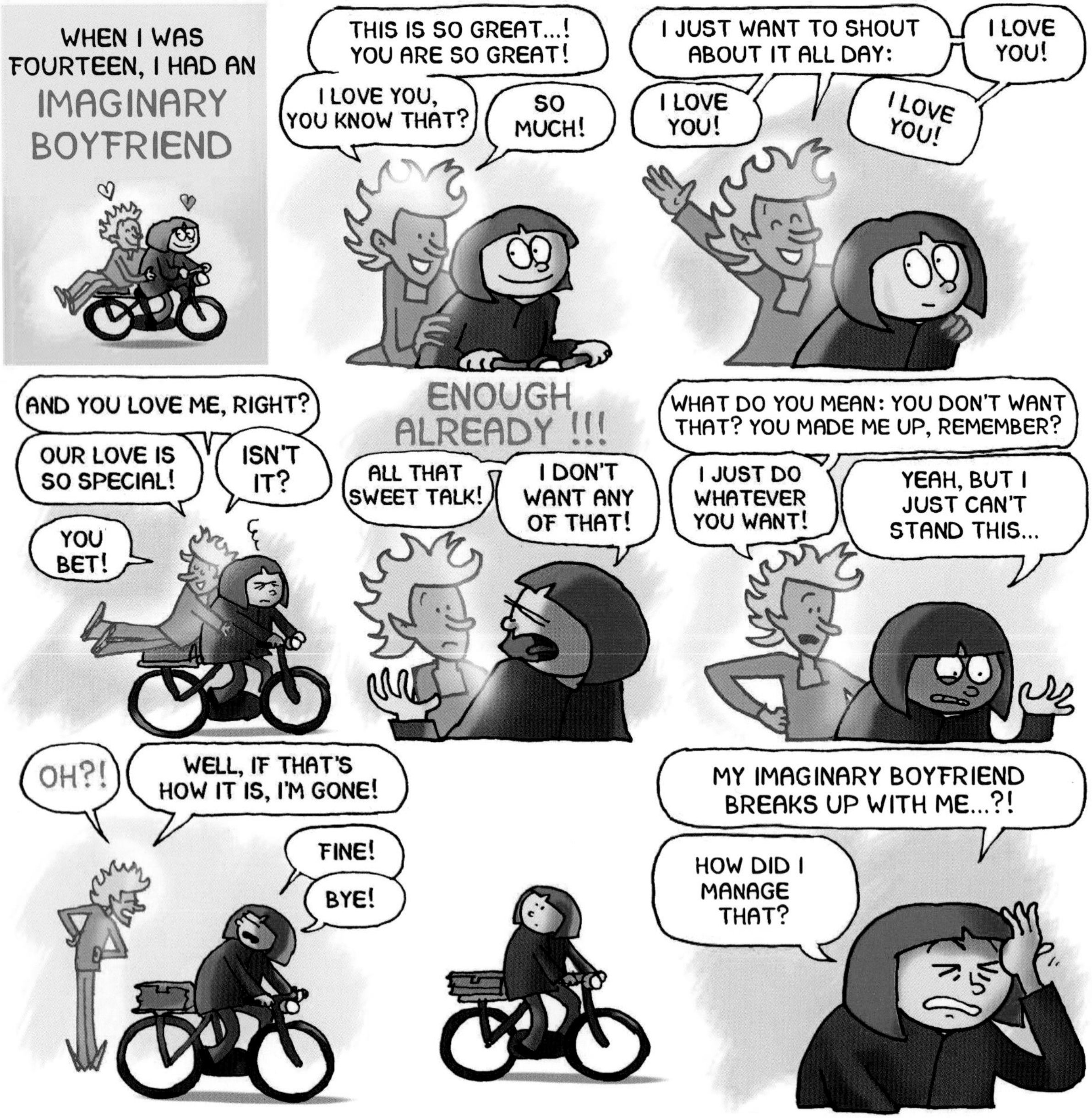
WHEN I WAS FOURTEEN, I HAD AN IMAGINARY BOYFRIEND
THIS IS SO GREAT...! YOU ARE SO GREAT!
I LOVE YOU, YOU KNOW THAT?
SO MUCH!
I JUST WANT TO SHOUT ABOUT IT ALL DAY:
I LOVE YOU!
I LOVE YOU!
I LOVE YOU!
AND YOU LOVE ME, RIGHT?
OUR LOVE IS SO SPECIAL!
ISN'T IT?
YOU BET!
ENOUGH ALREADY !!!
ALL THAT SWEET TALK!
I DON'T WANT ANY OF THAT!
WHAT DO YOU MEAN: YOU DON'T WANT THAT? YOU MADE ME UP, REMEMBER?
I JUST DO WHATEVER YOU WANT!
YEAH, BUT I JUST CAN'T STAND THIS...
OH?!
WELL, IF THAT'S HOW IT IS, I'M GONE!
FINE!
BYE!
MY IMAGINARY BOYFRIEND BREAKS UP WITH ME...?!
HOW DID I MANAGE THAT?

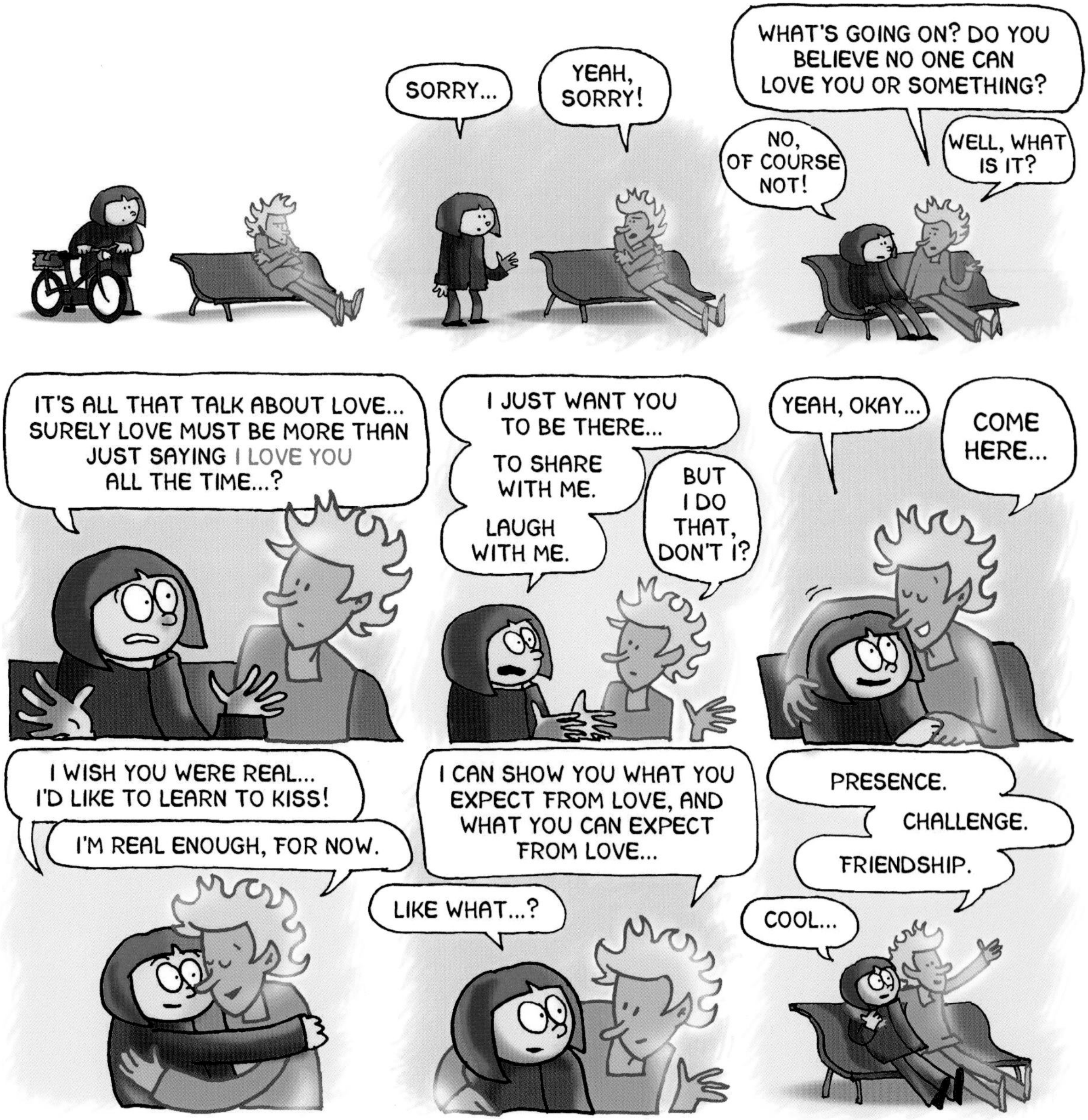
SORRY...
YEAH, SORRY!
WHAT'S GOING ON? DO YOU BELIEVE NO ONE CAN LOVE YOU OR SOMETHING?
NO, OF COURSE NOT!
WELL, WHAT IS IT?
IT'S ALL THAT TALK ABOUT LOVE... SURELY LOVE MUST BE MORE THAN JUST SAYING I LOVE YOU ALL THE TIME...?
I JUST WANT YOU TO BE THERE...
TO SHARE WITH ME.
LAUGH WITH ME.
BUT I DO THAT, DON'T I?
YEAH, OKAY...
COME HERE...
I WISH YOU WERE REAL... I'D LIKE TO LEARN TO KISS!
I'M REAL ENOUGH, FOR NOW.
I CAN SHOW YOU WHAT YOU EXPECT FROM LOVE, AND WHAT YOU CAN EXPECT FROM LOVE...
LIKE WHAT...?
PRESENCE.
CHALLENGE.
FRIENDSHIP.
COOL...

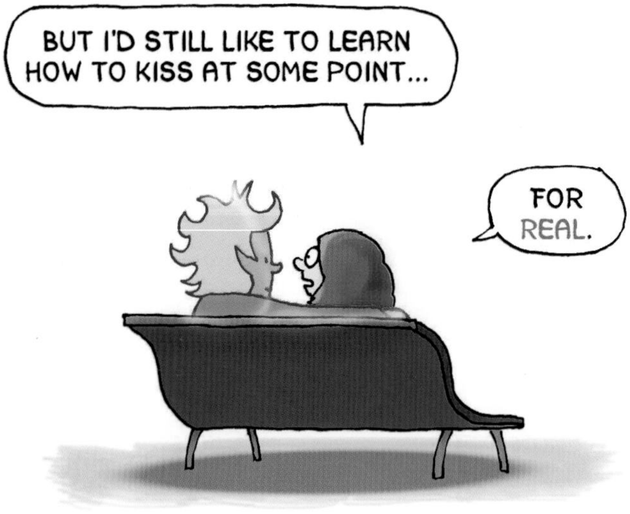
BUT I'D STILL LIKE TO LEARN HOW TO KISS AT SOME POINT...
FOR REAL.

SEX

SEX HAS NOTHING TO DO WITH LOVE!
SEX HAS EVERYTHING TO DO WITH LOVE!

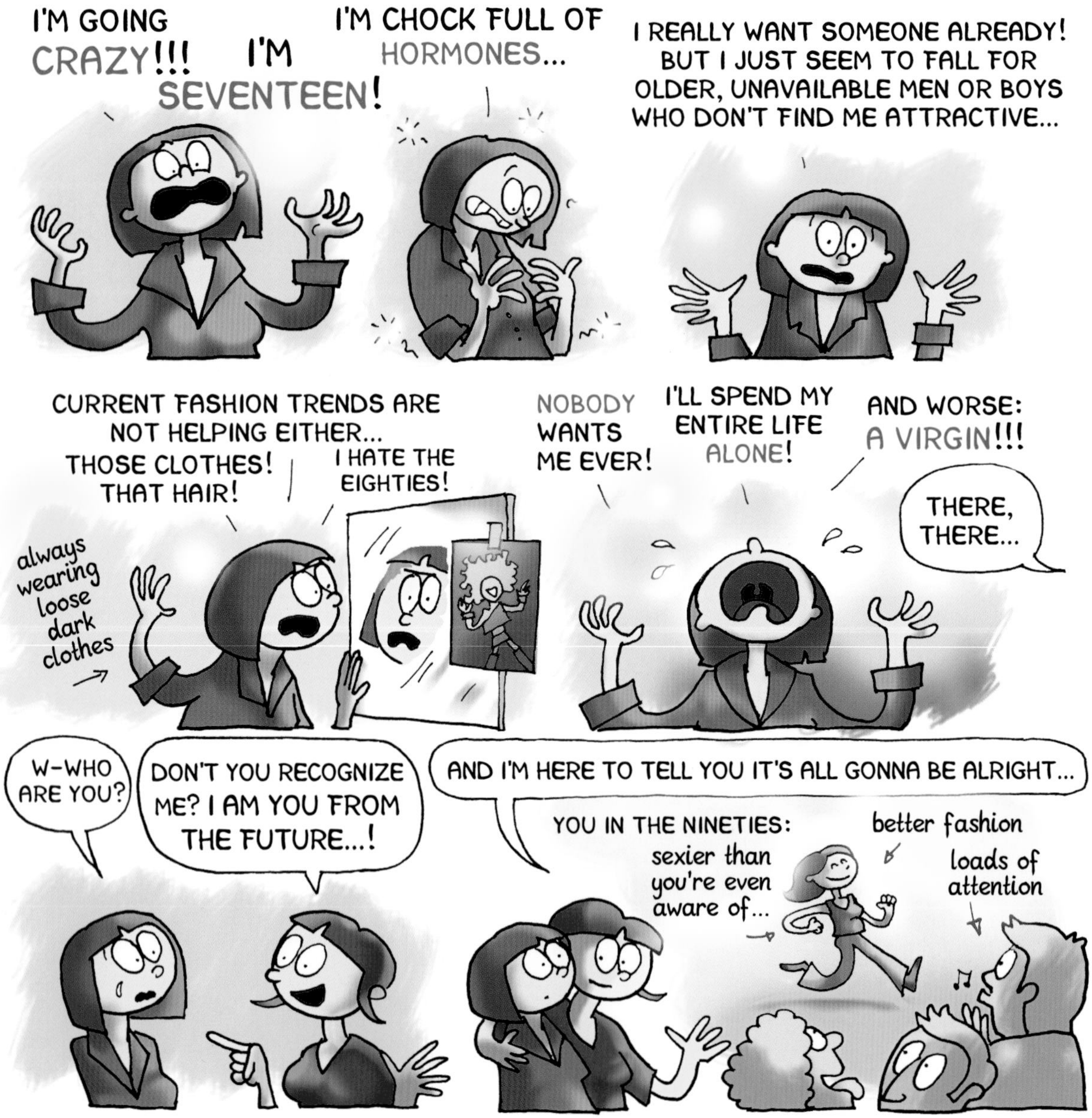
I'M GOING CRAZY!!!
I'M SEVENTEEN!
I'M CHOCK FULL OF HORMONES...
I REALLY WANT SOMEONE ALREADY! BUT I JUST SEEM TO FALL FOR OLDER, UNAVAILABLE MEN OR BOYS WHO DON'T FIND ME ATTRACTIVE...
CURRENT FASHION TRENDS ARE NOT HELPING EITHER...
THOSE CLOTHES! THAT HAIR!
I HATE THE EIGHTIES!
always wearing loose dark clothes
NOBODY WANTS ME EVER!
I'LL SPEND MY ENTIRE LIFE ALONE!
AND WORSE: A VIRGIN!!!
THERE, THERE...
W-WHO ARE YOU?
DON'T YOU RECOGNIZE ME? I AM YOU FROM THE FUTURE...!
AND I'M HERE TO TELL YOU IT'S ALL GONNA BE ALRIGHT...
YOU IN THE NINETIES:
sexier than you're even aware of...
better fashion
loads of attention

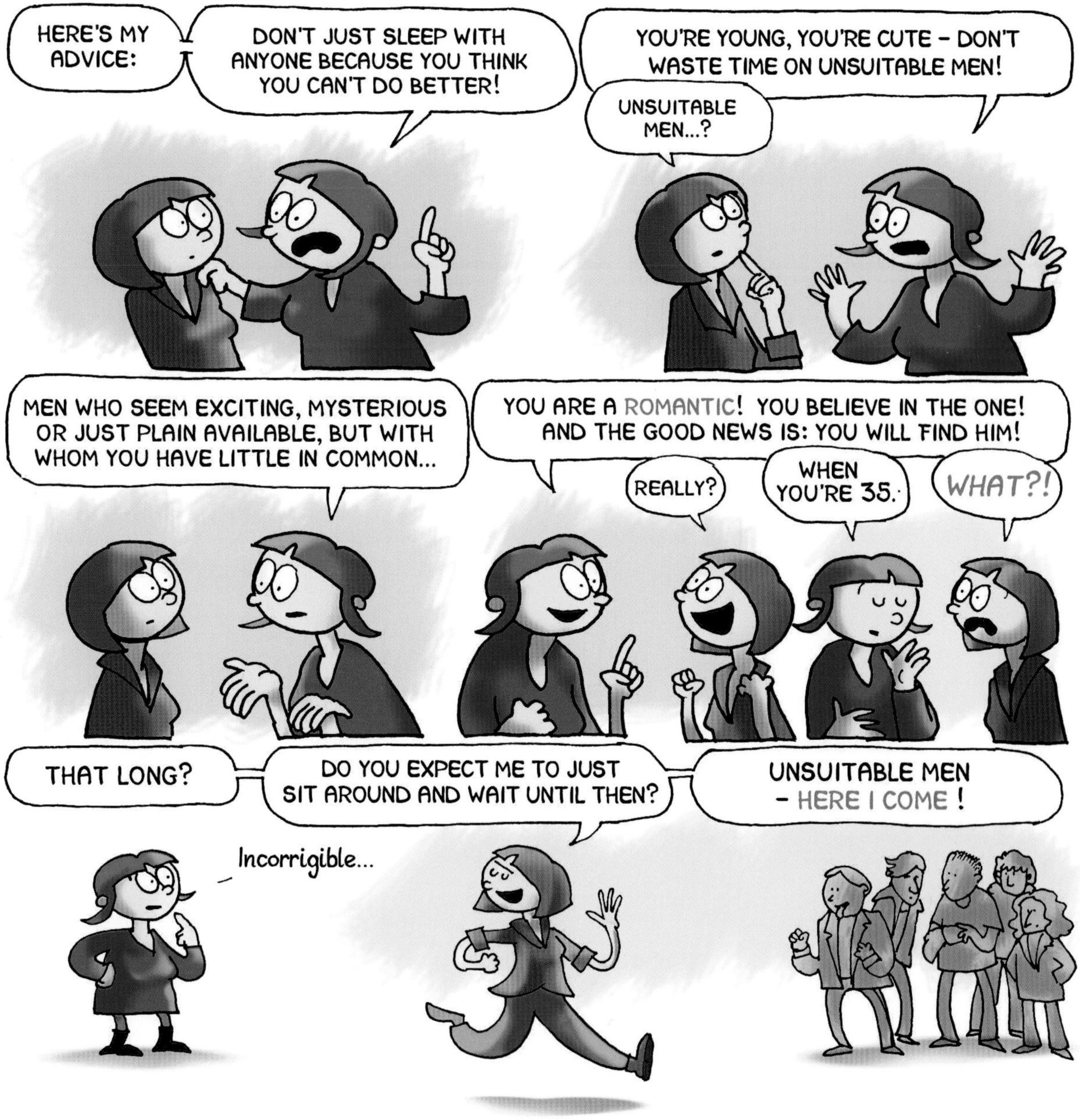
HERE'S MY ADVICE:
DON'T JUST SLEEP WITH ANYONE BECAUSE YOU THINK YOU CAN'T DO BETTER!
YOU'RE YOUNG, YOU'RE CUTE – DON'T WASTE TIME ON UNSUITABLE MEN!
UNSUITABLE MEN...?
MEN WHO SEEM EXCITING, MYSTERIOUS OR JUST PLAIN AVAILABLE, BUT WITH WHOM YOU HAVE LITTLE IN COMMON...
YOU ARE A ROMANTIC! YOU BELIEVE IN THE ONE! AND THE GOOD NEWS IS: YOU WILL FIND HIM!
REALLY?
WHEN YOU'RE 35.
WHAT?!
THAT LONG?
DO YOU EXPECT ME TO JUST SIT AROUND AND WAIT UNTIL THEN?
UNSUITABLE MEN – HERE I COME !
Incorrigible...

IN THE USA, SEX IS OFTEN EXPLAINED IN TERMS OF BASEBALL:

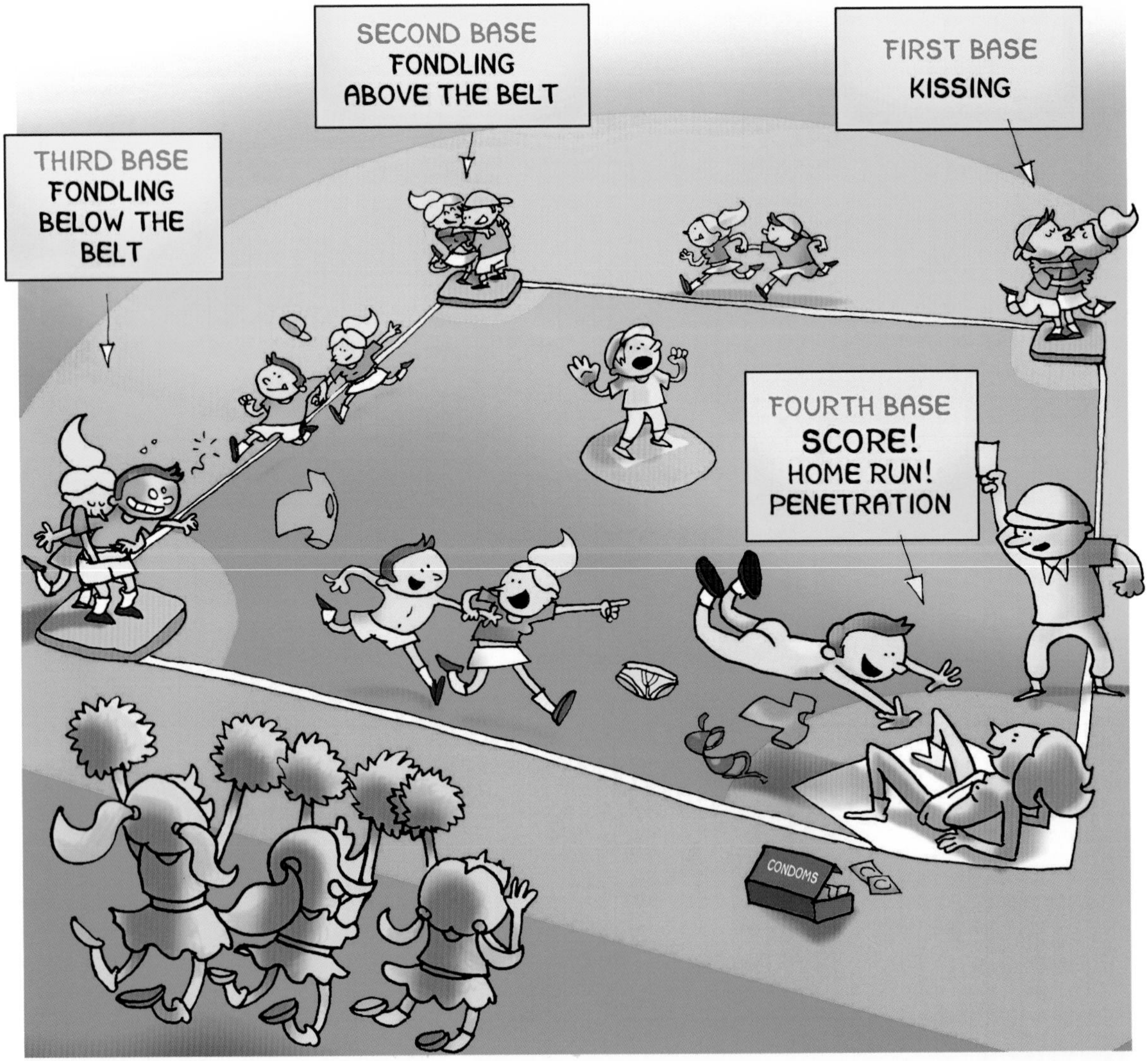
SECOND BASE
FONDLING
ABOVE THE BELT
FIRST BASE
KISSING
THIRD BASE
FONDLING
BELOW THE
BELT
FOURTH BASE
SCORE!
HOME RUN!
PENETRATION
CONDOMS

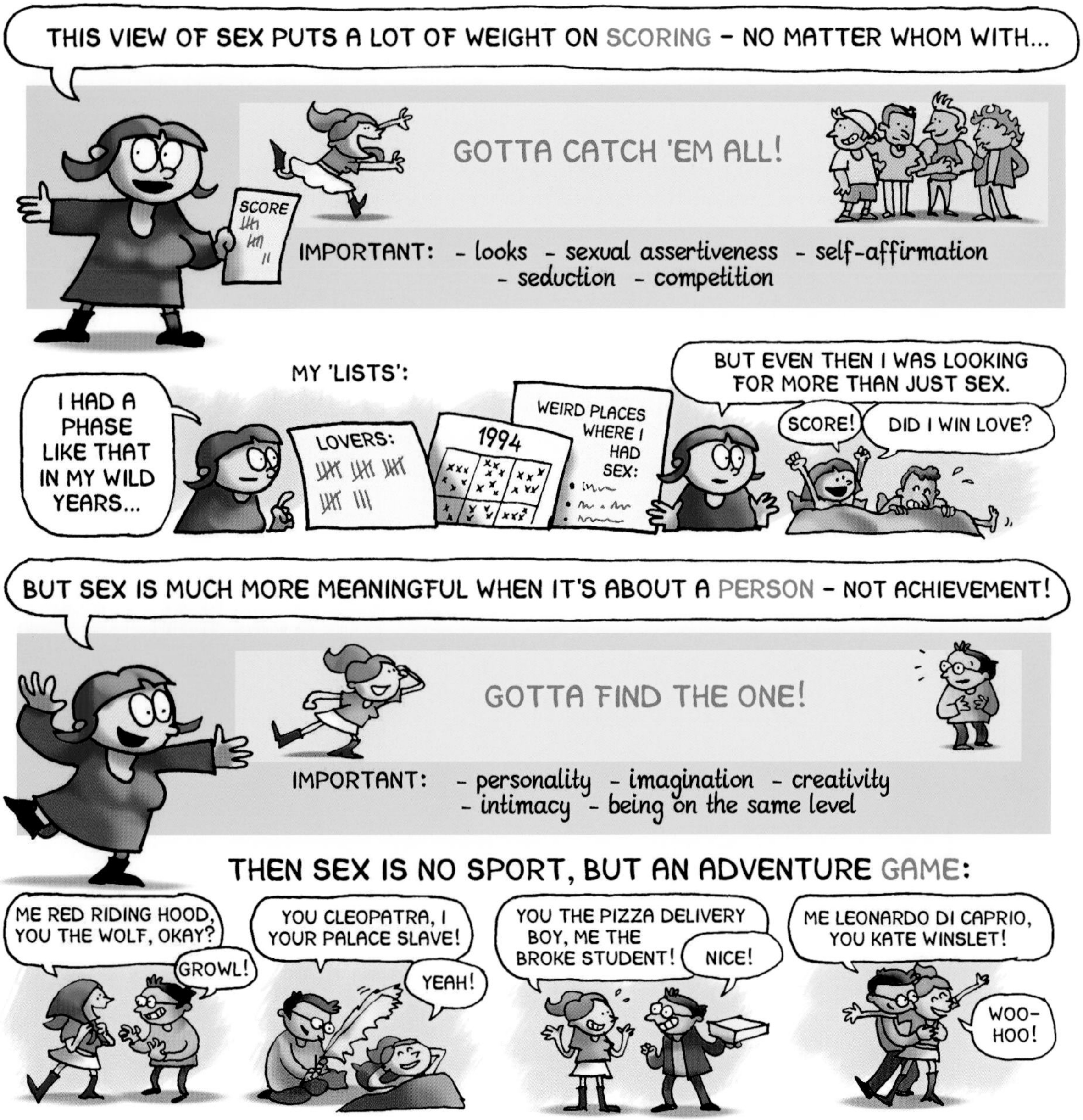
THIS VIEW OF SEX PUTS A LOT OF WEIGHT ON SCORING – NO MATTER WHOM WITH...
SCORE
GOTTA CATCH 'EM ALL!
IMPORTANT: - looks - sexual assertiveness - self-affirmation - seduction - competition
I HAD A PHASE LIKE THAT IN MY WILD YEARS...
MY 'LISTS':
LOVERS:
1994
WEIRD PLACES WHERE I HAD SEX:
BUT EVEN THEN I WAS LOOKING FOR MORE THAN JUST SEX.
SCORE!
DID I WIN LOVE?
BUT SEX IS MUCH MORE MEANINGFUL WHEN IT'S ABOUT A PERSON – NOT ACHIEVEMENT!
GOTTA FIND THE ONE!
IMPORTANT: - personality - imagination - creativity - intimacy - being on the same level
THEN SEX IS NO SPORT, BUT AN ADVENTURE GAME:
ME RED RIDING HOOD, YOU THE WOLF, OKAY?
GROWL!
YOU CLEOPATRA, I YOUR PALACE SLAVE!
YEAH!
YOU THE PIZZA DELIVERY BOY, ME THE BROKE STUDENT!
NICE!
ME LEONARDO DI CAPRIO, YOU KATE WINSLET!
WOO-HOO!

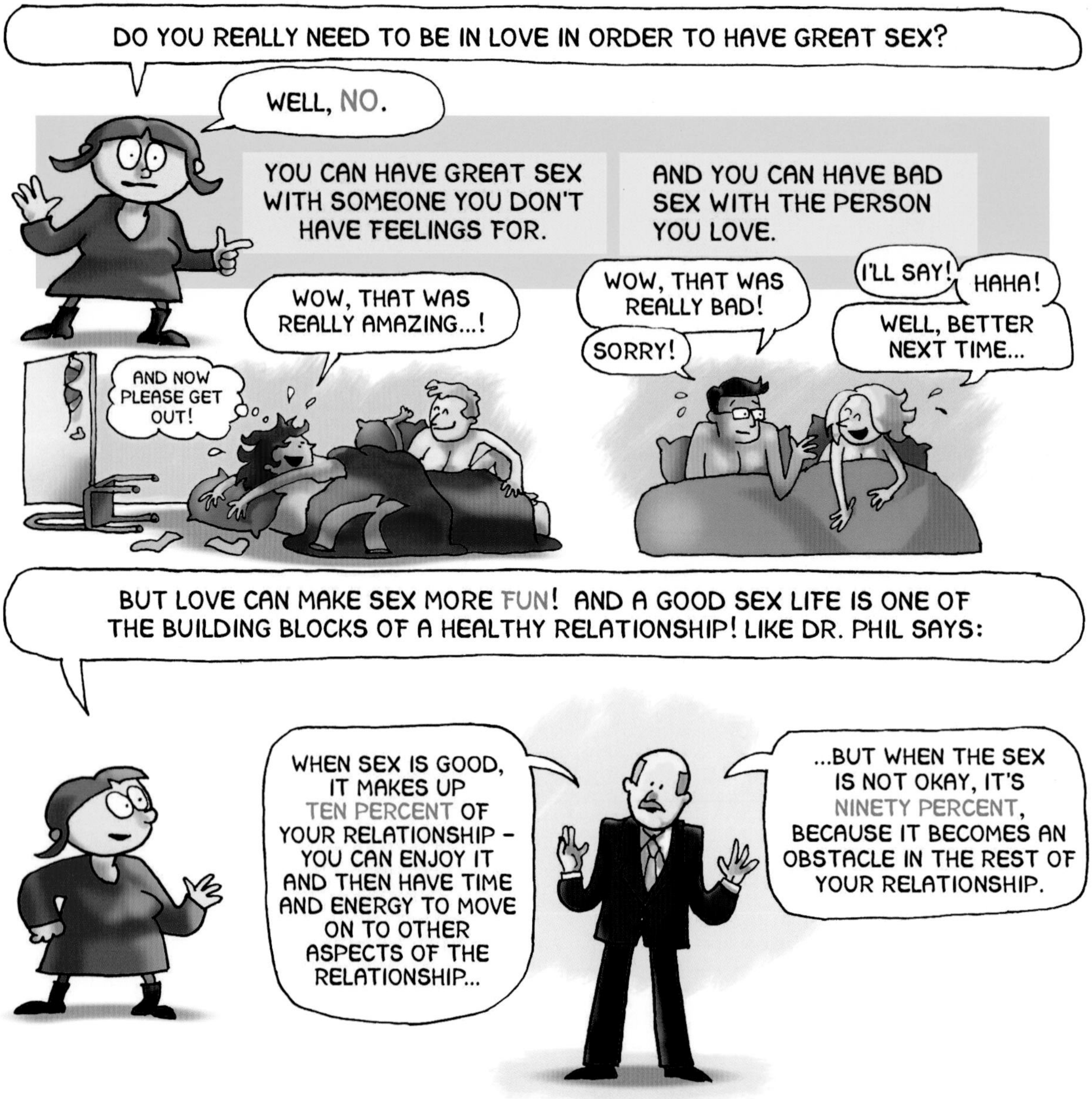
DO YOU REALLY NEED TO BE IN LOVE IN ORDER TO HAVE GREAT SEX?
WELL, NO.
YOU CAN HAVE GREAT SEX WITH SOMEONE YOU DON'T HAVE FEELINGS FOR.
AND YOU CAN HAVE BAD SEX WITH THE PERSON YOU LOVE.
WOW, THAT WAS REALLY AMAZING...!
AND NOW PLEASE GET OUT!
WOW, THAT WAS REALLY BAD!
SORRY!
I'LL SAY!
HAHA!
WELL, BETTER NEXT TIME...
BUT LOVE CAN MAKE SEX MORE FUN! AND A GOOD SEX LIFE IS ONE OF THE BUILDING BLOCKS OF A HEALTHY RELATIONSHIP! LIKE DR. PHIL SAYS:
WHEN SEX IS GOOD, IT MAKES UP TEN PERCENT OF YOUR RELATIONSHIP – YOU CAN ENJOY IT AND THEN HAVE TIME AND ENERGY TO MOVE ON TO OTHER ASPECTS OF THE RELATIONSHIP...
...BUT WHEN THE SEX IS NOT OKAY, IT'S NINETY PERCENT, BECAUSE IT BECOMES AN OBSTACLE IN THE REST OF YOUR RELATIONSHIP.

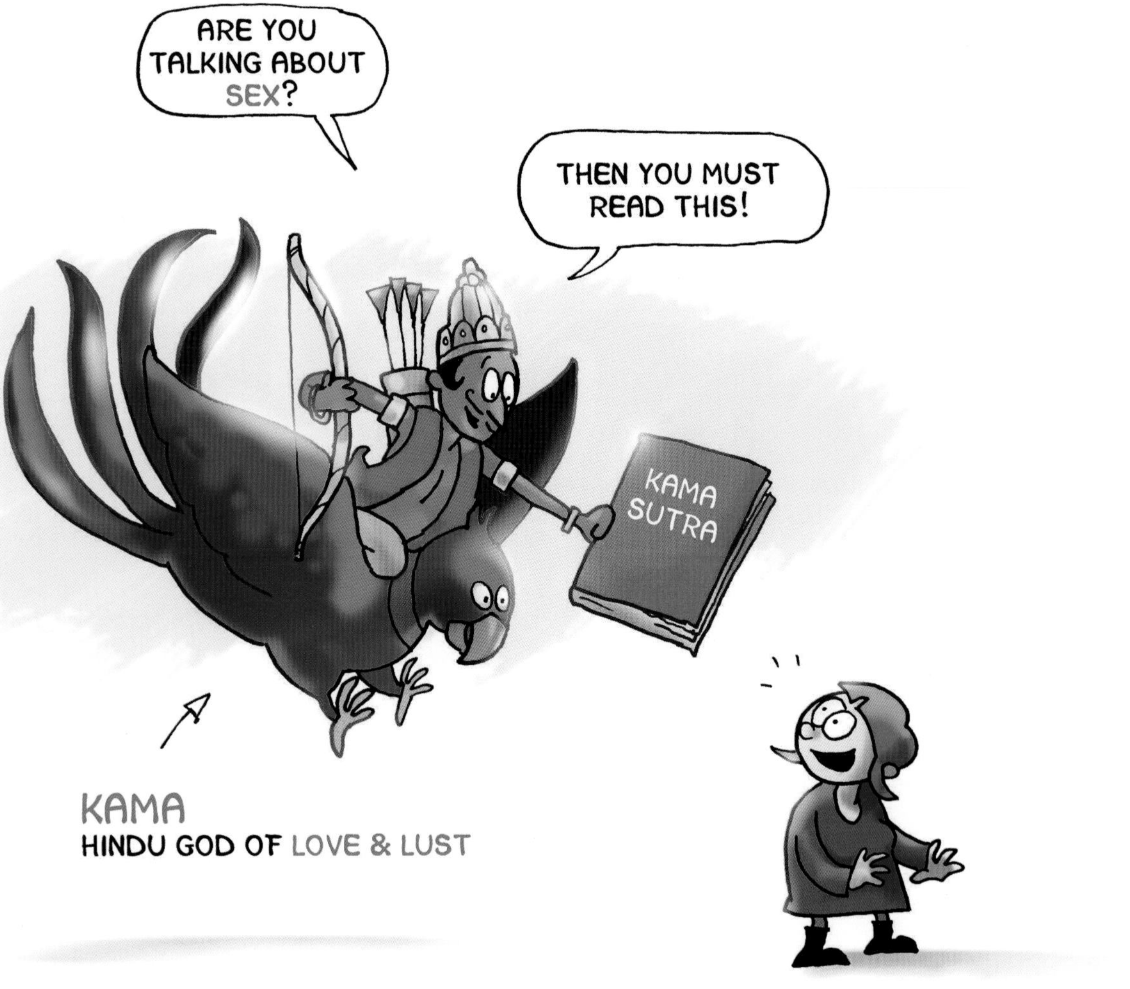
ARE YOU TALKING ABOUT SEX?
THEN YOU MUST READ THIS!
KAMA SUTRA
KAMA
HINDU GOD OF LOVE & LUST

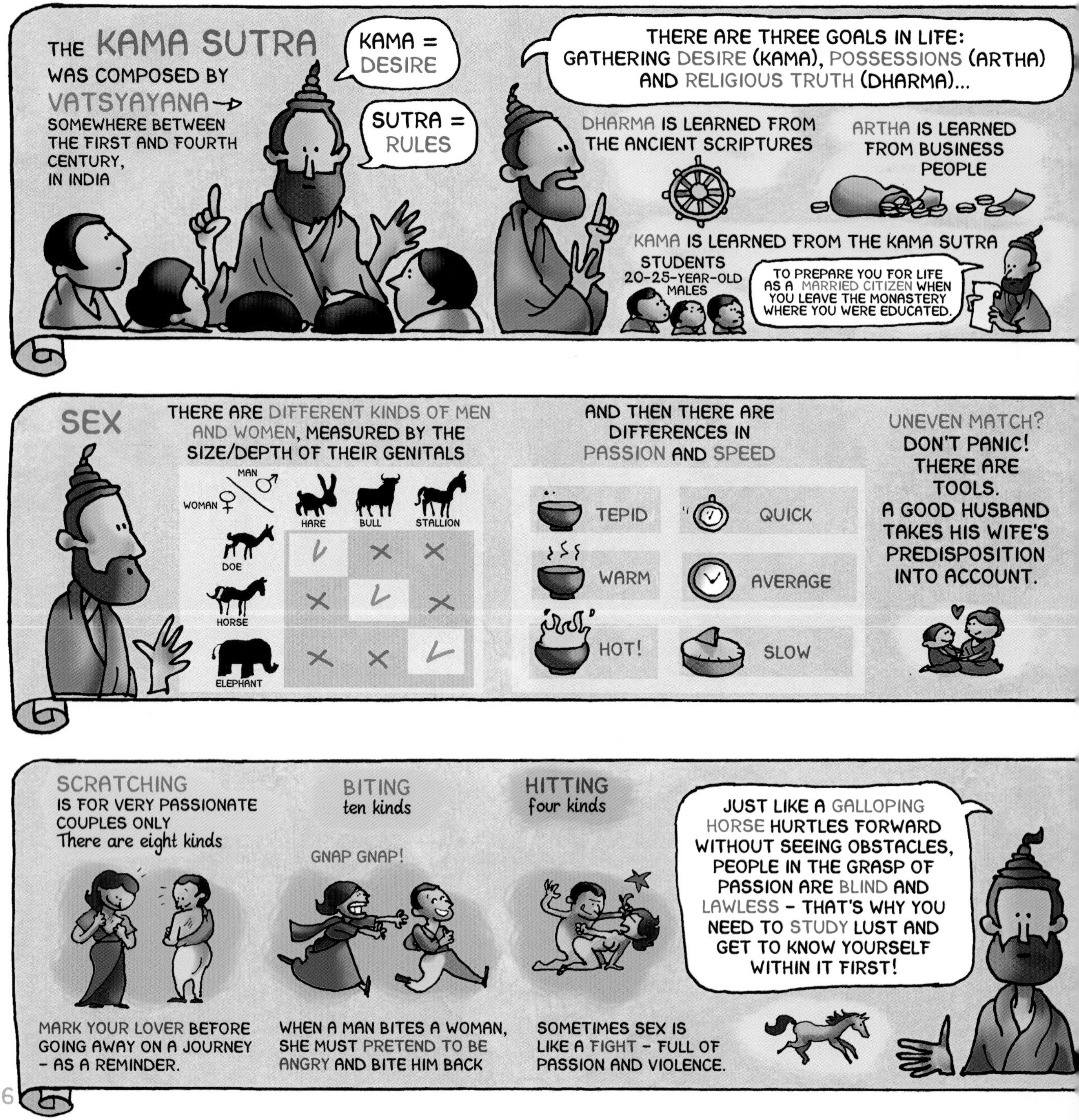
THE KAMA SUTRA WAS COMPOSED BY VATSYAYANA SOMEWHERE BETWEEN THE FIRST AND FOURTH CENTURY, IN INDIA
KAMA = DESIRE
SUTRA = RULES
THERE ARE THREE GOALS IN LIFE: GATHERING DESIRE (KAMA), POSSESSIONS (ARTHA) AND RELIGIOUS TRUTH (DHARMA)...
DHARMA IS LEARNED FROM THE ANCIENT SCRIPTURES
ARTHA IS LEARNED FROM BUSINESS PEOPLE
KAMA IS LEARNED FROM THE KAMA SUTRA
STUDENTS 20-25-YEAR-OLD MALES
TO PREPARE YOU FOR LIFE AS A MARRIED CITIZEN WHEN YOU LEAVE THE MONASTERY WHERE YOU WERE EDUCATED.
SEX
THERE ARE DIFFERENT KINDS OF MEN AND WOMEN, MEASURED BY THE SIZE/DEPTH OF THEIR GENITALS
MAN ♂
WOMAN ♀
HARE
BULL
STALLION
DOE
HORSE
ELEPHANT
AND THEN THERE ARE DIFFERENCES IN PASSION AND SPEED
TEPID
QUICK
WARM
AVERAGE
HOT!
SLOW
UNEVEN MATCH? DON'T PANIC! THERE ARE TOOLS. A GOOD HUSBAND TAKES HIS WIFE'S PREDISPOSITION INTO ACCOUNT.
SCRATCHING IS FOR VERY PASSIONATE COUPLES ONLY There are eight kinds
BITING ten kinds
HITTING four kinds
GNAP GNAP!
JUST LIKE A GALLOPING HORSE HURTLES FORWARD WITHOUT SEEING OBSTACLES, PEOPLE IN THE GRASP OF PASSION ARE BLIND AND LAWLESS – THAT'S WHY YOU NEED TO STUDY LUST AND GET TO KNOW YOURSELF WITHIN IT FIRST!
MARK YOUR LOVER BEFORE GOING AWAY ON A JOURNEY – AS A REMINDER.
WHEN A MAN BITES A WOMAN, SHE MUST PRETEND TO BE ANGRY AND BITE HIM BACK
SOMETIMES SEX IS LIKE A FIGHT – FULL OF PASSION AND VIOLENCE.

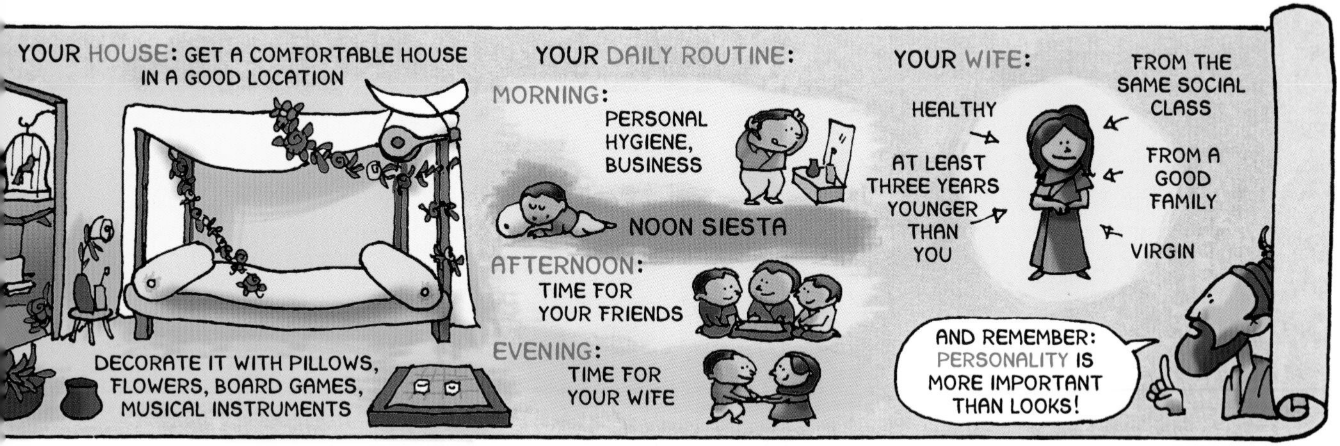
YOUR HOUSE: GET A COMFORTABLE HOUSE IN A GOOD LOCATION
DECORATE IT WITH PILLOWS, FLOWERS, BOARD GAMES, MUSICAL INSTRUMENTS
YOUR DAILY ROUTINE:
MORNING:
PERSONAL HYGIENE, BUSINESS
NOON SIESTA
AFTERNOON:
TIME FOR YOUR FRIENDS
EVENING:
TIME FOR YOUR WIFE
YOUR WIFE:
HEALTHY
AT LEAST THREE YEARS YOUNGER THAN YOU
FROM THE SAME SOCIAL CLASS
FROM A GOOD FAMILY
VIRGIN
AND REMEMBER: PERSONALITY IS MORE IMPORTANT THAN LOOKS!

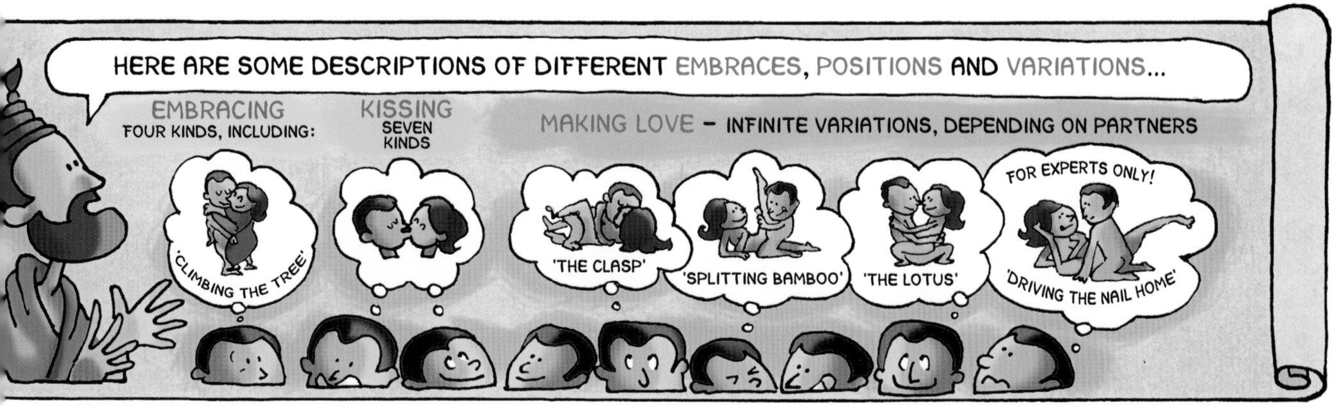
HERE ARE SOME DESCRIPTIONS OF DIFFERENT EMBRACES, POSITIONS AND VARIATIONS...
EMBRACING
FOUR KINDS, INCLUDING:
KISSING
SEVEN KINDS
MAKING LOVE – INFINITE VARIATIONS, DEPENDING ON PARTNERS
'CLIMBING THE TREE'
'THE CLASP'
'SPLITTING BAMBOO'
'THE LOTUS'
FOR EXPERTS ONLY!
'DRIVING THE NAIL HOME'

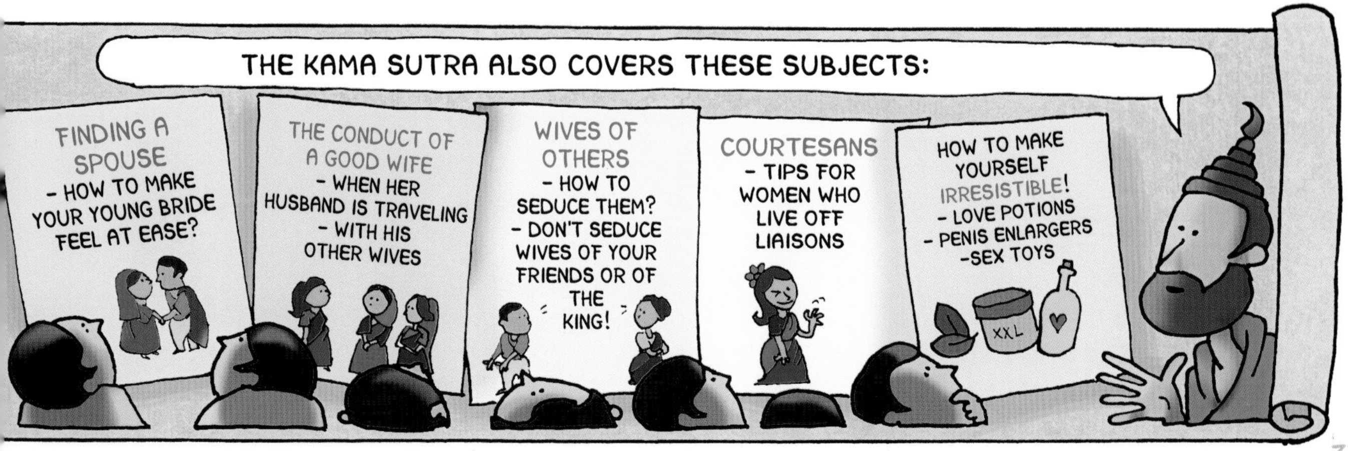
THE KAMA SUTRA ALSO COVERS THESE SUBJECTS:
FINDING A SPOUSE
- HOW TO MAKE YOUR YOUNG BRIDE FEEL AT EASE?
THE CONDUCT OF A GOOD WIFE
- WHEN HER HUSBAND IS TRAVELING
- WITH HIS OTHER WIVES
WIVES OF OTHERS
- HOW TO SEDUCE THEM?
- DON'T SEDUCE WIVES OF YOUR FRIENDS OR OF THE KING!
COURTESANS
- TIPS FOR WOMEN WHO LIVE OFF LIAISONS
HOW TO MAKE YOURSELF IRRESISTIBLE!
- LOVE POTIONS
- PENIS ENLARGERS
-SEX TOYS
XXL

TANTRIC SEX

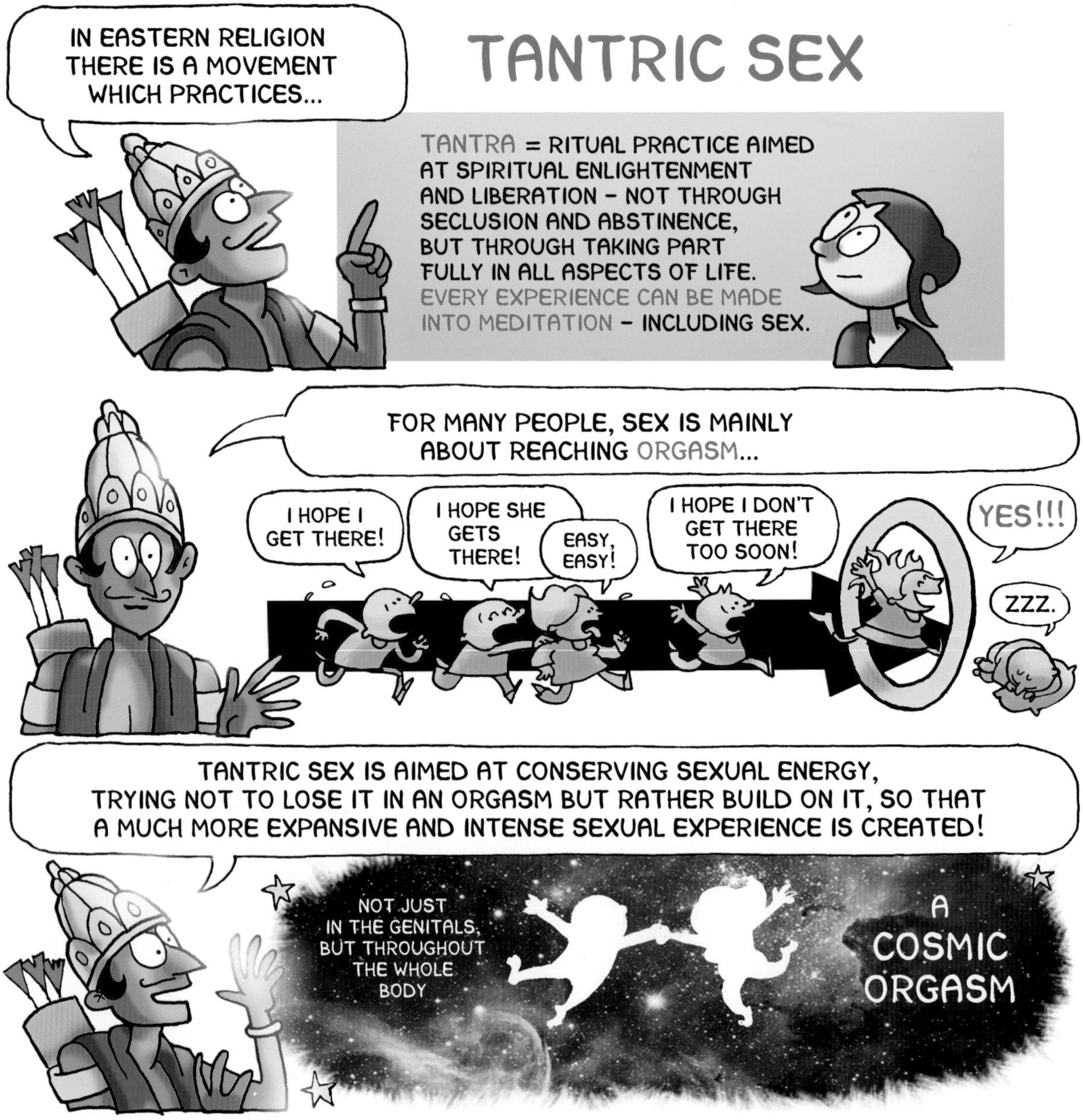
IN EASTERN RELIGION THERE IS A MOVEMENT WHICH PRACTICES...
TANTRA = RITUAL PRACTICE AIMED AT SPIRITUAL ENLIGHTENMENT AND LIBERATION – NOT THROUGH SECLUSION AND ABSTINENCE, BUT THROUGH TAKING PART FULLY IN ALL ASPECTS OF LIFE. EVERY EXPERIENCE CAN BE MADE INTO MEDITATION – INCLUDING SEX.
FOR MANY PEOPLE, SEX IS MAINLY ABOUT REACHING ORGASM...
I HOPE I GET THERE!
I HOPE SHE GETS THERE!
EASY, EASY!
I HOPE I DON'T GET THERE TOO SOON!
YES!!!
ZZZ.
TANTRIC SEX IS AIMED AT CONSERVING SEXUAL ENERGY, TRYING NOT TO LOSE IT IN AN ORGASM BUT RATHER BUILD ON IT, SO THAT A MUCH MORE EXPANSIVE AND INTENSE SEXUAL EXPERIENCE IS CREATED!
NOT JUST IN THE GENITALS, BUT THROUGHOUT THE WHOLE BODY
A COSMIC ORGASM

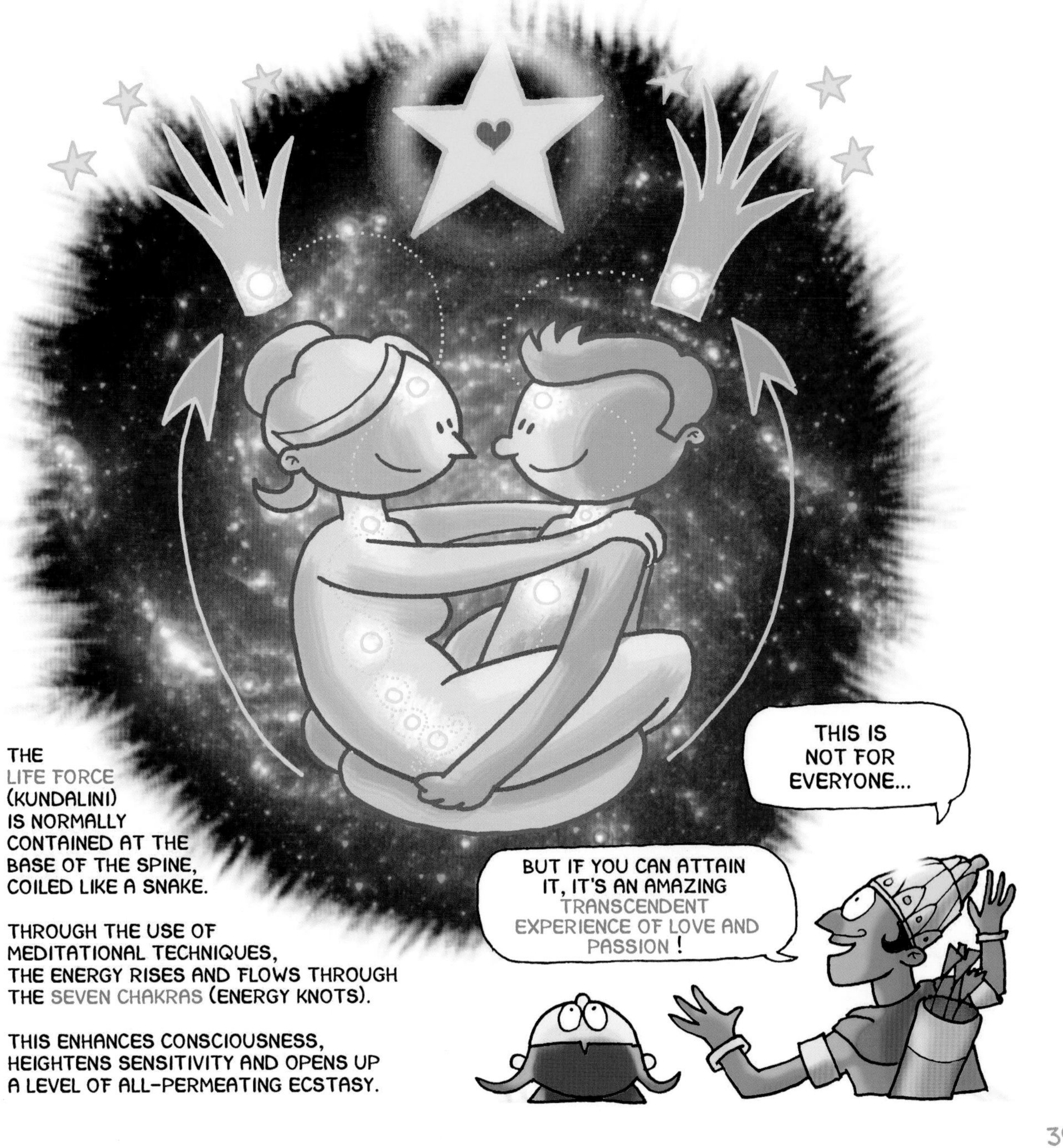
THE LIFE FORCE (KUNDALINI) IS NORMALLY CONTAINED AT THE BASE OF THE SPINE, COILED LIKE A SNAKE.
THROUGH THE USE OF MEDITATIONAL TECHNIQUES, THE ENERGY RISES AND FLOWS THROUGH THE SEVEN CHAKRAS (ENERGY KNOTS).
THIS ENHANCES CONSCIOUSNESS, HEIGHTENS SENSITIVITY AND OPENS UP A LEVEL OF ALL-PERMEATING ECSTASY.
THIS IS NOT FOR EVERYONE...
BUT IF YOU CAN ATTAIN IT, IT'S AN AMAZING TRANSCENDENT EXPERIENCE OF LOVE AND PASSION!

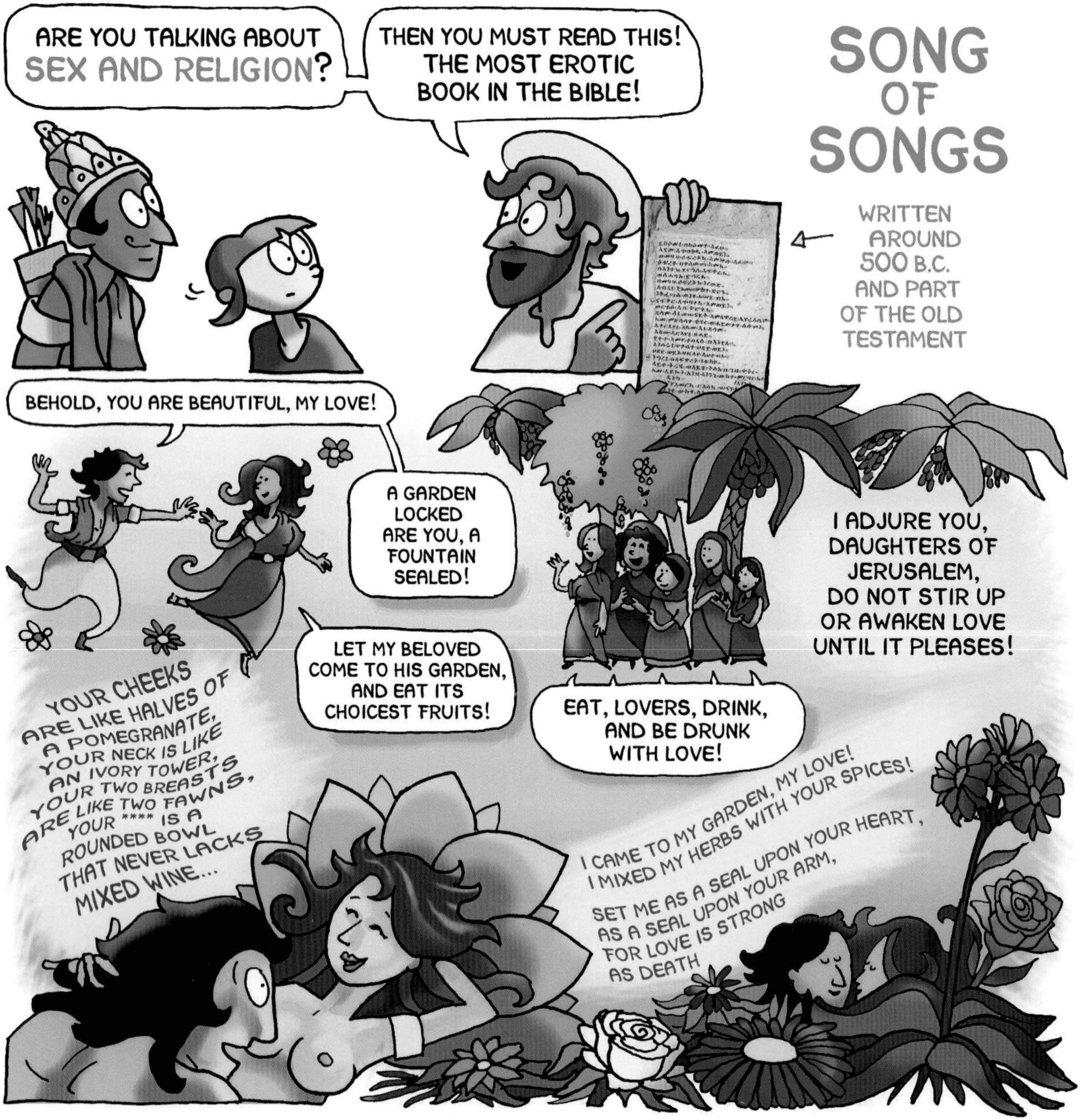

ARE YOU TALKING ABOUT SEX AND RELIGION?
THEN YOU MUST READ THIS! THE MOST EROTIC BOOK IN THE BIBLE!
SONG OF SONGS
WRITTEN AROUND 500 B.C. AND PART OF THE OLD TESTAMENT
BEHOLD, YOU ARE BEAUTIFUL, MY LOVE!
A GARDEN LOCKED ARE YOU, A FOUNTAIN SEALED!
LET MY BELOVED COME TO HIS GARDEN, AND EAT ITS CHOICEST FRUITS!
I ADJURE YOU, DAUGHTERS OF JERUSALEM, DO NOT STIR UP OR AWAKEN LOVE UNTIL IT PLEASES!
EAT, LOVERS, DRINK, AND BE DRUNK WITH LOVE!
YOUR CHEEKS ARE LIKE HALVES OF A POMEGRANATE, YOUR NECK IS LIKE AN IVORY TOWER, YOUR TWO BREASTS ARE LIKE TWO FAWNS, YOUR **** IS A ROUNDED BOWL THAT NEVER LACKS MIXED WINE...
I CAME TO MY GARDEN, MY LOVE! I MIXED MY HERBS WITH YOUR SPICES!
SET ME AS A SEAL UPON YOUR HEART, AS A SEAL UPON YOUR ARM, FOR LOVE IS STRONG AS DEATH

 SEX IN THE BIBLE?

REALLY?

I LEARNED DURING MY STUDIES THAT SONG OF SONGS SHOULD BE READ AS AN ALLEGORY...!

 HA!

IT'S REALLY ABOUT THE LOVE OF GOD FOR THE PEOPLE OF ISRAEL!

NO – ABOUT THE LOVE OF JESUS FOR THE CHURCH!

IT'S ALMOST LIKE SOME SCHOLARS WANT TO EXPLAIN AWAY THE SEX IN THIS BIBLE BOOK...

AS IF HUMAN PHYSICAL LOVE AND SPIRITUALITY CAN'T GO TOGETHER!

DUALITY DIVIDES THE WORLD INTO SEPARATE, INCOMPATIBLE CATEGORIES

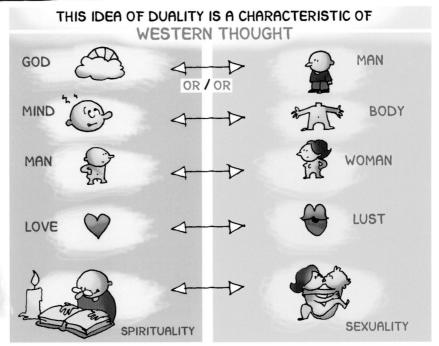

THIS IDEA OF DUALITY IS A CHARACTERISTIC OF WESTERN THOUGHT

	OR / OR	
GOD	⟷	MAN
MIND	⟷	BODY
MAN	⟷	WOMAN
LOVE	⟷	LUST
SPIRITUALITY	⟷	SEXUALITY

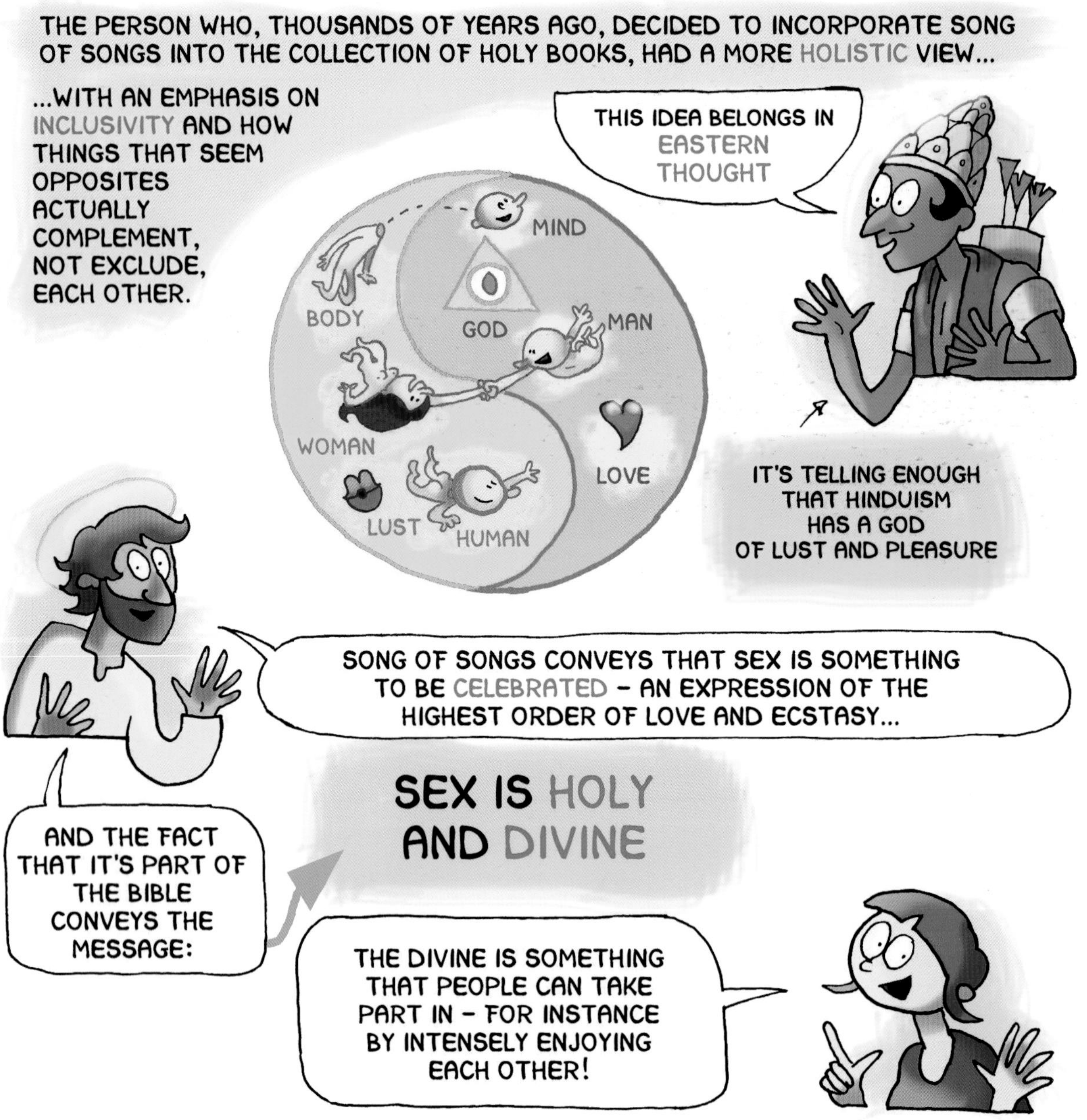
THE PERSON WHO, THOUSANDS OF YEARS AGO, DECIDED TO INCORPORATE SONG OF SONGS INTO THE COLLECTION OF HOLY BOOKS, HAD A MORE HOLISTIC VIEW...
...WITH AN EMPHASIS ON INCLUSIVITY AND HOW THINGS THAT SEEM OPPOSITES ACTUALLY COMPLEMENT, NOT EXCLUDE, EACH OTHER.
THIS IDEA BELONGS IN EASTERN THOUGHT
MIND
BODY
GOD
MAN
WOMAN
LOVE
LUST
HUMAN
IT'S TELLING ENOUGH THAT HINDUISM HAS A GOD OF LUST AND PLEASURE
SONG OF SONGS CONVEYS THAT SEX IS SOMETHING TO BE CELEBRATED – AN EXPRESSION OF THE HIGHEST ORDER OF LOVE AND ECSTASY...
AND THE FACT THAT IT'S PART OF THE BIBLE CONVEYS THE MESSAGE:
SEX IS HOLY AND DIVINE
THE DIVINE IS SOMETHING THAT PEOPLE CAN TAKE PART IN – FOR INSTANCE BY INTENSELY ENJOYING EACH OTHER!

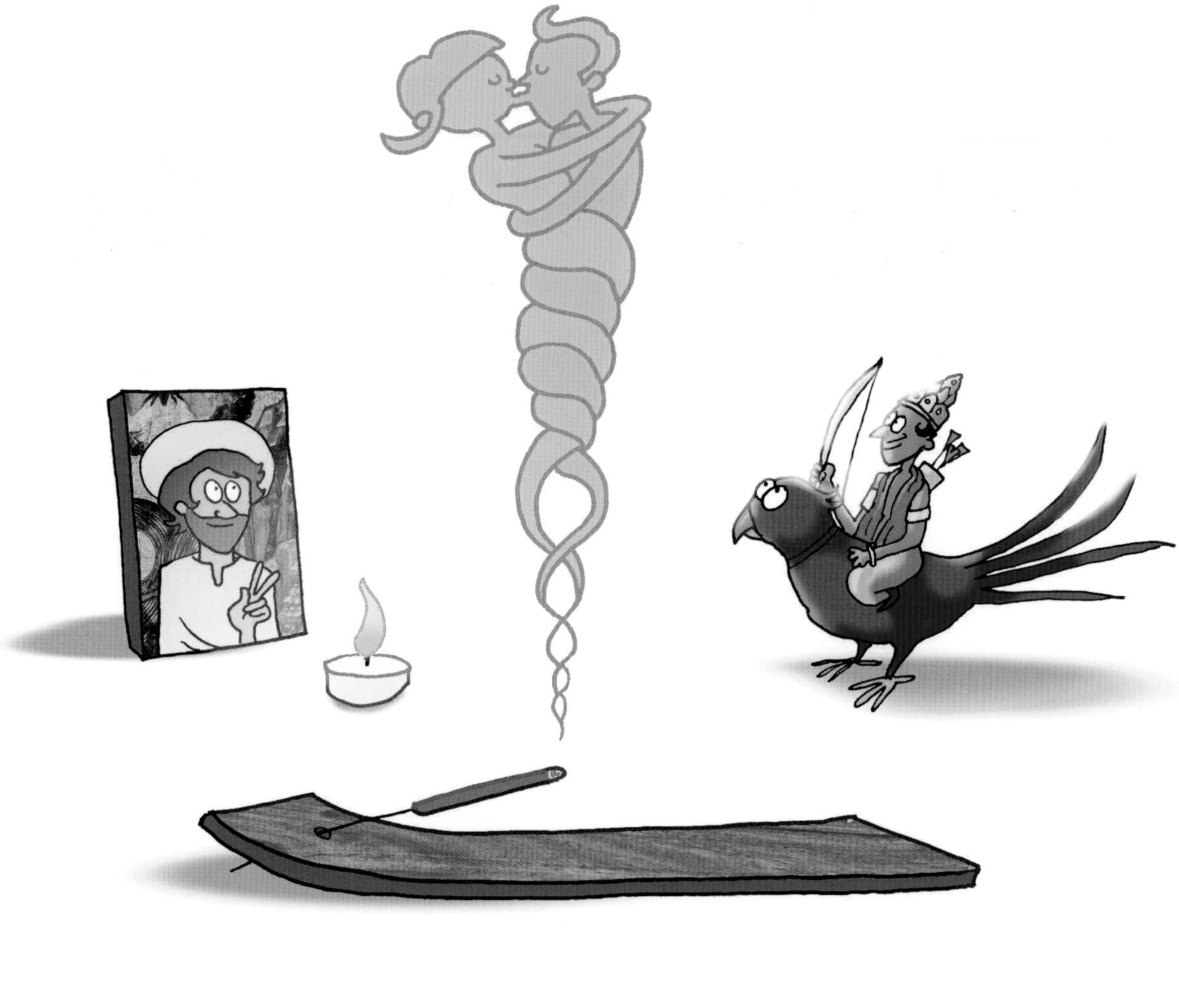

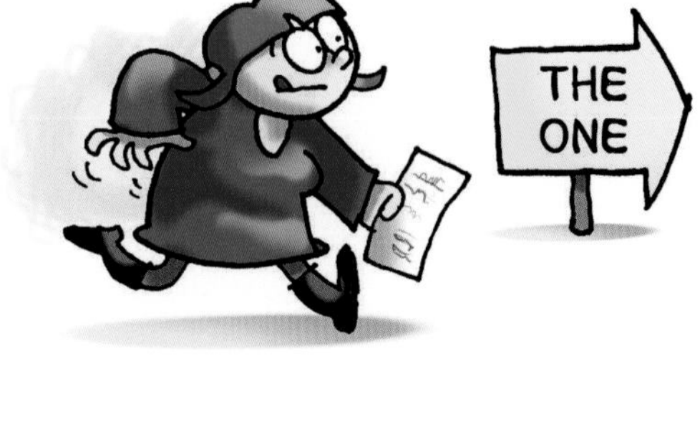
THE
ONE

IN CHINESE MYTHOLOGY IT'S THE GOD YUE LAO
WHO CONNECTS FATED LOVERS WITH A RED THREAD...

YUE LAO IS DEPICTED
AS AN OLD MAN WITH
A SACK OF THREAD.
HE WALKS THE
EARTH, BUT
HIS HOME IS
THE MOON.

THE 'RED THREAD
OF DESTINY'
NOT ONLY
CONNECTS
LOVERS, BUT
EVERYONE
WHOSE FATES
ARE INTERTWINED:
ALL PEOPLE WHO
ARE DESTINED TO
PLAY AN IMPORTANT
ROLE IN EACH
OTHER'S LIVES.

THE THREAD CAN
NOT BE BROKEN AND
KEEPS GETTING
SHORTER, UNTIL
AT LAST DESTINED
LOVERS MEET.

IN CHINESE LEGEND
THE THREAD IS
CONNECTED TO
THE ANKLE.

IN JAPAN
THE THREAD
IS CONNECTED
TO THE
PINKIE
FINGER.

45

IS THERE SUCH A THING AS 'THE ONE'?

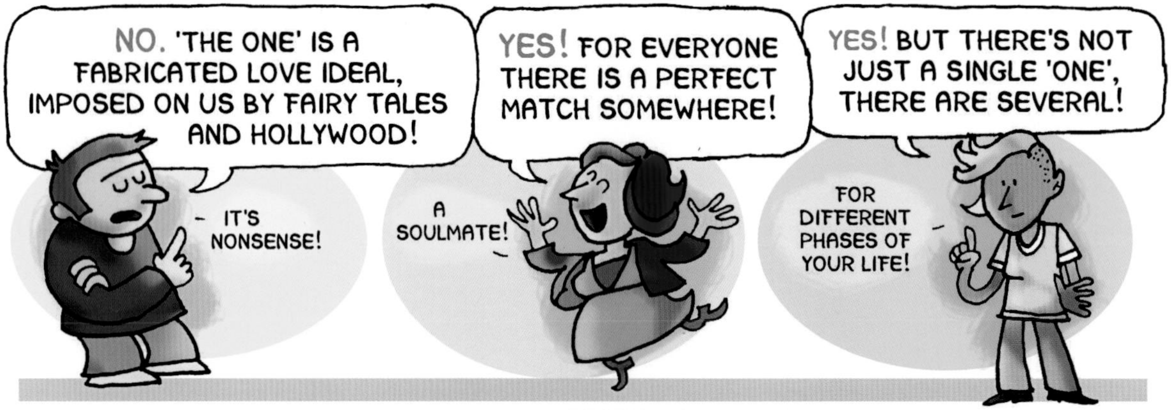
NO. 'THE ONE' IS A FABRICATED LOVE IDEAL, IMPOSED ON US BY FAIRY TALES AND HOLLYWOOD!
- IT'S NONSENSE!
YES! FOR EVERYONE THERE IS A PERFECT MATCH SOMEWHERE!
A SOULMATE!
YES! BUT THERE'S NOT JUST A SINGLE 'ONE', THERE ARE SEVERAL!
FOR DIFFERENT PHASES OF YOUR LIFE!

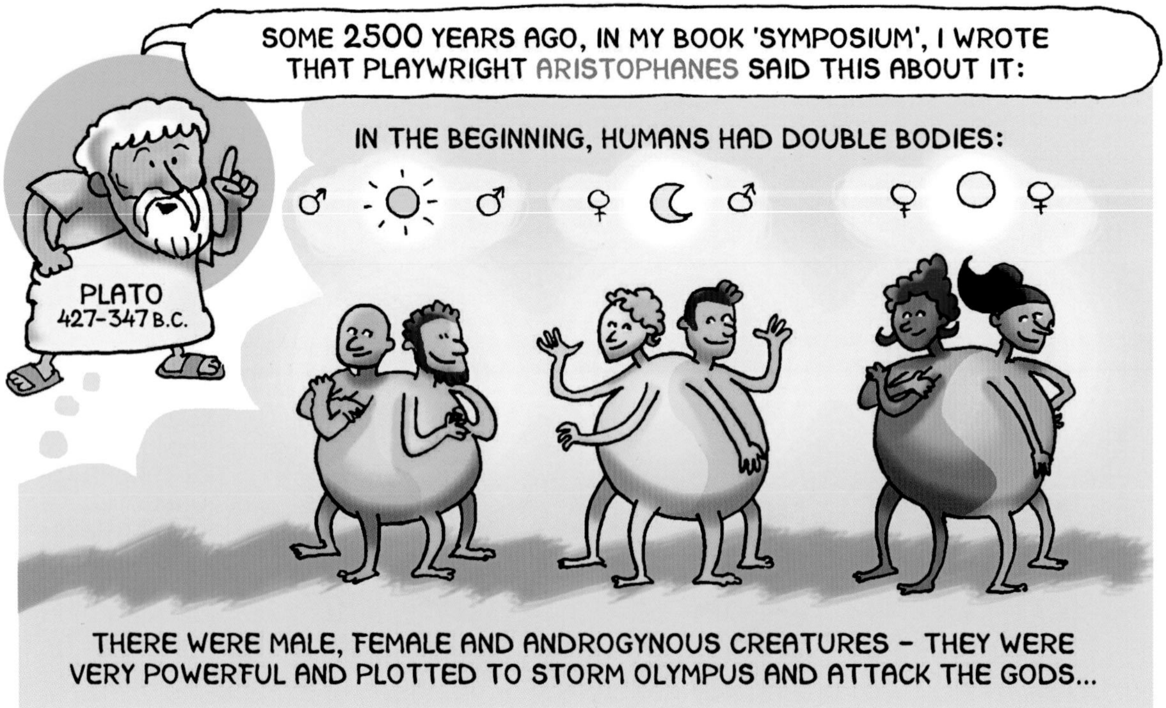
SOME 2500 YEARS AGO, IN MY BOOK 'SYMPOSIUM', I WROTE THAT PLAYWRIGHT ARISTOPHANES SAID THIS ABOUT IT:
PLATO
427–347 B.C.
IN THE BEGINNING, HUMANS HAD DOUBLE BODIES:
♂ ♂ ♀ ♂ ♀ ♀
THERE WERE MALE, FEMALE AND ANDROGYNOUS CREATURES – THEY WERE VERY POWERFUL AND PLOTTED TO STORM OLYMPUS AND ATTACK THE GODS...

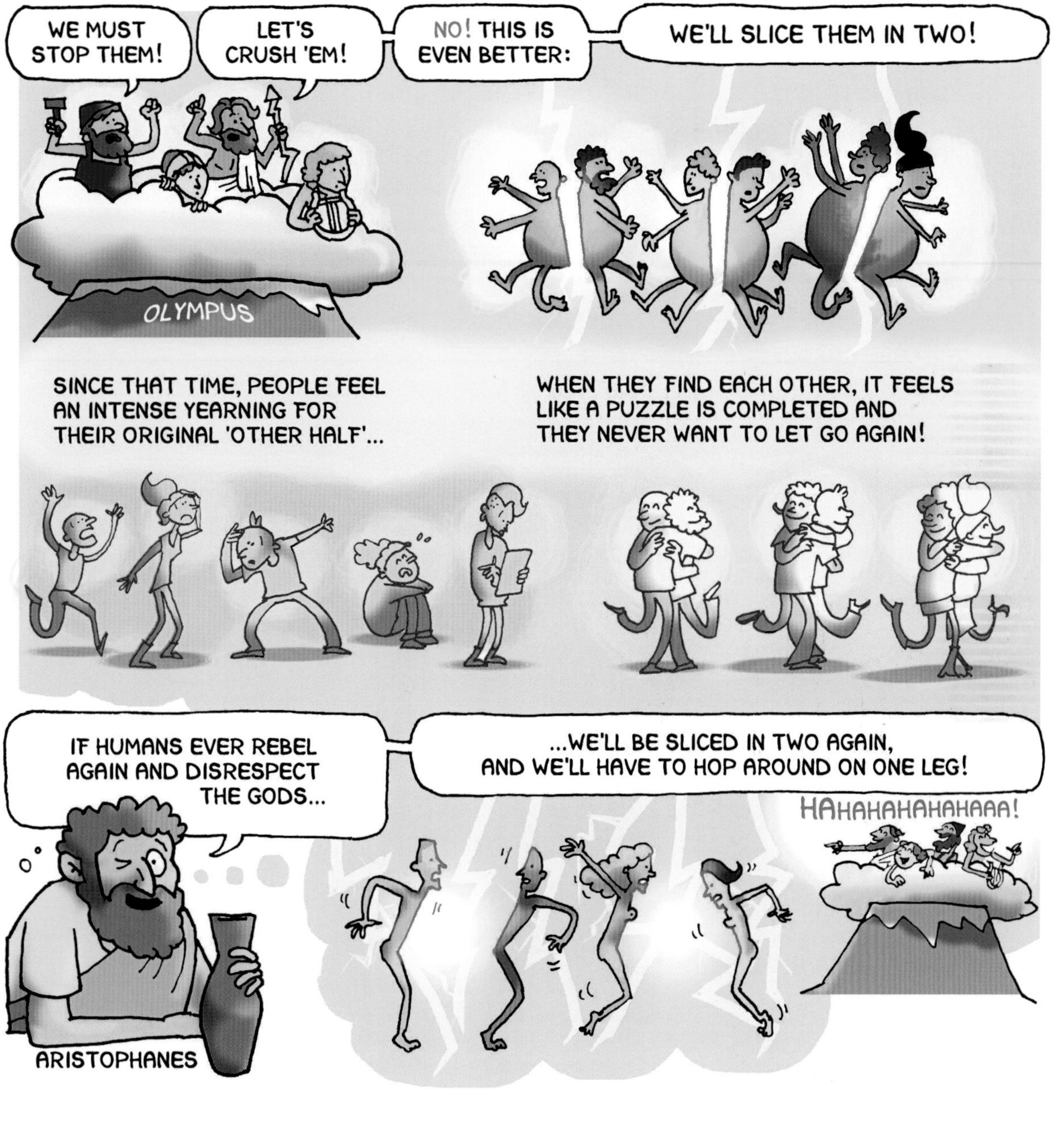
WE MUST STOP THEM!
LET'S CRUSH 'EM!
NO! THIS IS EVEN BETTER:
WE'LL SLICE THEM IN TWO!
OLYMPUS
SINCE THAT TIME, PEOPLE FEEL AN INTENSE YEARNING FOR THEIR ORIGINAL 'OTHER HALF'...
WHEN THEY FIND EACH OTHER, IT FEELS LIKE A PUZZLE IS COMPLETED AND THEY NEVER WANT TO LET GO AGAIN!
IF HUMANS EVER REBEL AGAIN AND DISRESPECT THE GODS...
...WE'LL BE SLICED IN TWO AGAIN, AND WE'LL HAVE TO HOP AROUND ON ONE LEG!
HAHAHAHAHAHAAA!
ARISTOPHANES

SOME SAY THAT EVERYONE GETS NOT ONE, BUT THREE GREAT LOVES:

1. YOUR FIRST LOVE	THE ONE WITH WHOM YOU EXPERIENCE LOVE FOR THE FIRST TIME, WHEN YOU THINK LOVE WILL LAST FOREVER....	CHARACTERISTICS: PASSION DRAMA IN THE MOMENT SHORT-TERM VISION LOTS OF SEX
2. THE LOVE YOU BUILD A FAMILY WITH	YOUR 'BUSINESS PARTNER' WITH WHOM YOU WORK TOWARD CREATING AND SUSTAINING YOUR OWN CLAN (WITH OR WITHOUT KIDS)	LONG-TERM VISION COMPROMISES GIVE + TAKE YOU GOTTA WORK ON IT COMMITMENT APPRECIATION GROWTH
3. THE LOVE YOU GROW OLD WITH	YOUR 'MATE' WITH WHOM YOU ENJOY LIFE AFTER FAMILY AND CAREER CEASE TO BE PRIORITIES	HARMONY ENJOYMENT FONDNESS DOING THINGS TOGETHER

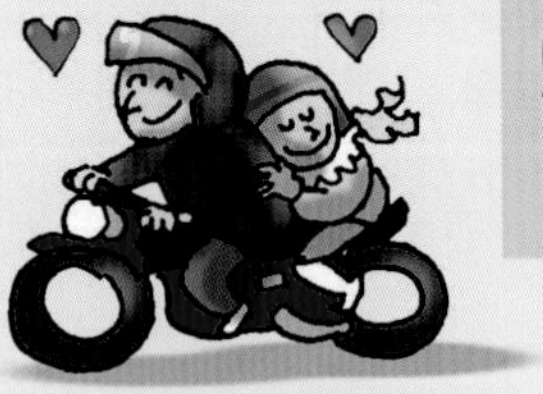

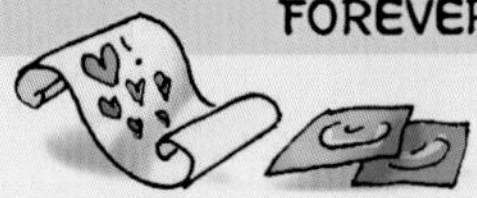

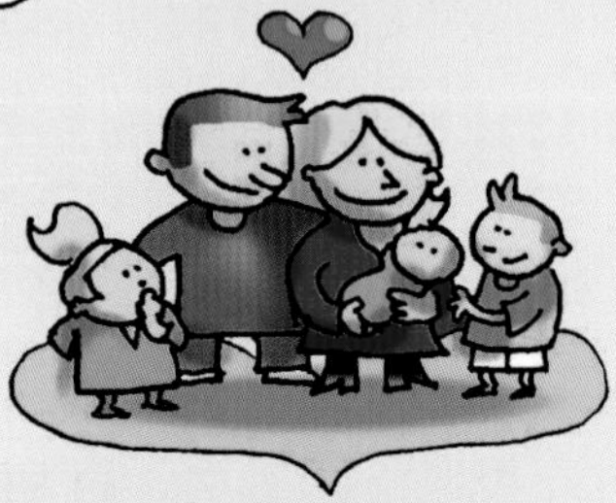

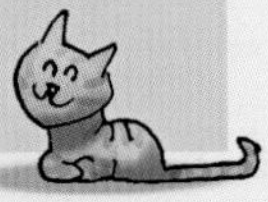

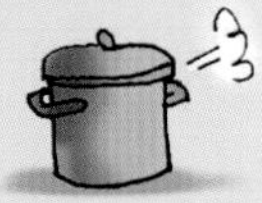

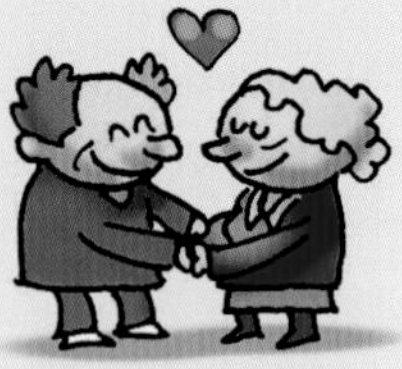

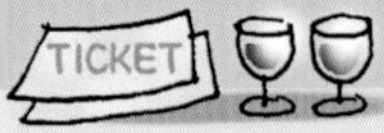
TICKET

OF COURSE, THESE THREE LOVES MIGHT TURN OUT TO BE THE SAME PERSON!

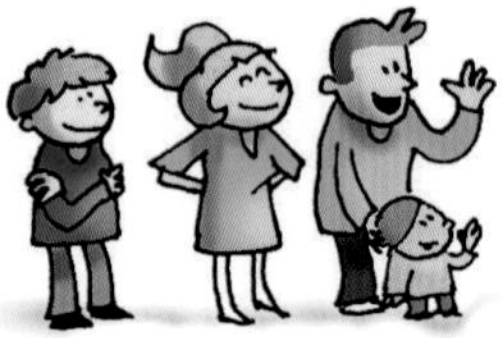

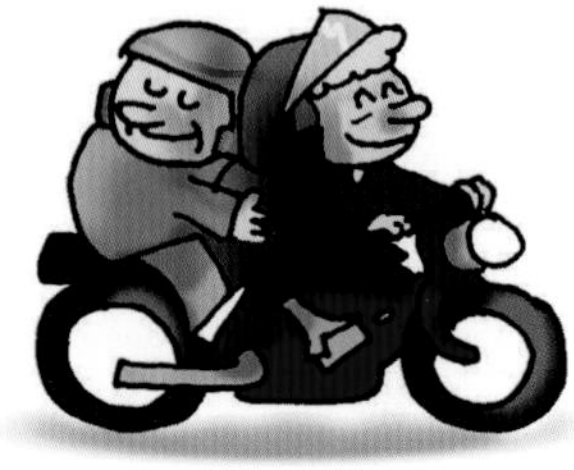

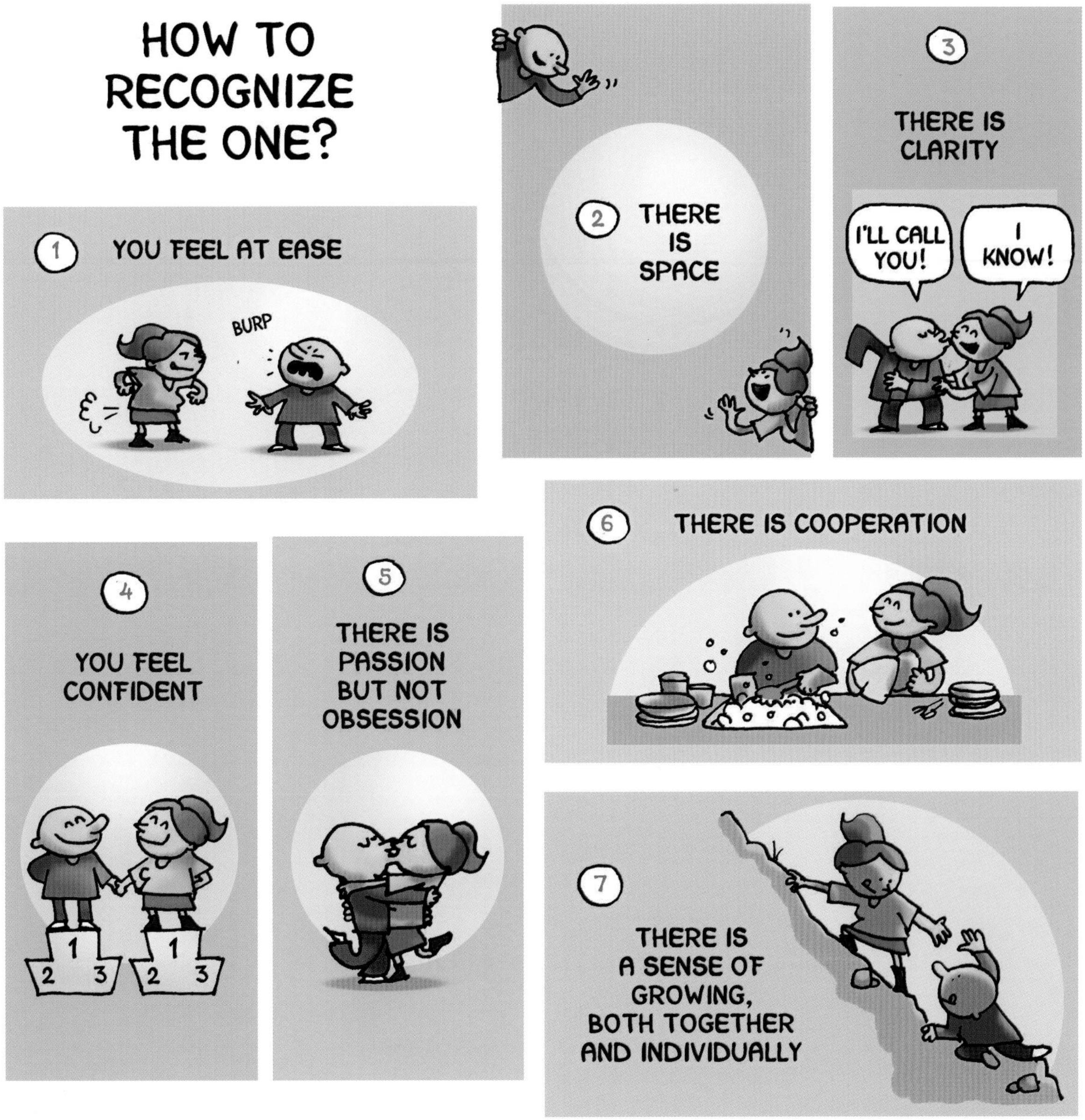
HOW TO RECOGNIZE THE ONE?
1 YOU FEEL AT EASE
BURP
2 THERE IS SPACE
3 THERE IS CLARITY
I'LL CALL YOU!
I KNOW!
4 YOU FEEL CONFIDENT
1 2 3
1 2 3
5 THERE IS PASSION BUT NOT OBSESSION
6 THERE IS COOPERATION
7 THERE IS A SENSE OF GROWING, BOTH TOGETHER AND INDIVIDUALLY

THE PERFECT MOMENT

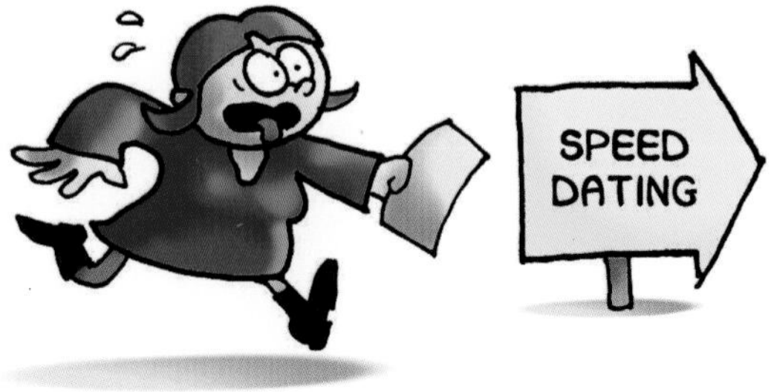
SPEED
DATING

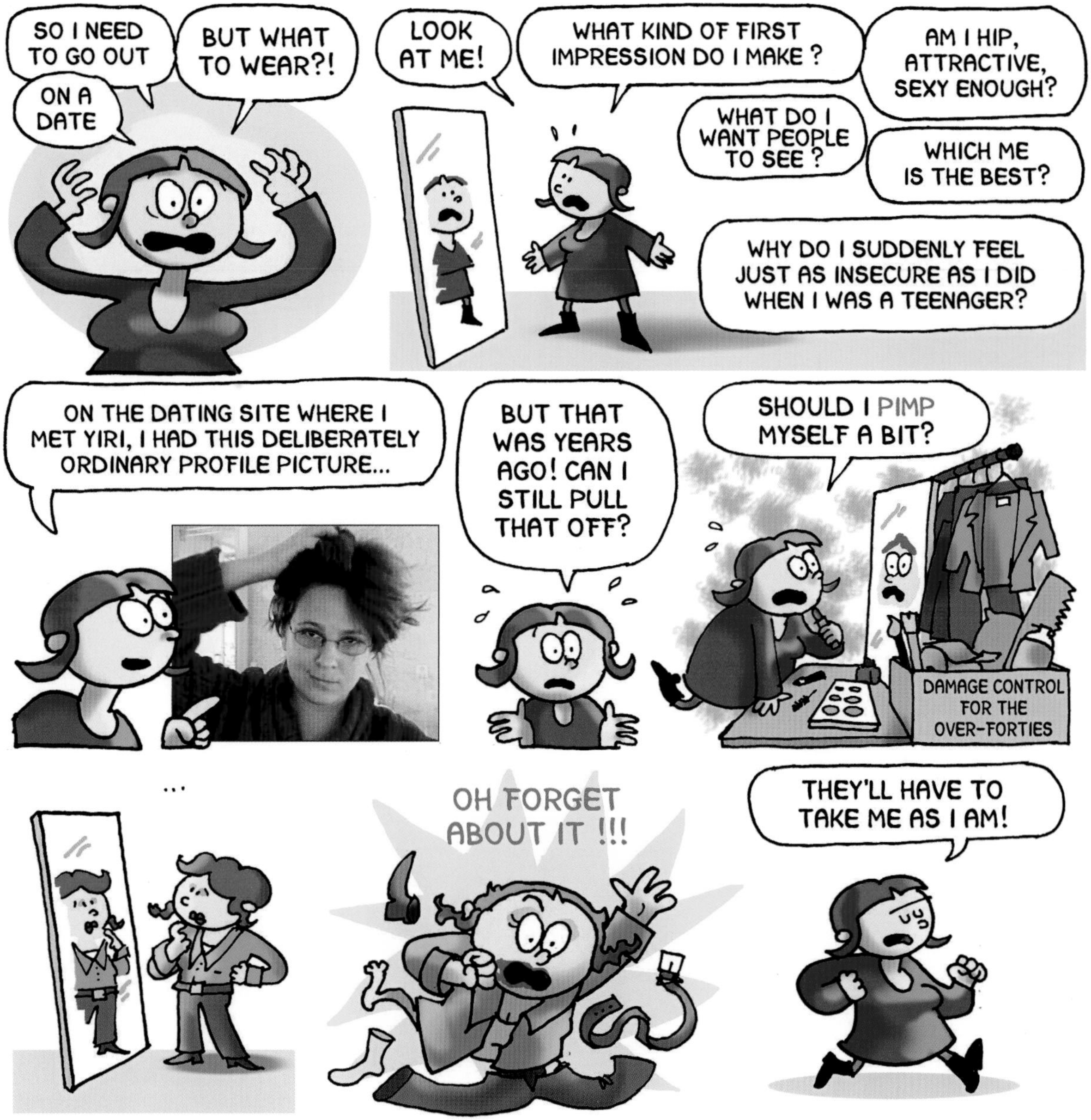
SO I NEED TO GO OUT
ON A DATE
BUT WHAT TO WEAR?!
LOOK AT ME!
WHAT KIND OF FIRST IMPRESSION DO I MAKE ?
AM I HIP, ATTRACTIVE, SEXY ENOUGH?
WHAT DO I WANT PEOPLE TO SEE ?
WHICH ME IS THE BEST?
WHY DO I SUDDENLY FEEL JUST AS INSECURE AS I DID WHEN I WAS A TEENAGER?
ON THE DATING SITE WHERE I MET YIRI, I HAD THIS DELIBERATELY ORDINARY PROFILE PICTURE...
BUT THAT WAS YEARS AGO! CAN I STILL PULL THAT OFF?
SHOULD I PIMP MYSELF A BIT?
DAMAGE CONTROL FOR THE OVER-FORTIES
...
OH FORGET ABOUT IT !!!
THEY'LL HAVE TO TAKE ME AS I AM!

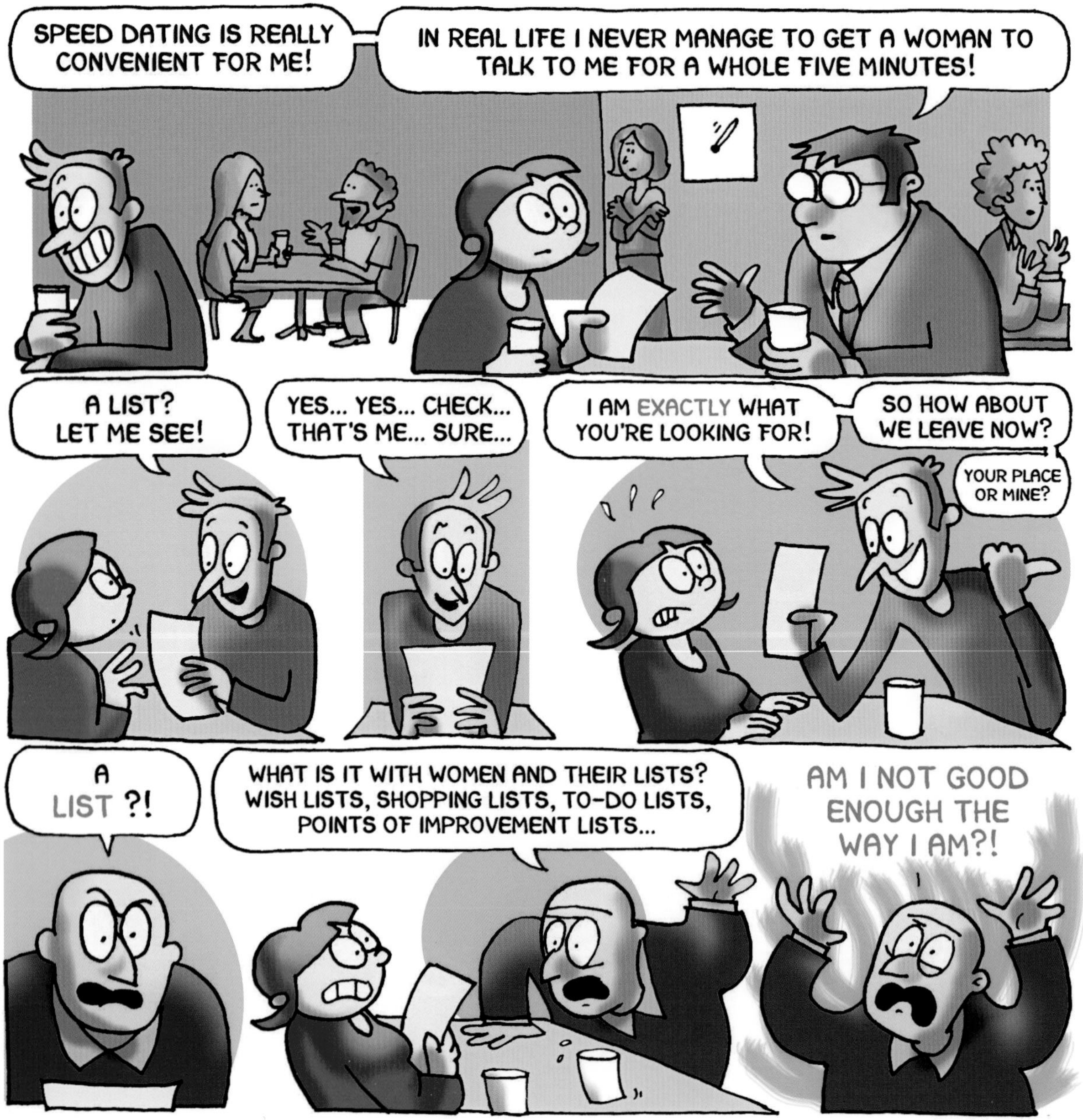
SPEED DATING IS REALLY CONVENIENT FOR ME!
IN REAL LIFE I NEVER MANAGE TO GET A WOMAN TO TALK TO ME FOR A WHOLE FIVE MINUTES!
A LIST? LET ME SEE!
YES... YES... CHECK... THAT'S ME... SURE...
I AM EXACTLY WHAT YOU'RE LOOKING FOR!
SO HOW ABOUT WE LEAVE NOW?
YOUR PLACE OR MINE?
A LIST ?!
WHAT IS IT WITH WOMEN AND THEIR LISTS? WISH LISTS, SHOPPING LISTS, TO-DO LISTS, POINTS OF IMPROVEMENT LISTS...
AM I NOT GOOD ENOUGH THE WAY I AM?!

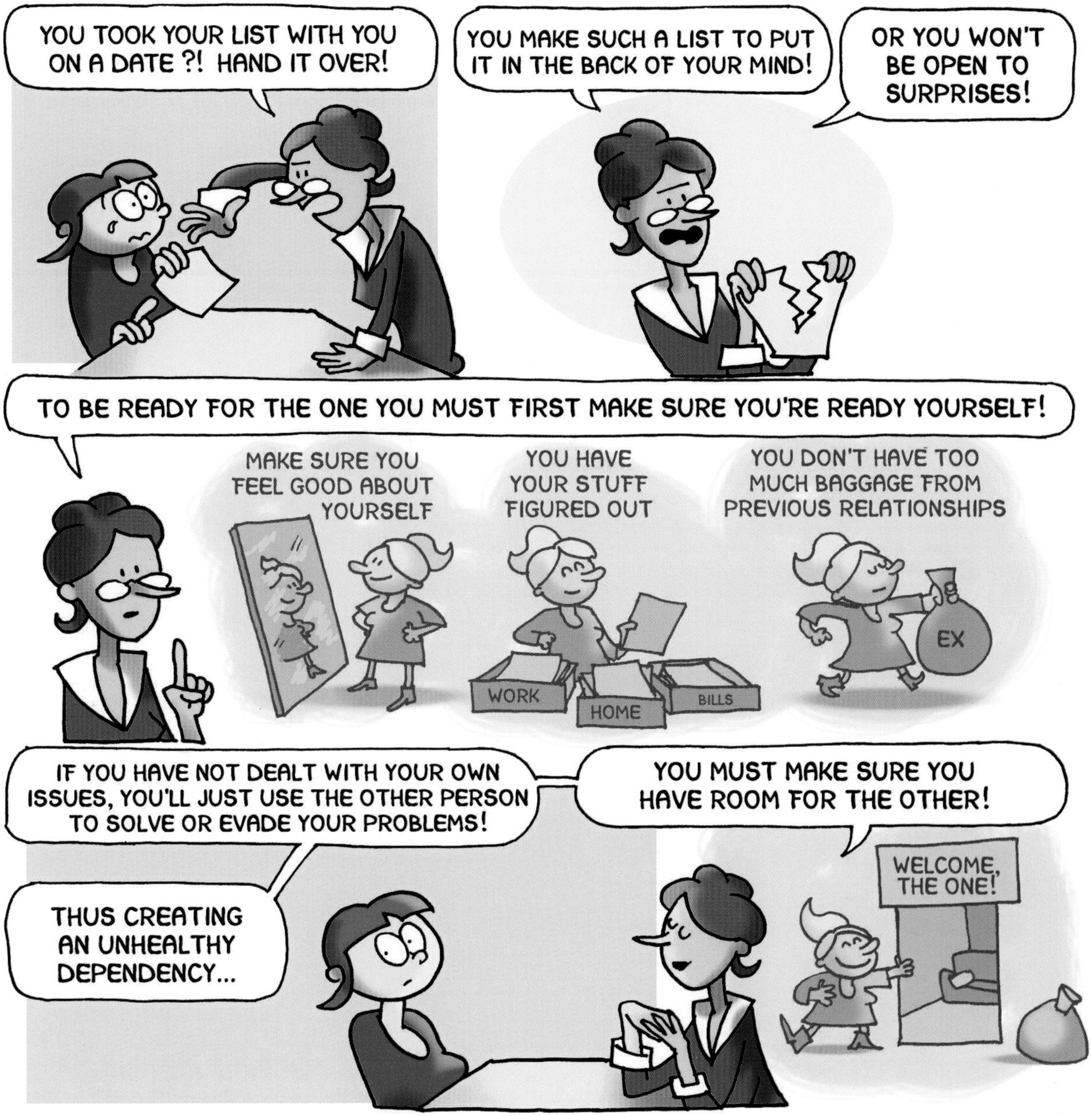
YOU TOOK YOUR LIST WITH YOU ON A DATE ?! HAND IT OVER!
YOU MAKE SUCH A LIST TO PUT IT IN THE BACK OF YOUR MIND!
OR YOU WON'T BE OPEN TO SURPRISES!
TO BE READY FOR THE ONE YOU MUST FIRST MAKE SURE YOU'RE READY YOURSELF!
MAKE SURE YOU FEEL GOOD ABOUT YOURSELF
YOU HAVE YOUR STUFF FIGURED OUT
WORK
HOME
BILLS
YOU DON'T HAVE TOO MUCH BAGGAGE FROM PREVIOUS RELATIONSHIPS
EX
IF YOU HAVE NOT DEALT WITH YOUR OWN ISSUES, YOU'LL JUST USE THE OTHER PERSON TO SOLVE OR EVADE YOUR PROBLEMS!
THUS CREATING AN UNHEALTHY DEPENDENCY...
YOU MUST MAKE SURE YOU HAVE ROOM FOR THE OTHER!
WELCOME, THE ONE!

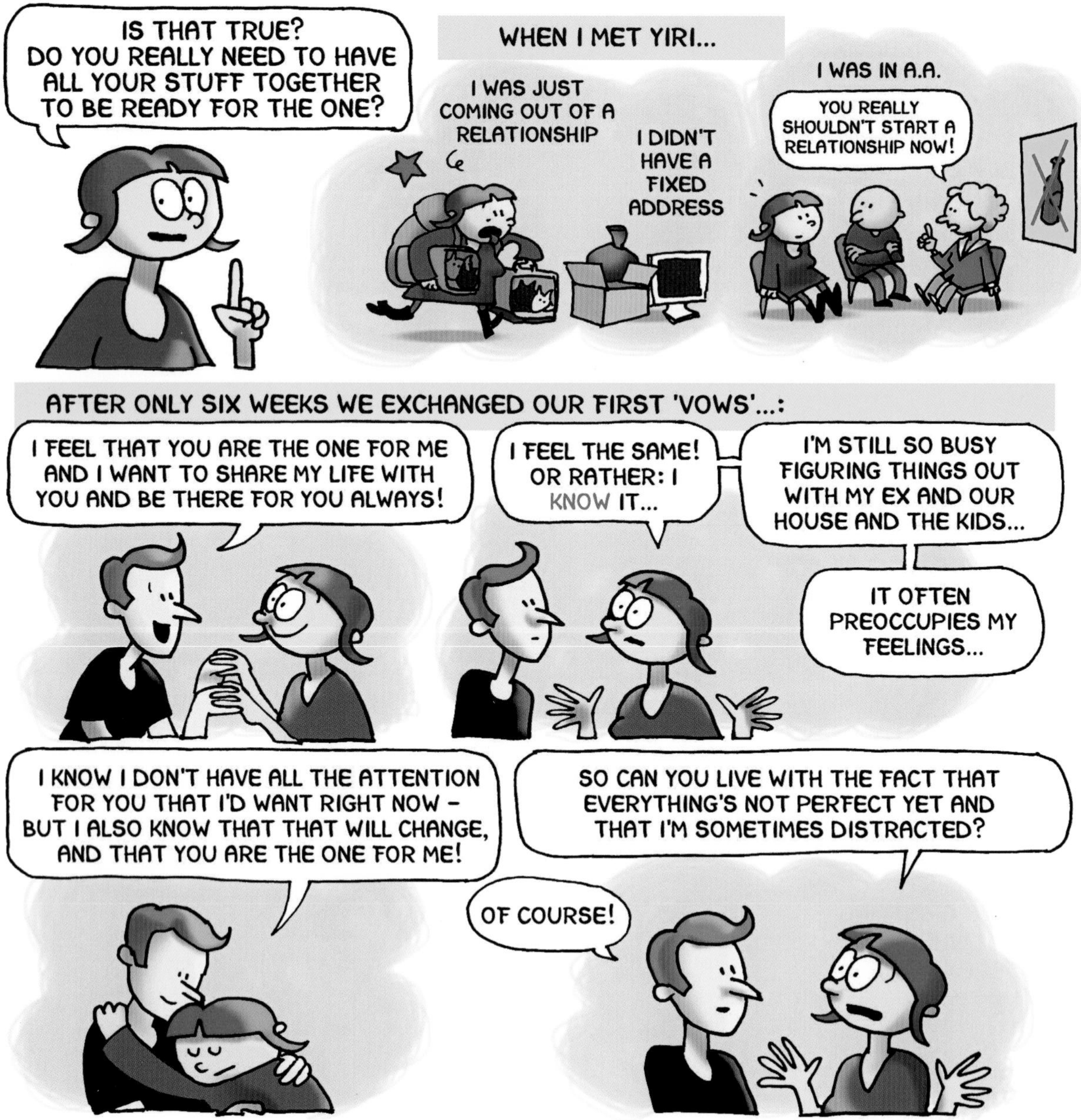
IS THAT TRUE? DO YOU REALLY NEED TO HAVE ALL YOUR STUFF TOGETHER TO BE READY FOR THE ONE?
WHEN I MET YIRI...
I WAS JUST COMING OUT OF A RELATIONSHIP
I DIDN'T HAVE A FIXED ADDRESS
I WAS IN A.A.
YOU REALLY SHOULDN'T START A RELATIONSHIP NOW!
AFTER ONLY SIX WEEKS WE EXCHANGED OUR FIRST 'VOWS'...:
I FEEL THAT YOU ARE THE ONE FOR ME AND I WANT TO SHARE MY LIFE WITH YOU AND BE THERE FOR YOU ALWAYS!
I FEEL THE SAME! OR RATHER: I KNOW IT...
I'M STILL SO BUSY FIGURING THINGS OUT WITH MY EX AND OUR HOUSE AND THE KIDS...
IT OFTEN PREOCCUPIES MY FEELINGS...
I KNOW I DON'T HAVE ALL THE ATTENTION FOR YOU THAT I'D WANT RIGHT NOW – BUT I ALSO KNOW THAT THAT WILL CHANGE, AND THAT YOU ARE THE ONE FOR ME!
SO CAN YOU LIVE WITH THE FACT THAT EVERYTHING'S NOT PERFECT YET AND THAT I'M SOMETIMES DISTRACTED?
OF COURSE!

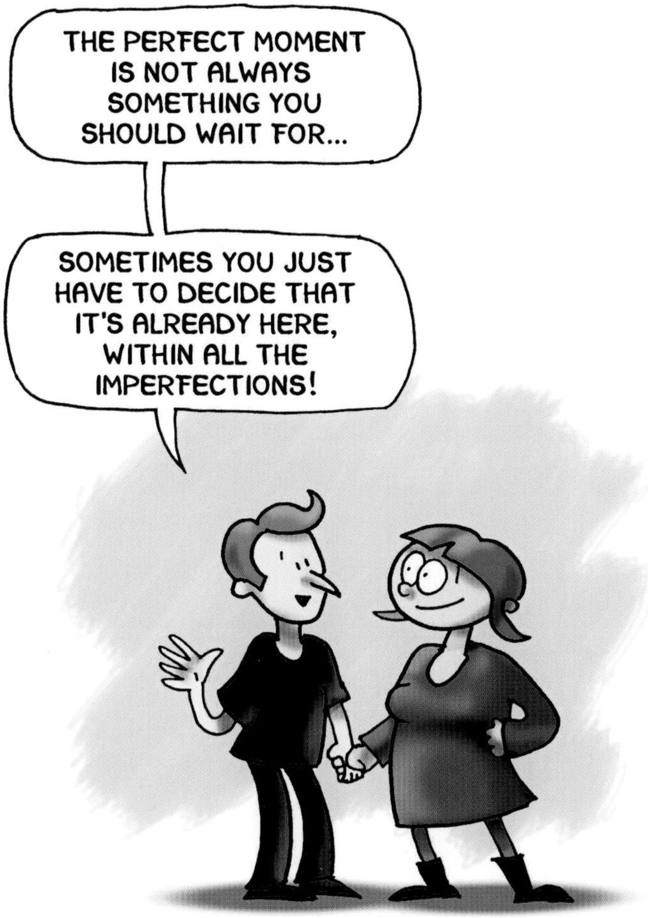
THE PERFECT MOMENT IS NOT ALWAYS SOMETHING YOU SHOULD WAIT FOR...
SOMETIMES YOU JUST HAVE TO DECIDE THAT IT'S ALREADY HERE, WITHIN ALL THE IMPERFECTIONS!

THE TRAGEDY OF ROMANCE

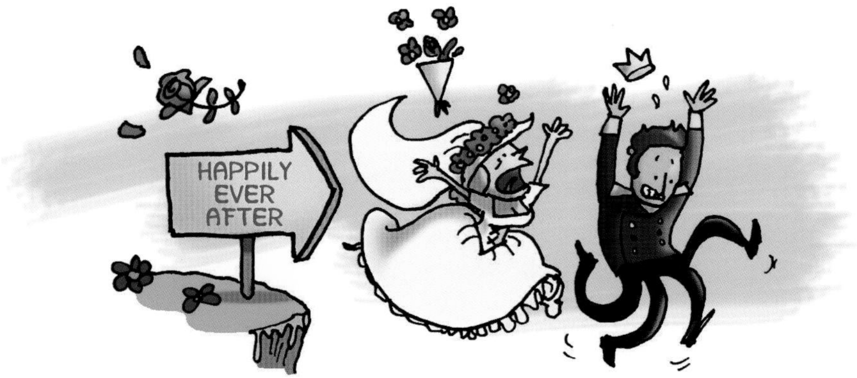
HAPPILY
EVER
AFTER

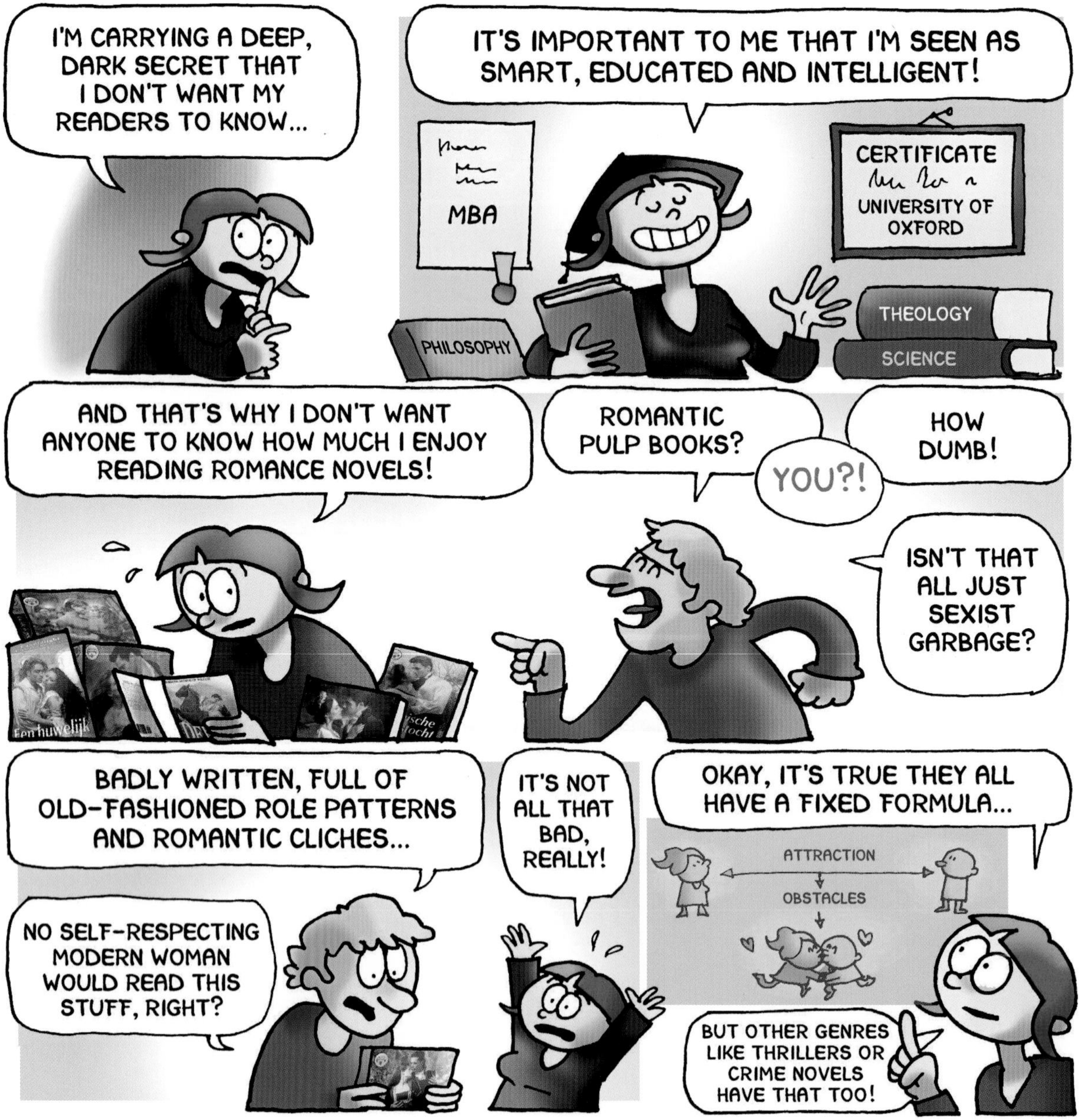
I'M CARRYING A DEEP, DARK SECRET THAT I DON'T WANT MY READERS TO KNOW...
IT'S IMPORTANT TO ME THAT I'M SEEN AS SMART, EDUCATED AND INTELLIGENT!
MBA
CERTIFICATE
UNIVERSITY OF OXFORD
PHILOSOPHY
THEOLOGY
SCIENCE
AND THAT'S WHY I DON'T WANT ANYONE TO KNOW HOW MUCH I ENJOY READING ROMANCE NOVELS!
ROMANTIC PULP BOOKS?
YOU?!
HOW DUMB!
ISN'T THAT ALL JUST SEXIST GARBAGE?
Een huwelijk
BADLY WRITTEN, FULL OF OLD-FASHIONED ROLE PATTERNS AND ROMANTIC CLICHES...
NO SELF-RESPECTING MODERN WOMAN WOULD READ THIS STUFF, RIGHT?
IT'S NOT ALL THAT BAD, REALLY!
OKAY, IT'S TRUE THEY ALL HAVE A FIXED FORMULA...
ATTRACTION
OBSTACLES
BUT OTHER GENRES LIKE THRILLERS OR CRIME NOVELS HAVE THAT TOO!

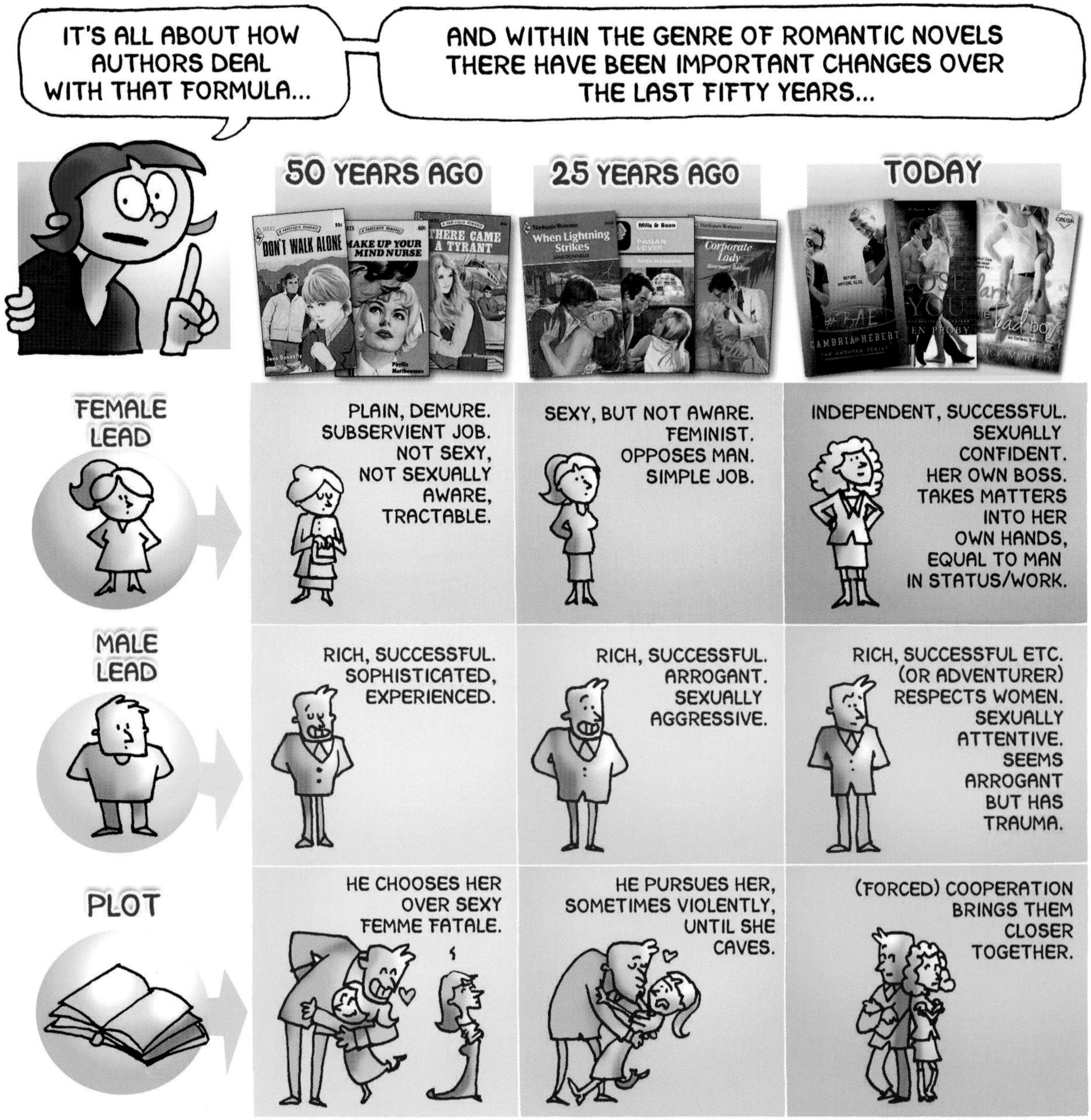
IT'S ALL ABOUT HOW AUTHORS DEAL WITH THAT FORMULA...
AND WITHIN THE GENRE OF ROMANTIC NOVELS THERE HAVE BEEN IMPORTANT CHANGES OVER THE LAST FIFTY YEARS...
50 YEARS AGO
25 YEARS AGO
TODAY
DON'T WALK ALONE
MAKE UP YOUR MIND NURSE
THERE CAME A TYRANT
When Lightning Strikes
Corporate Lady
FEMALE LEAD
PLAIN, DEMURE. SUBSERVIENT JOB. NOT SEXY, NOT SEXUALLY AWARE, TRACTABLE.
SEXY, BUT NOT AWARE. FEMINIST. OPPOSES MAN. SIMPLE JOB.
INDEPENDENT, SUCCESSFUL. SEXUALLY CONFIDENT. HER OWN BOSS. TAKES MATTERS INTO HER OWN HANDS, EQUAL TO MAN IN STATUS/WORK.
MALE LEAD
RICH, SUCCESSFUL. SOPHISTICATED, EXPERIENCED.
RICH, SUCCESSFUL. ARROGANT. SEXUALLY AGGRESSIVE.
RICH, SUCCESSFUL ETC. (OR ADVENTURER) RESPECTS WOMEN. SEXUALLY ATTENTIVE. SEEMS ARROGANT BUT HAS TRAUMA.
PLOT
HE CHOOSES HER OVER SEXY FEMME FATALE.
HE PURSUES HER, SOMETIMES VIOLENTLY, UNTIL SHE CAVES.
(FORCED) COOPERATION BRINGS THEM CLOSER TOGETHER.

I THINK IT'S FASCINATING HOW THESE NOVELS REFLECT THEIR CONTEMPORARY CULTURAL NOTIONS OF ROMANCE!

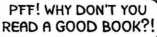

AND I JUST LIKE TO READ ABOUT LOVE! RATHER THAN ABOUT CRIME OR HORROR.

PFF! WHY DON'T YOU READ A GOOD BOOK?!

I DO READ OTHER BOOKS, YOU KNOW! IT'S JUST THAT I LIKE THESE OCCASIONALLY!

COMPARE IT WITH FOOD!

IF TRUE LITERATURE IS THE SAME AS A FOUR-COURSE MEAL...

...THEN THIS IS CHOCOLATE!

NOT NECESSARILY GOOD, BUT DEFINITELY A SWEET, DELECTABLE TREAT!

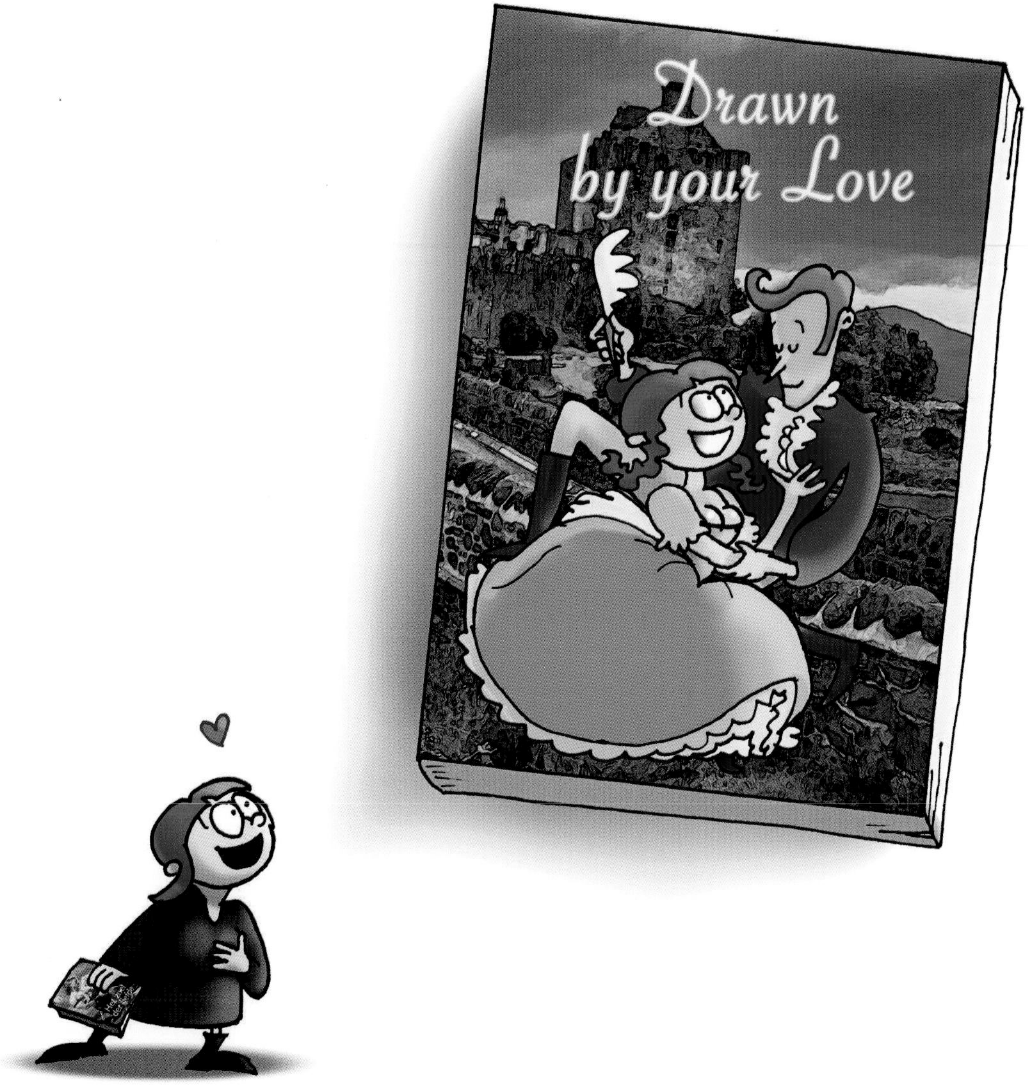
Drawn
by your Love

FAIRY TALE

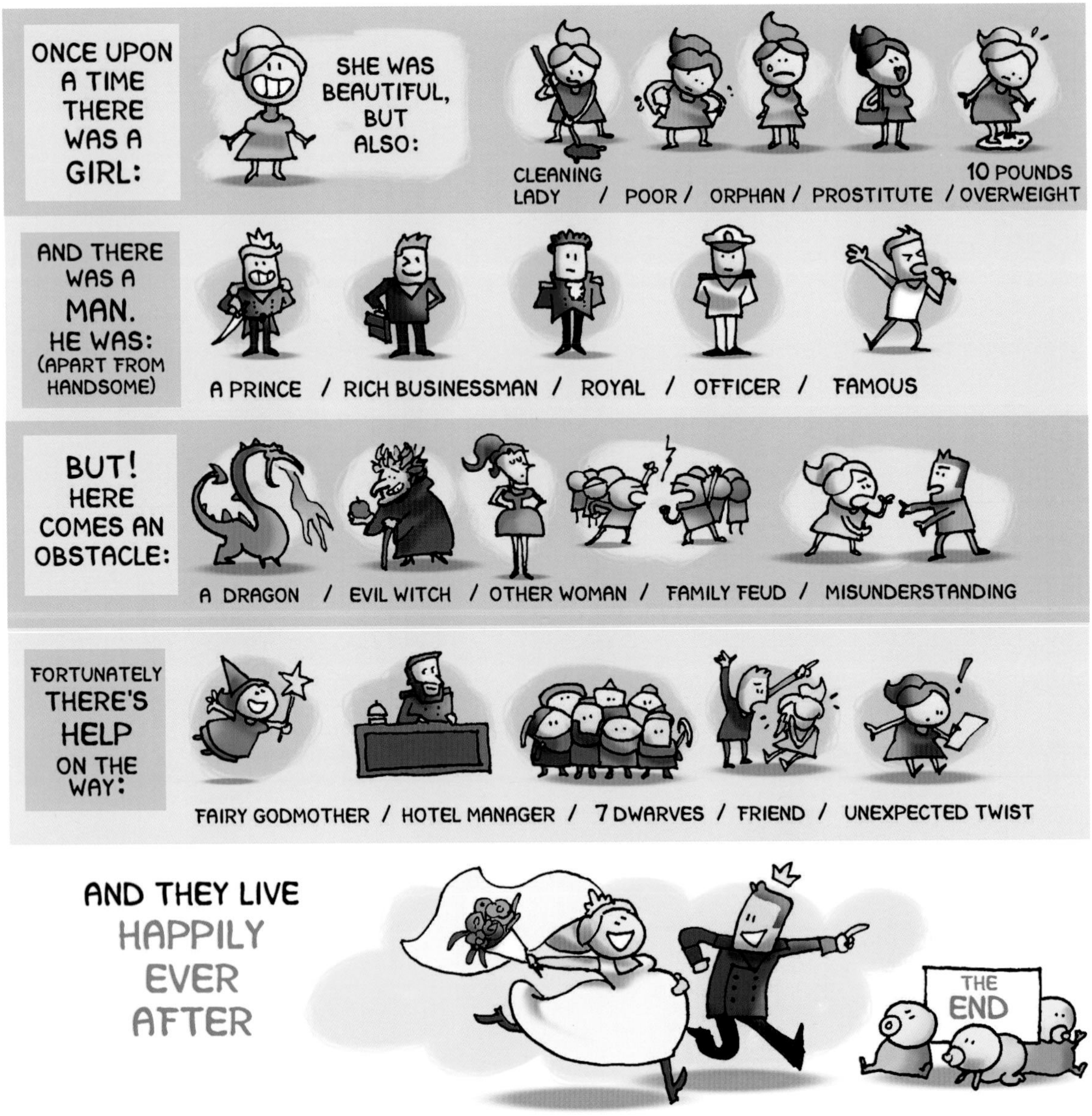
ONCE UPON A TIME THERE WAS A GIRL:
SHE WAS BEAUTIFUL, BUT ALSO:
CLEANING LADY / POOR / ORPHAN / PROSTITUTE / 10 POUNDS OVERWEIGHT
AND THERE WAS A MAN. HE WAS: (APART FROM HANDSOME)
A PRINCE / RICH BUSINESSMAN / ROYAL / OFFICER / FAMOUS
BUT! HERE COMES AN OBSTACLE:
A DRAGON / EVIL WITCH / OTHER WOMAN / FAMILY FEUD / MISUNDERSTANDING
FORTUNATELY THERE'S HELP ON THE WAY:
FAIRY GODMOTHER / HOTEL MANAGER / 7 DWARVES / FRIEND / UNEXPECTED TWIST
AND THEY LIVE HAPPILY EVER AFTER
THE END

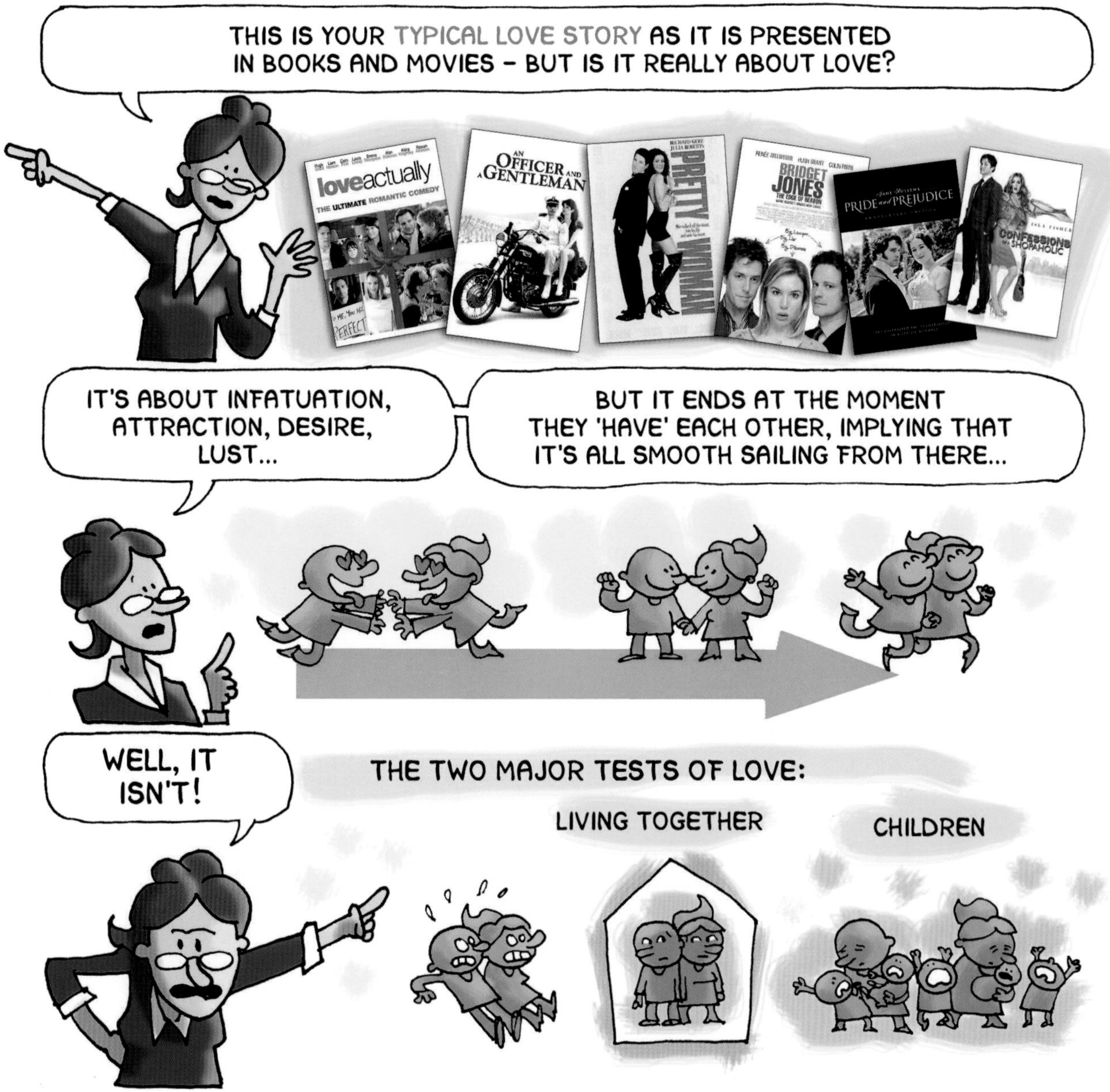
THIS IS YOUR TYPICAL LOVE STORY AS IT IS PRESENTED IN BOOKS AND MOVIES – BUT IS IT REALLY ABOUT LOVE?
love actually
THE ULTIMATE ROMANTIC COMEDY
AN OFFICER AND A GENTLEMAN
PRETTY WOMAN
BRIDGET JONES
THE EDGE OF REASON
PRIDE and PREJUDICE
CONFESSIONS OF A SHOPAHOLIC
IT'S ABOUT INFATUATION, ATTRACTION, DESIRE, LUST...
BUT IT ENDS AT THE MOMENT THEY 'HAVE' EACH OTHER, IMPLYING THAT IT'S ALL SMOOTH SAILING FROM THERE...
WELL, IT ISN'T!
THE TWO MAJOR TESTS OF LOVE:
LIVING TOGETHER
CHILDREN

THE DANGERS OF LIVING TOGETHER

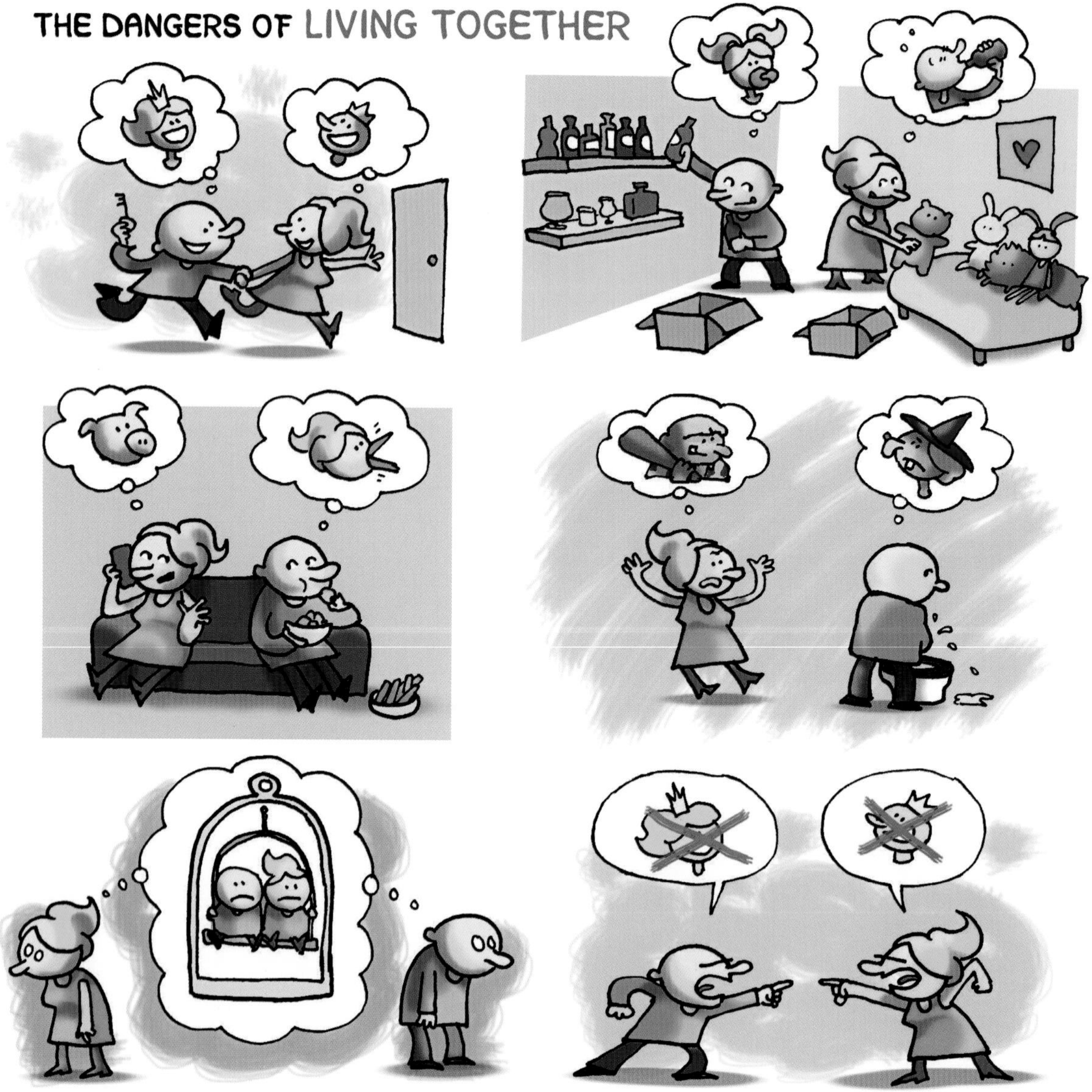

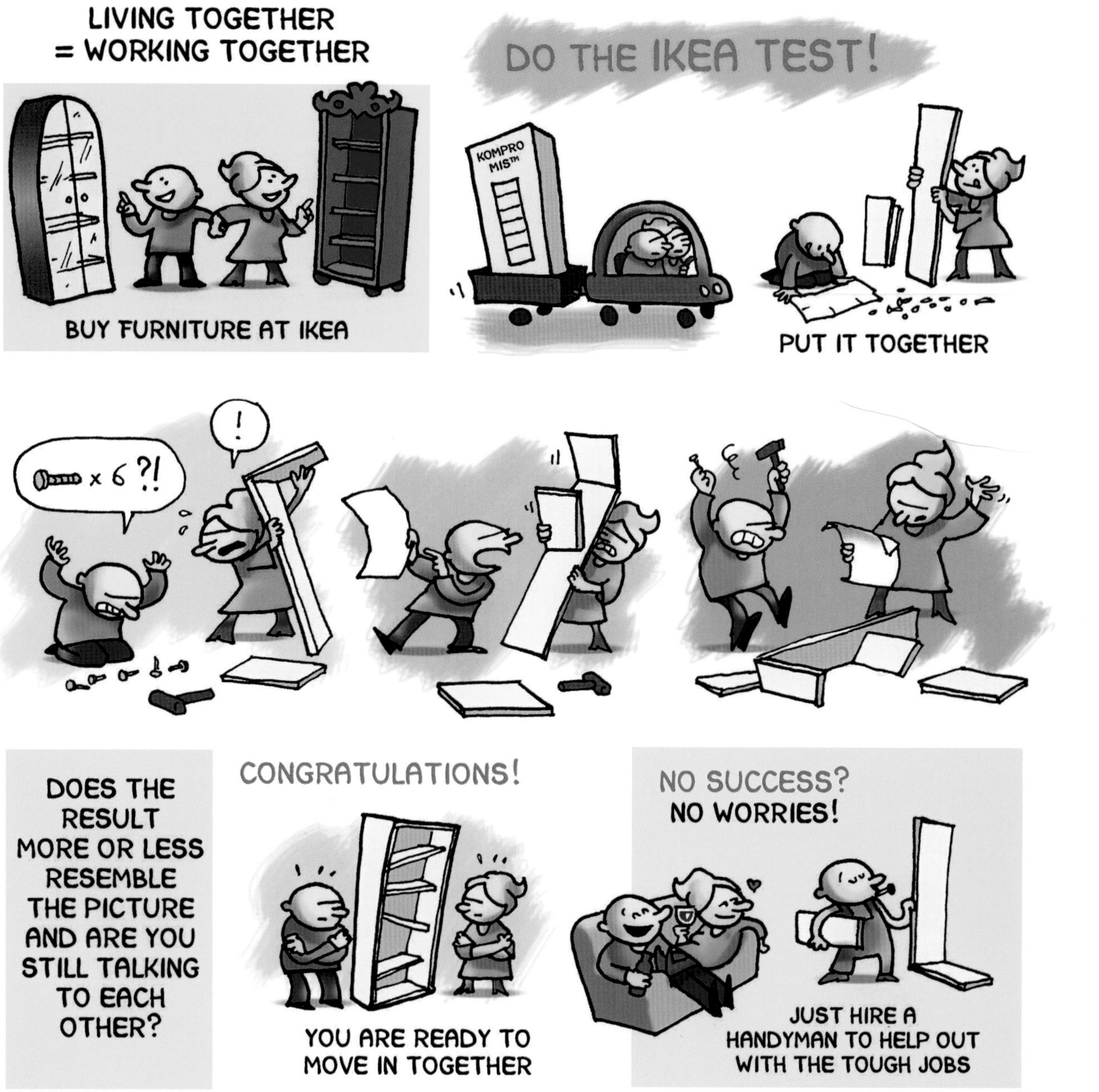
LIVING TOGETHER
= WORKING TOGETHER
BUY FURNITURE AT IKEA
DO THE IKEA TEST!
KOMPRO MIS™
PUT IT TOGETHER
x 6 ?!
!
DOES THE RESULT MORE OR LESS RESEMBLE THE PICTURE AND ARE YOU STILL TALKING TO EACH OTHER?
CONGRATULATIONS!
YOU ARE READY TO MOVE IN TOGETHER
NO SUCCESS?
NO WORRIES!
JUST HIRE A HANDYMAN TO HELP OUT WITH THE TOUGH JOBS

THE DANGER OF HAVING CHILDREN

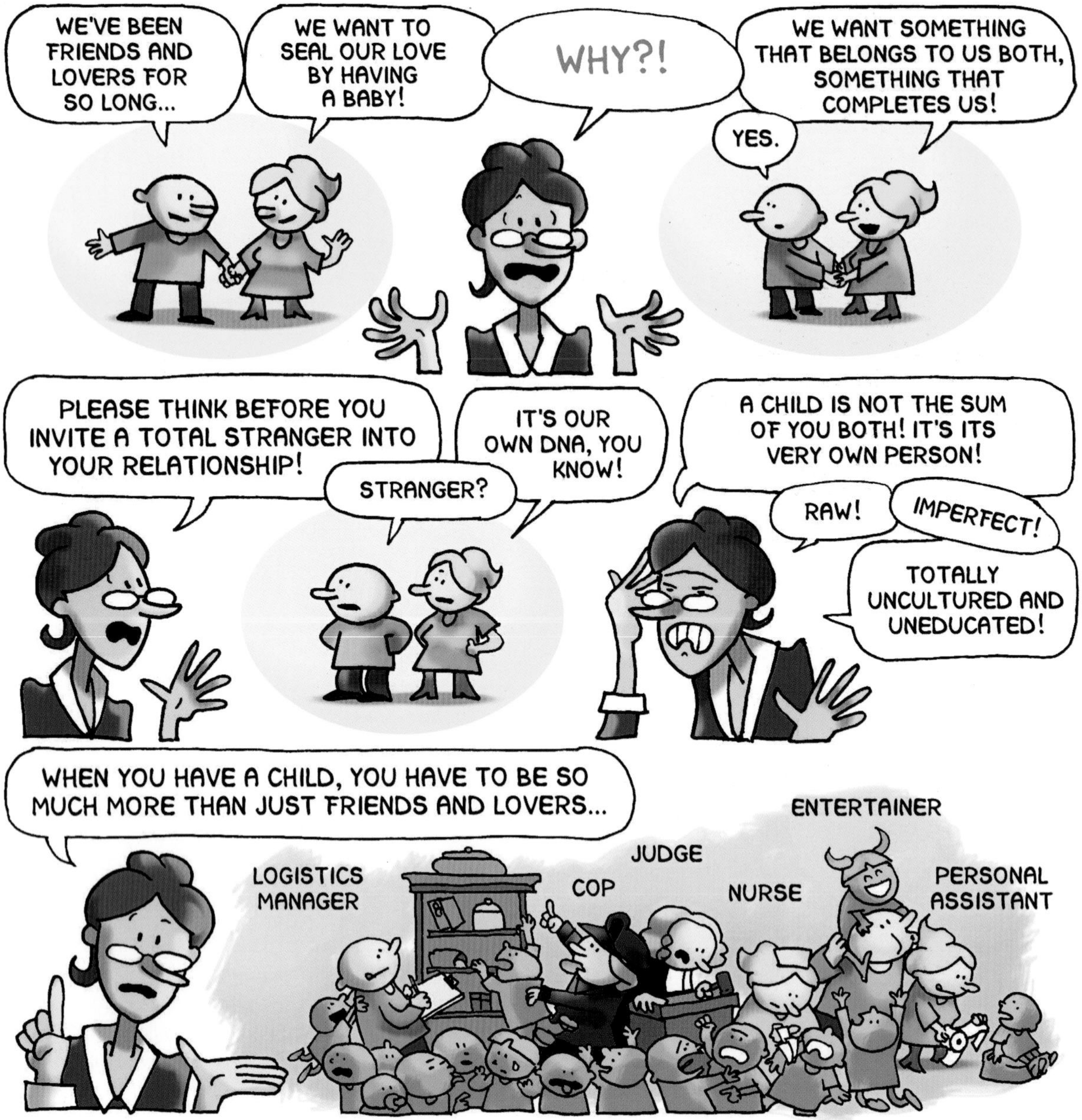

WE'VE BEEN FRIENDS AND LOVERS FOR SO LONG...
WE WANT TO SEAL OUR LOVE BY HAVING A BABY!
WHY?!
WE WANT SOMETHING THAT BELONGS TO US BOTH, SOMETHING THAT COMPLETES US!
YES.
PLEASE THINK BEFORE YOU INVITE A TOTAL STRANGER INTO YOUR RELATIONSHIP!
STRANGER?
IT'S OUR OWN DNA, YOU KNOW!
A CHILD IS NOT THE SUM OF YOU BOTH! IT'S ITS VERY OWN PERSON!
RAW!
IMPERFECT!
TOTALLY UNCULTURED AND UNEDUCATED!
WHEN YOU HAVE A CHILD, YOU HAVE TO BE SO MUCH MORE THAN JUST FRIENDS AND LOVERS...
LOGISTICS MANAGER
COP
JUDGE
NURSE
ENTERTAINER
PERSONAL ASSISTANT

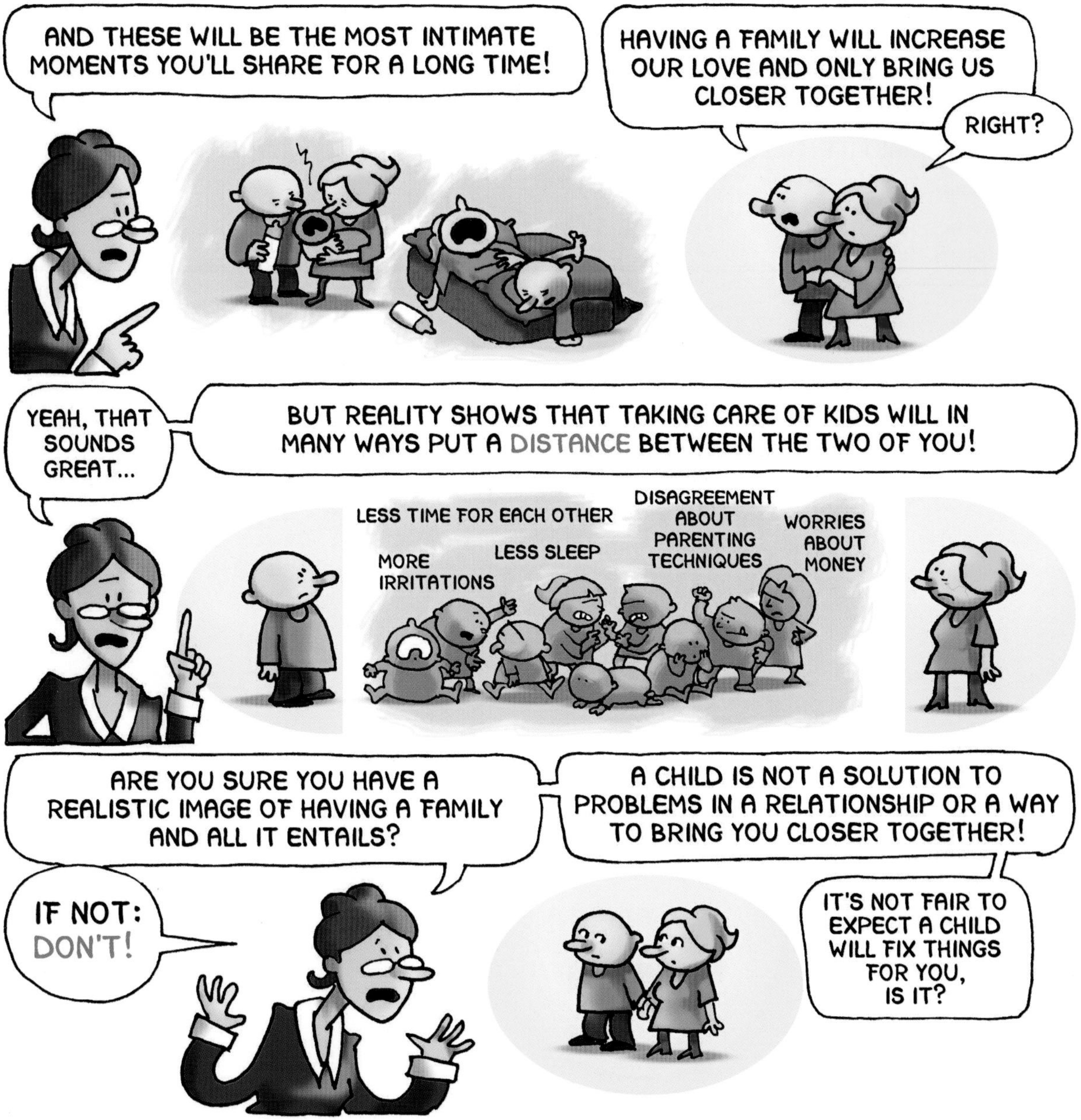
AND THESE WILL BE THE MOST INTIMATE MOMENTS YOU'LL SHARE FOR A LONG TIME!
HAVING A FAMILY WILL INCREASE OUR LOVE AND ONLY BRING US CLOSER TOGETHER!
RIGHT?
YEAH, THAT SOUNDS GREAT...
BUT REALITY SHOWS THAT TAKING CARE OF KIDS WILL IN MANY WAYS PUT A DISTANCE BETWEEN THE TWO OF YOU!
LESS TIME FOR EACH OTHER
MORE IRRITATIONS
LESS SLEEP
DISAGREEMENT ABOUT PARENTING TECHNIQUES
WORRIES ABOUT MONEY
ARE YOU SURE YOU HAVE A REALISTIC IMAGE OF HAVING A FAMILY AND ALL IT ENTAILS?
A CHILD IS NOT A SOLUTION TO PROBLEMS IN A RELATIONSHIP OR A WAY TO BRING YOU CLOSER TOGETHER!
IF NOT: DON'T!
IT'S NOT FAIR TO EXPECT A CHILD WILL FIX THINGS FOR YOU, IS IT?

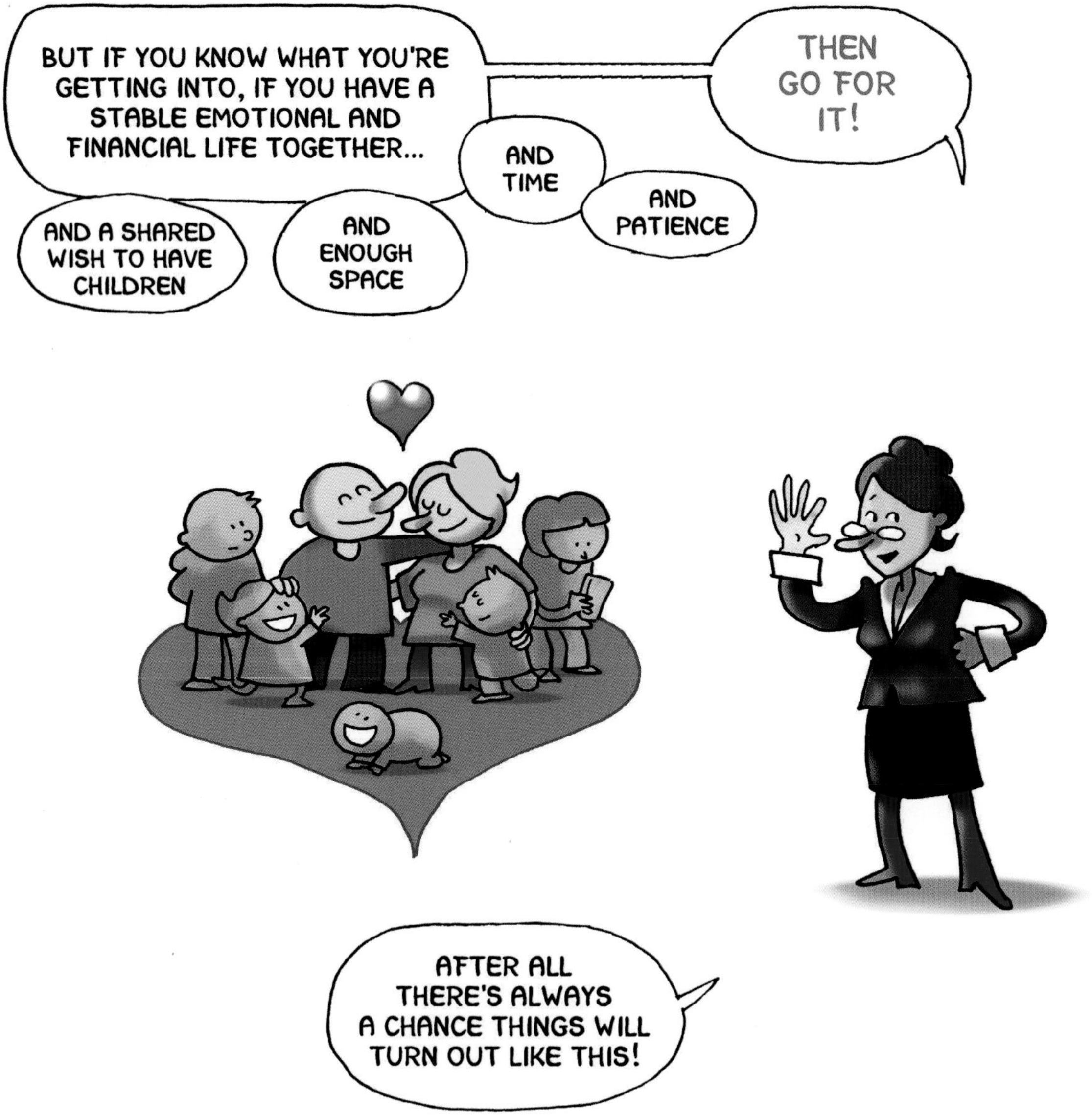
BUT IF YOU KNOW WHAT YOU'RE GETTING INTO, IF YOU HAVE A STABLE EMOTIONAL AND FINANCIAL LIFE TOGETHER...
AND A SHARED WISH TO HAVE CHILDREN
AND ENOUGH SPACE
AND TIME
AND PATIENCE
THEN GO FOR IT!
AFTER ALL THERE'S ALWAYS A CHANCE THINGS WILL TURN OUT LIKE THIS!

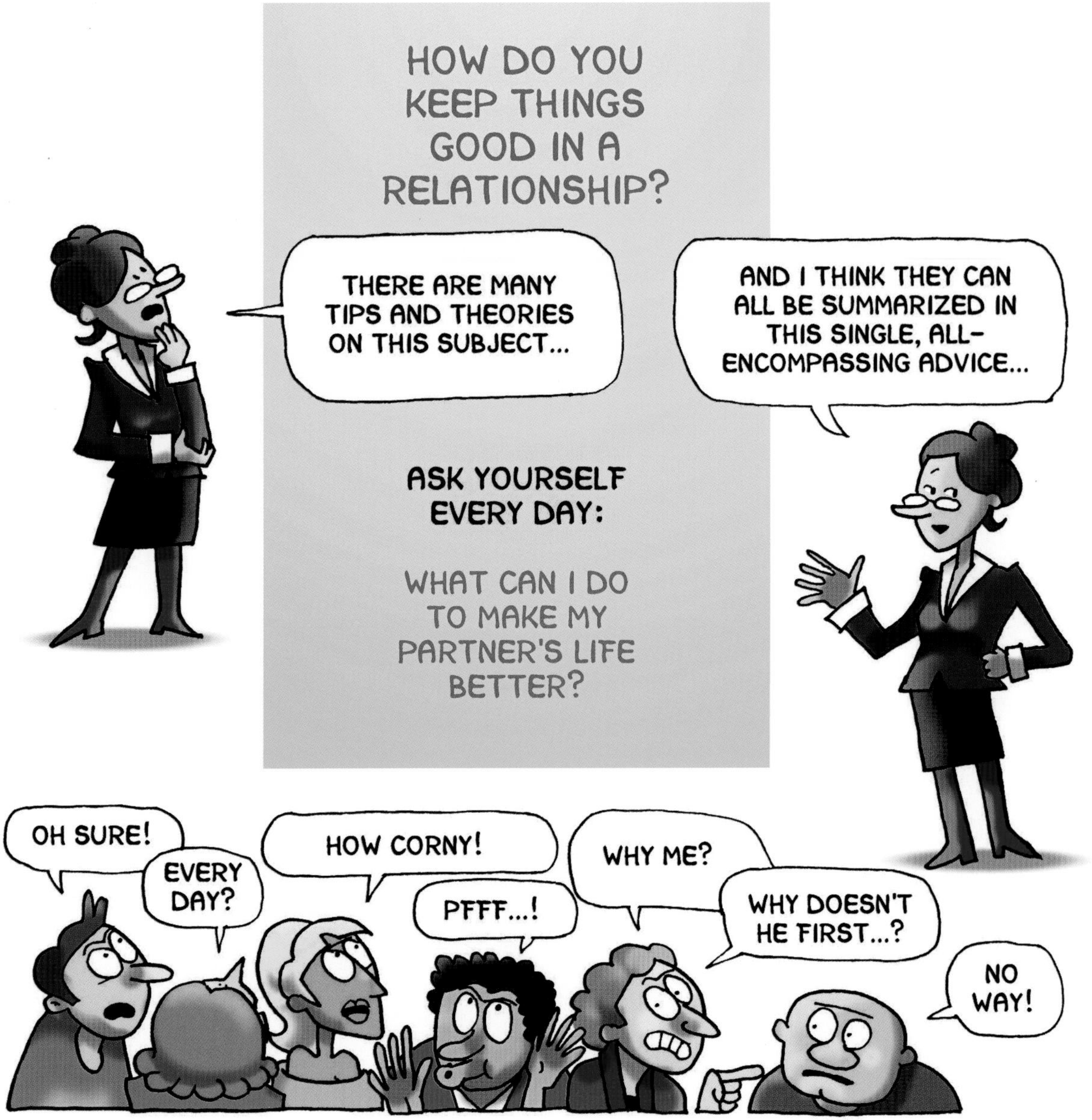
HOW DO YOU KEEP THINGS GOOD IN A RELATIONSHIP?
THERE ARE MANY TIPS AND THEORIES ON THIS SUBJECT...
AND I THINK THEY CAN ALL BE SUMMARIZED IN THIS SINGLE, ALL-ENCOMPASSING ADVICE...
ASK YOURSELF EVERY DAY:
WHAT CAN I DO TO MAKE MY PARTNER'S LIFE BETTER?
OH SURE!
EVERY DAY?
HOW CORNY!
PFFF...!
WHY ME?
WHY DOESN'T HE FIRST...?
NO WAY!

A TRUE STORY

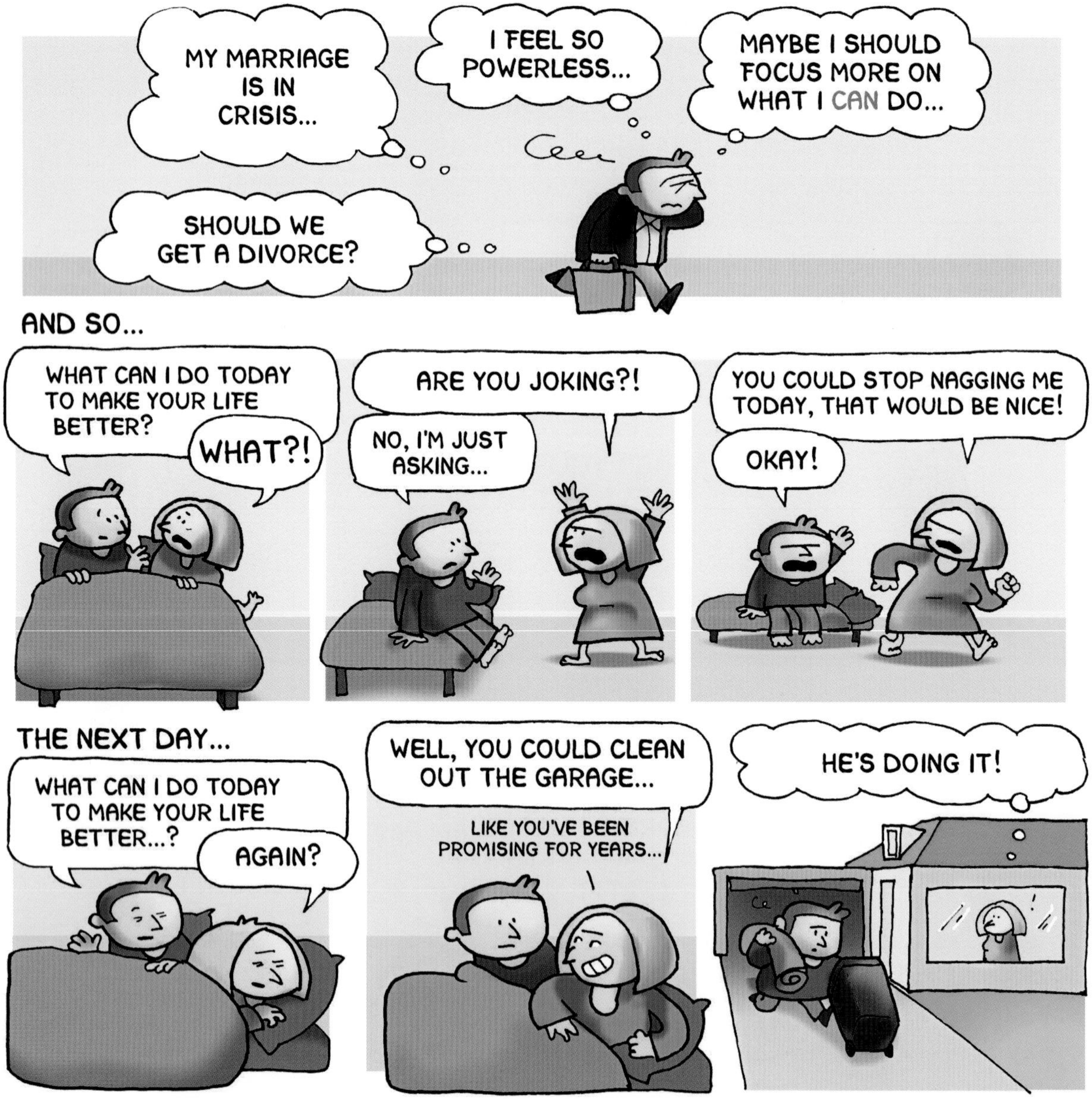
MY MARRIAGE IS IN CRISIS...
SHOULD WE GET A DIVORCE?
I FEEL SO POWERLESS...
MAYBE I SHOULD FOCUS MORE ON WHAT I CAN DO...
AND SO...
WHAT CAN I DO TODAY TO MAKE YOUR LIFE BETTER?
WHAT?!
ARE YOU JOKING?!
NO, I'M JUST ASKING...
YOU COULD STOP NAGGING ME TODAY, THAT WOULD BE NICE!
OKAY!
THE NEXT DAY...
WHAT CAN I DO TODAY TO MAKE YOUR LIFE BETTER...?
AGAIN?
WELL, YOU COULD CLEAN OUT THE GARAGE...
LIKE YOU'VE BEEN PROMISING FOR YEARS...
HE'S DOING IT!

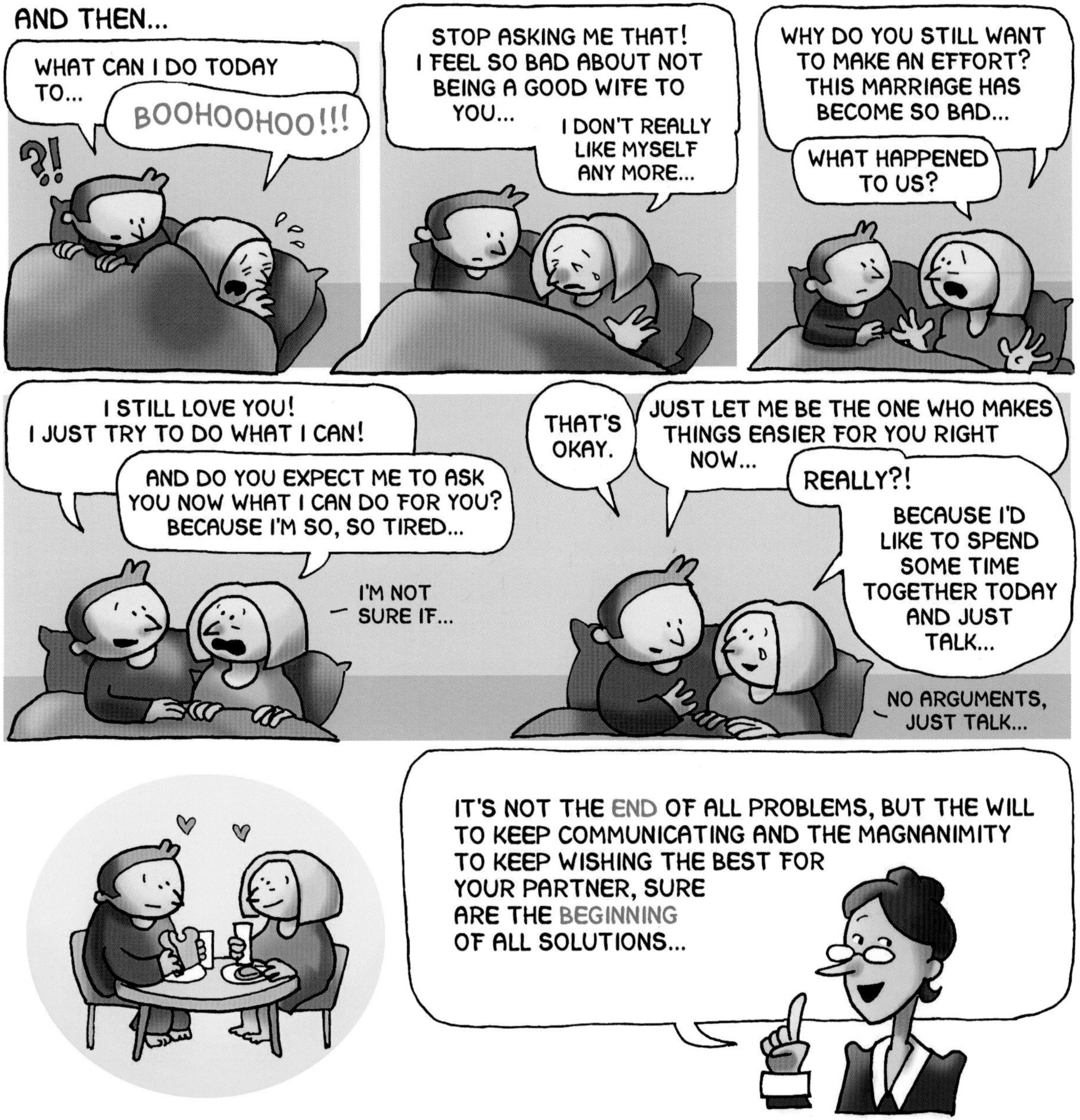
AND THEN...
WHAT CAN I DO TODAY TO...
BOOHOOHOO!!!
?!
STOP ASKING ME THAT! I FEEL SO BAD ABOUT NOT BEING A GOOD WIFE TO YOU...
I DON'T REALLY LIKE MYSELF ANY MORE...
WHY DO YOU STILL WANT TO MAKE AN EFFORT? THIS MARRIAGE HAS BECOME SO BAD...
WHAT HAPPENED TO US?
I STILL LOVE YOU! I JUST TRY TO DO WHAT I CAN!
AND DO YOU EXPECT ME TO ASK YOU NOW WHAT I CAN DO FOR YOU? BECAUSE I'M SO, SO TIRED...
I'M NOT SURE IF...
THAT'S OKAY.
JUST LET ME BE THE ONE WHO MAKES THINGS EASIER FOR YOU RIGHT NOW...
REALLY?!
BECAUSE I'D LIKE TO SPEND SOME TIME TOGETHER TODAY AND JUST TALK...
NO ARGUMENTS, JUST TALK...
IT'S NOT THE END OF ALL PROBLEMS, BUT THE WILL TO KEEP COMMUNICATING AND THE MAGNANIMITY TO KEEP WISHING THE BEST FOR YOUR PARTNER, SURE ARE THE BEGINNING OF ALL SOLUTIONS...

MARRIAGE

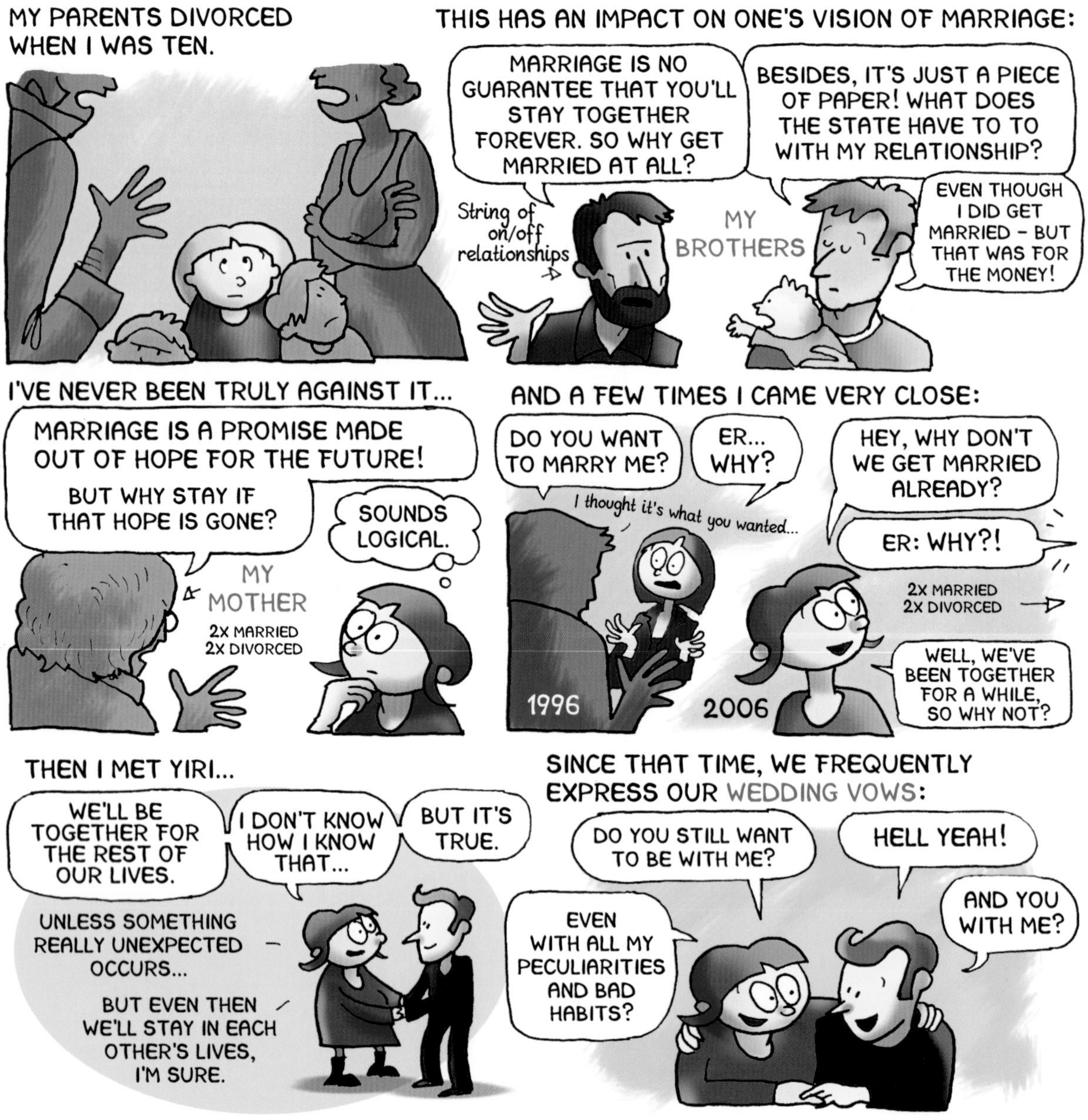
MY PARENTS DIVORCED WHEN I WAS TEN.
THIS HAS AN IMPACT ON ONE'S VISION OF MARRIAGE:
MARRIAGE IS NO GUARANTEE THAT YOU'LL STAY TOGETHER FOREVER. SO WHY GET MARRIED AT ALL?
String of on/off relationships
MY BROTHERS
BESIDES, IT'S JUST A PIECE OF PAPER! WHAT DOES THE STATE HAVE TO TO WITH MY RELATIONSHIP?
EVEN THOUGH I DID GET MARRIED – BUT THAT WAS FOR THE MONEY!
I'VE NEVER BEEN TRULY AGAINST IT...
MARRIAGE IS A PROMISE MADE OUT OF HOPE FOR THE FUTURE!
BUT WHY STAY IF THAT HOPE IS GONE?
MY MOTHER
2X MARRIED
2X DIVORCED
SOUNDS LOGICAL.
AND A FEW TIMES I CAME VERY CLOSE:
DO YOU WANT TO MARRY ME?
ER... WHY?
I thought it's what you wanted...
1996
HEY, WHY DON'T WE GET MARRIED ALREADY?
ER: WHY?!
2X MARRIED
2X DIVORCED
WELL, WE'VE BEEN TOGETHER FOR A WHILE, SO WHY NOT?
2006
THEN I MET YIRI...
WE'LL BE TOGETHER FOR THE REST OF OUR LIVES.
I DON'T KNOW HOW I KNOW THAT...
BUT IT'S TRUE.
UNLESS SOMETHING REALLY UNEXPECTED OCCURS...
BUT EVEN THEN WE'LL STAY IN EACH OTHER'S LIVES, I'M SURE.
SINCE THAT TIME, WE FREQUENTLY EXPRESS OUR WEDDING VOWS:
DO YOU STILL WANT TO BE WITH ME?
HELL YEAH!
EVEN WITH ALL MY PECULIARITIES AND BAD HABITS?
AND YOU WITH ME?

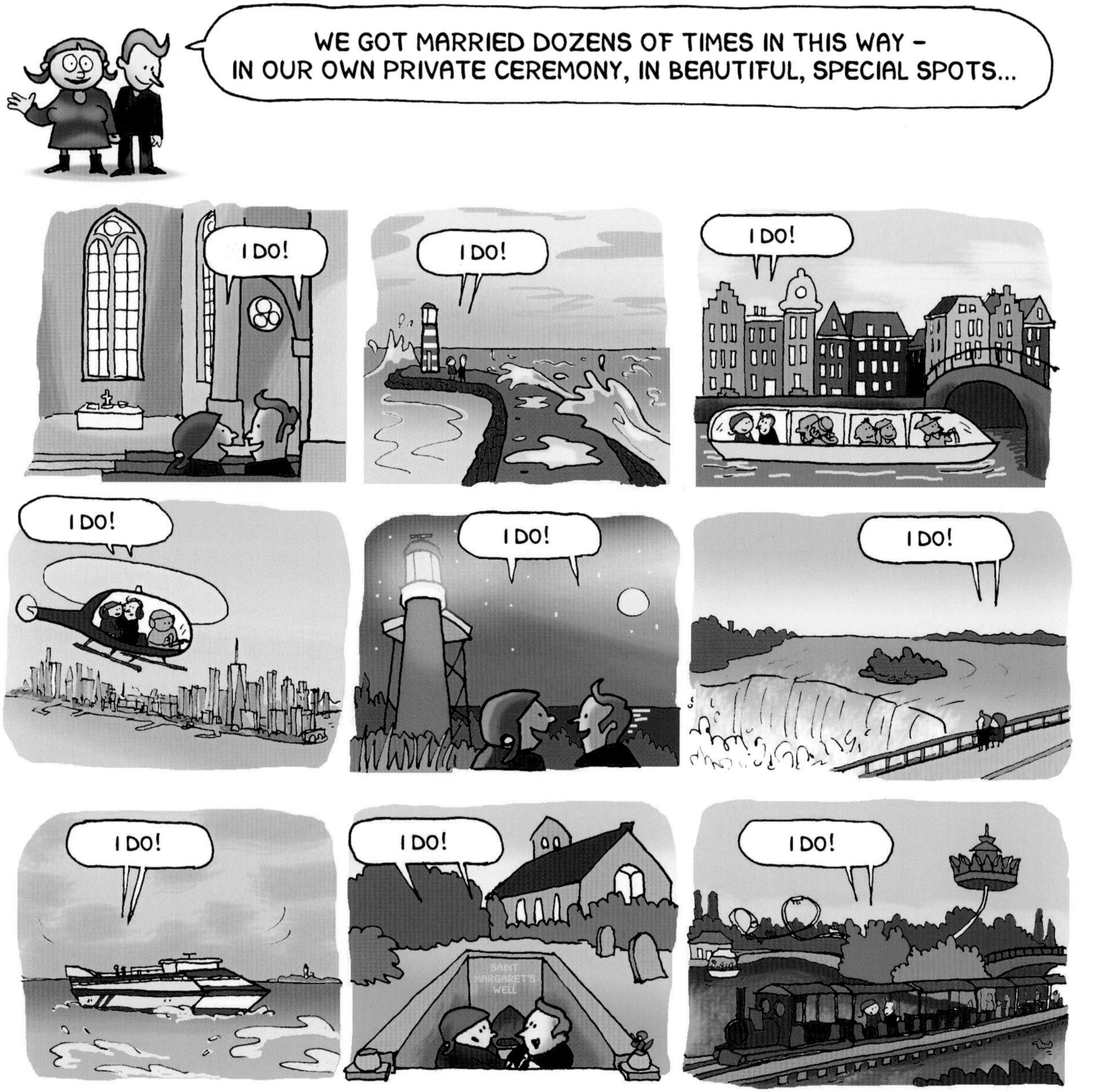
WE GOT MARRIED DOZENS OF TIMES IN THIS WAY –
IN OUR OWN PRIVATE CEREMONY, IN BEAUTIFUL, SPECIAL SPOTS...
I DO!
I DO!
I DO!
I DO!
I DO!
I DO!
I DO!
I DO!
SAINT MARGARET'S WELL
I DO!

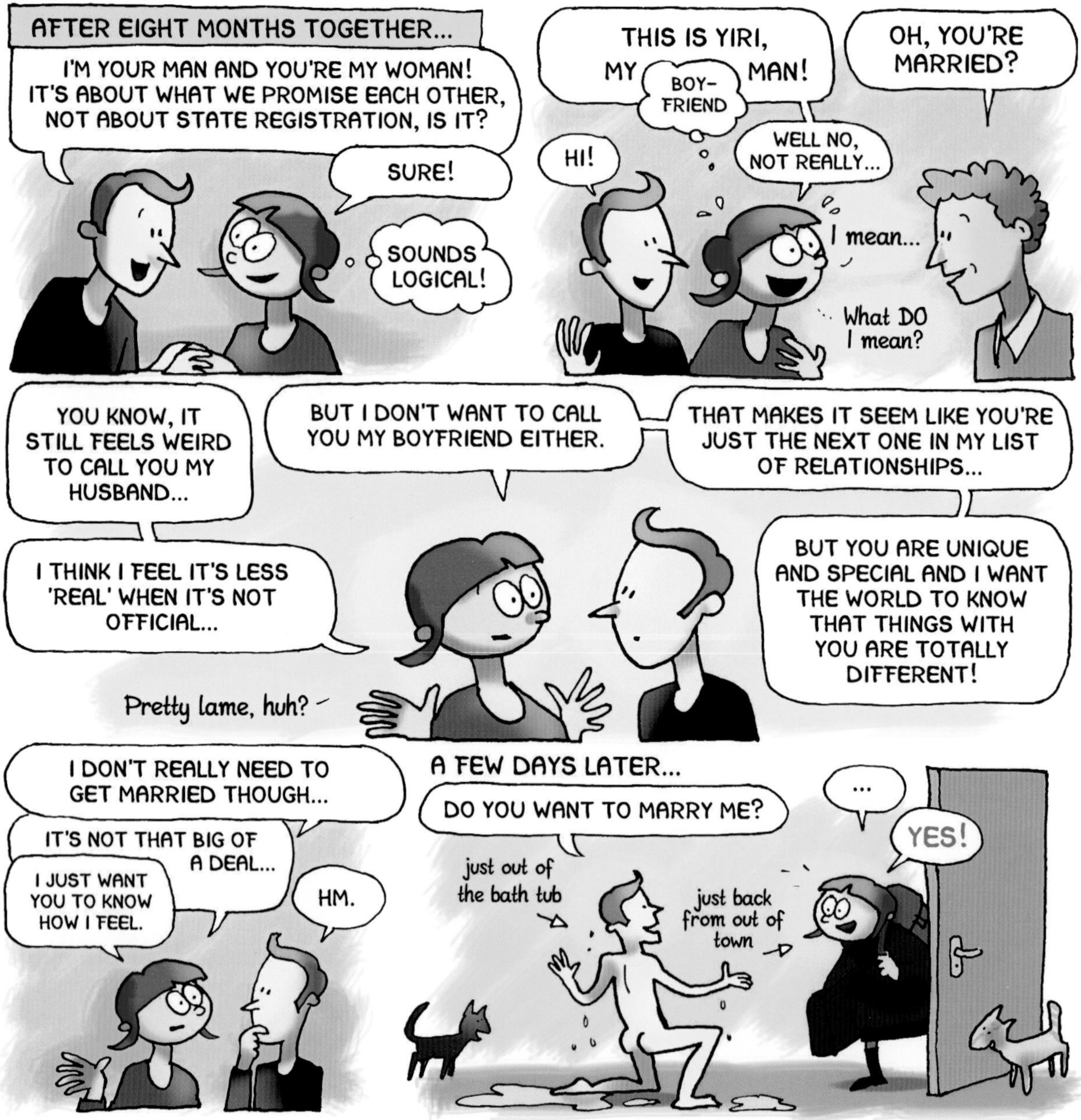

AFTER EIGHT MONTHS TOGETHER...
I'M YOUR MAN AND YOU'RE MY WOMAN! IT'S ABOUT WHAT WE PROMISE EACH OTHER, NOT ABOUT STATE REGISTRATION, IS IT?
SURE!
SOUNDS LOGICAL!
THIS IS YIRI, MY MAN!
BOY-FRIEND
HI!
OH, YOU'RE MARRIED?
WELL NO, NOT REALLY...
I mean...
What DO I mean?
YOU KNOW, IT STILL FEELS WEIRD TO CALL YOU MY HUSBAND...
BUT I DON'T WANT TO CALL YOU MY BOYFRIEND EITHER.
THAT MAKES IT SEEM LIKE YOU'RE JUST THE NEXT ONE IN MY LIST OF RELATIONSHIPS...
I THINK I FEEL IT'S LESS 'REAL' WHEN IT'S NOT OFFICIAL...
BUT YOU ARE UNIQUE AND SPECIAL AND I WANT THE WORLD TO KNOW THAT THINGS WITH YOU ARE TOTALLY DIFFERENT!
Pretty lame, huh?
I DON'T REALLY NEED TO GET MARRIED THOUGH...
IT'S NOT THAT BIG OF A DEAL...
I JUST WANT YOU TO KNOW HOW I FEEL.
HM.
A FEW DAYS LATER...
DO YOU WANT TO MARRY ME?
...
YES!
just out of the bath tub
just back from out of town

ON FRIDAY 23 JANUARY 2009
WE GOT MARRIED OFFICIALLY.

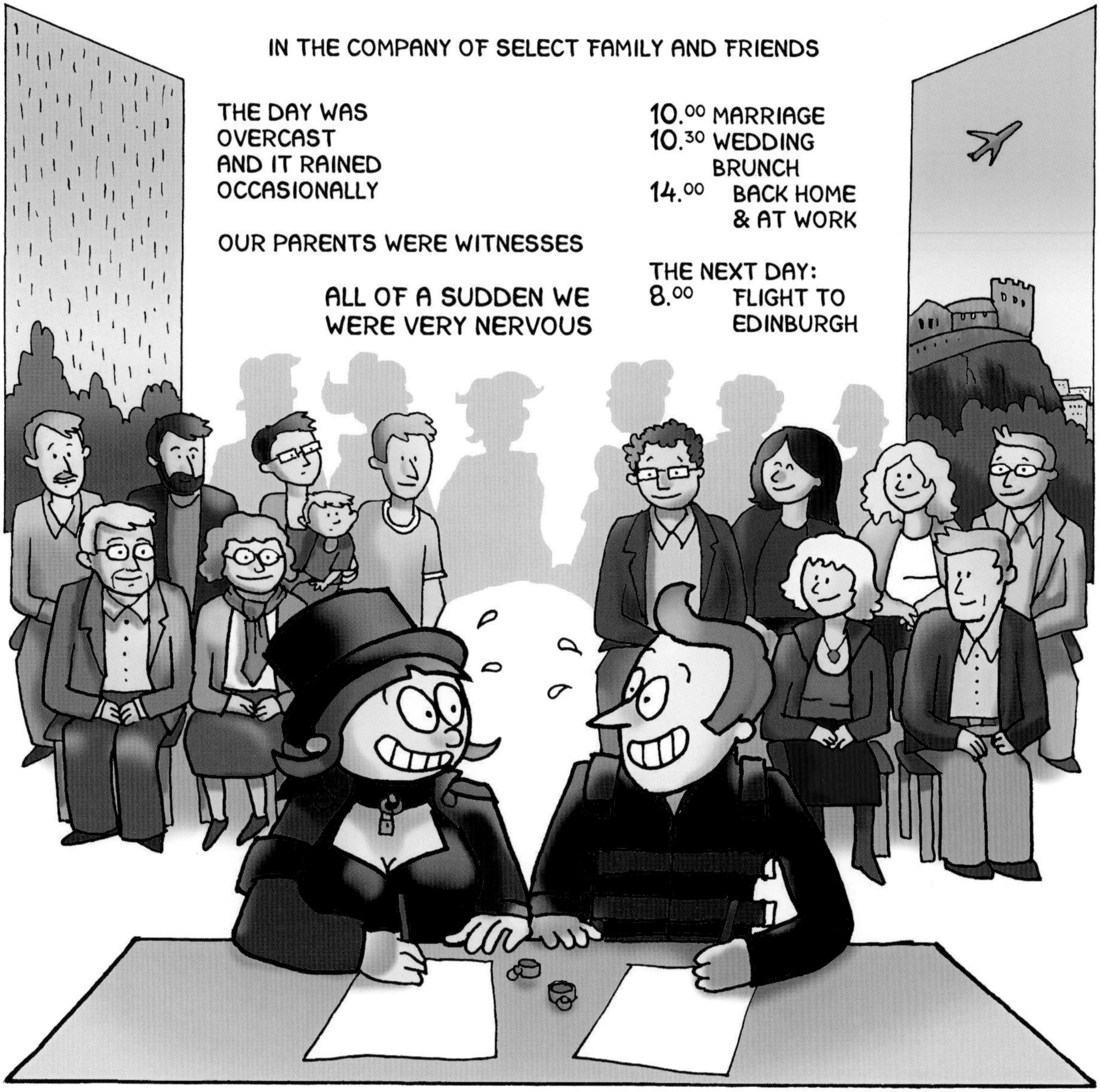
IN THE COMPANY OF SELECT FAMILY AND FRIENDS
THE DAY WAS OVERCAST AND IT RAINED OCCASIONALLY
OUR PARENTS WERE WITNESSES
ALL OF A SUDDEN WE WERE VERY NERVOUS
10.00 MARRIAGE
10.30 WEDDING BRUNCH
14.00 BACK HOME & AT WORK
THE NEXT DAY:
8.00 FLIGHT TO EDINBURGH

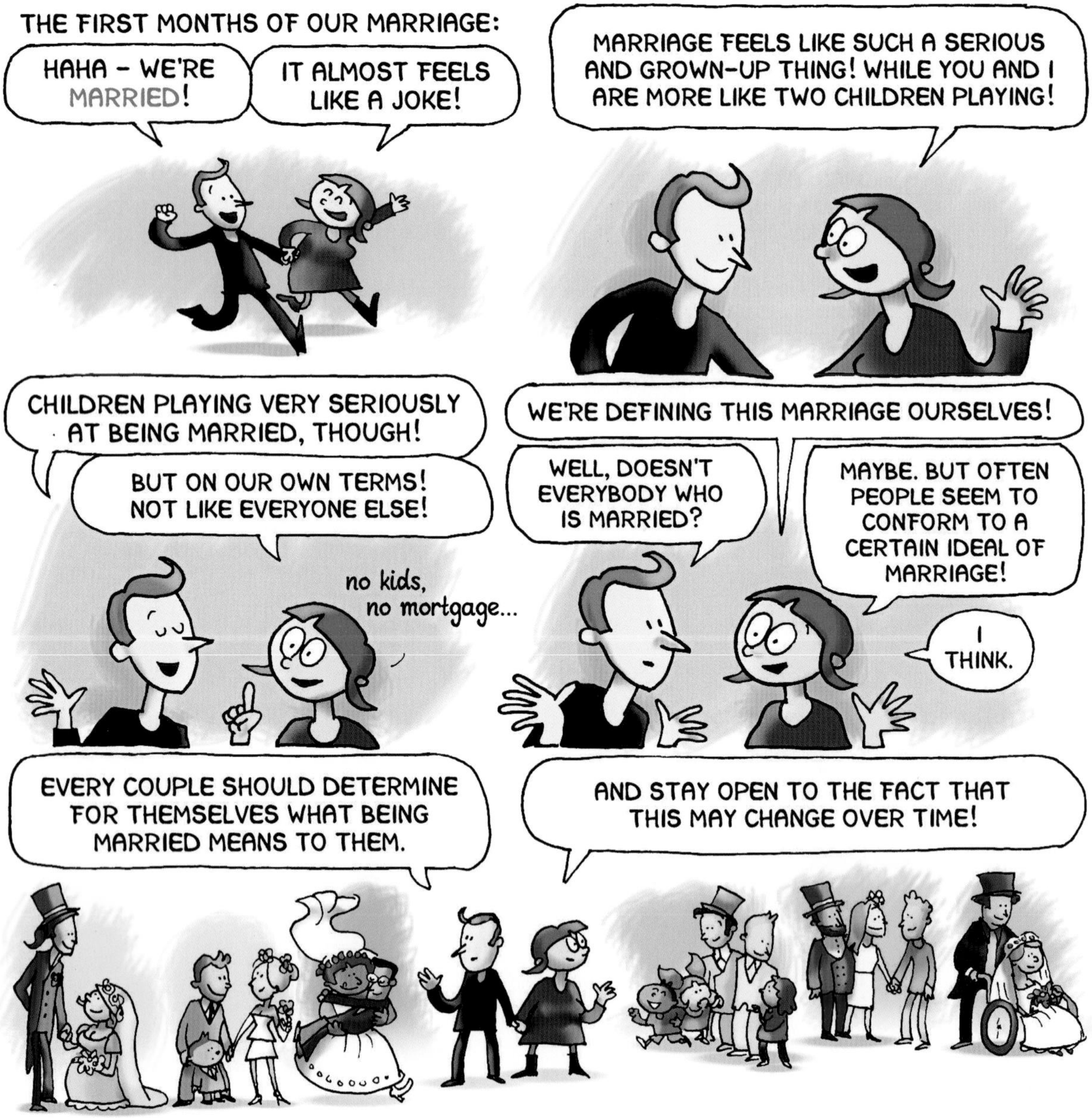
THE FIRST MONTHS OF OUR MARRIAGE:
HAHA – WE'RE MARRIED!
IT ALMOST FEELS LIKE A JOKE!
MARRIAGE FEELS LIKE SUCH A SERIOUS AND GROWN-UP THING! WHILE YOU AND I ARE MORE LIKE TWO CHILDREN PLAYING!
CHILDREN PLAYING VERY SERIOUSLY AT BEING MARRIED, THOUGH!
BUT ON OUR OWN TERMS! NOT LIKE EVERYONE ELSE!
no kids, no mortgage...
WE'RE DEFINING THIS MARRIAGE OURSELVES!
WELL, DOESN'T EVERYBODY WHO IS MARRIED?
MAYBE. BUT OFTEN PEOPLE SEEM TO CONFORM TO A CERTAIN IDEAL OF MARRIAGE!
I THINK.
EVERY COUPLE SHOULD DETERMINE FOR THEMSELVES WHAT BEING MARRIED MEANS TO THEM.
AND STAY OPEN TO THE FACT THAT THIS MAY CHANGE OVER TIME!

DIFFERENT KINDS OF MARRIAGE

FAMILY MARRIAGE

IS ALL ABOUT RAISING CHILDREN

BUSINESS MARRIAGE

IS ABOUT RUNNING A BUSINESS TOGETHER

CARE MARRIAGE

REVOLVES AROUND CHRONIC CARE

STATUS MARRIAGE

IS ALL ABOUT LOOKING GOOD TO THE OUTSIDE WORLD

MARRIAGE OF CONVENIENCE

IS BASED ON RATIONAL CONSIDERATIONS AND AGREEMENTS

FRIENDSHIP MARRIAGE

IS BASED ON FEELING SAFE AND COMFORTABLE

ARTISTIC MARRIAGE

REVOLVES AROUND CREATIVE PROJECTS

OPEN MARRIAGE

IS ABOUT A BALANCE BETWEEN SEXUAL FREEDOM AND COMMITMENT

ONE DOES NOT EXCLUDE THE OTHER!

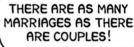
THERE ARE AS MANY MARRIAGES AS THERE ARE COUPLES!

79

SHORT HISTORY OF (WESTERN) MARRIAGE

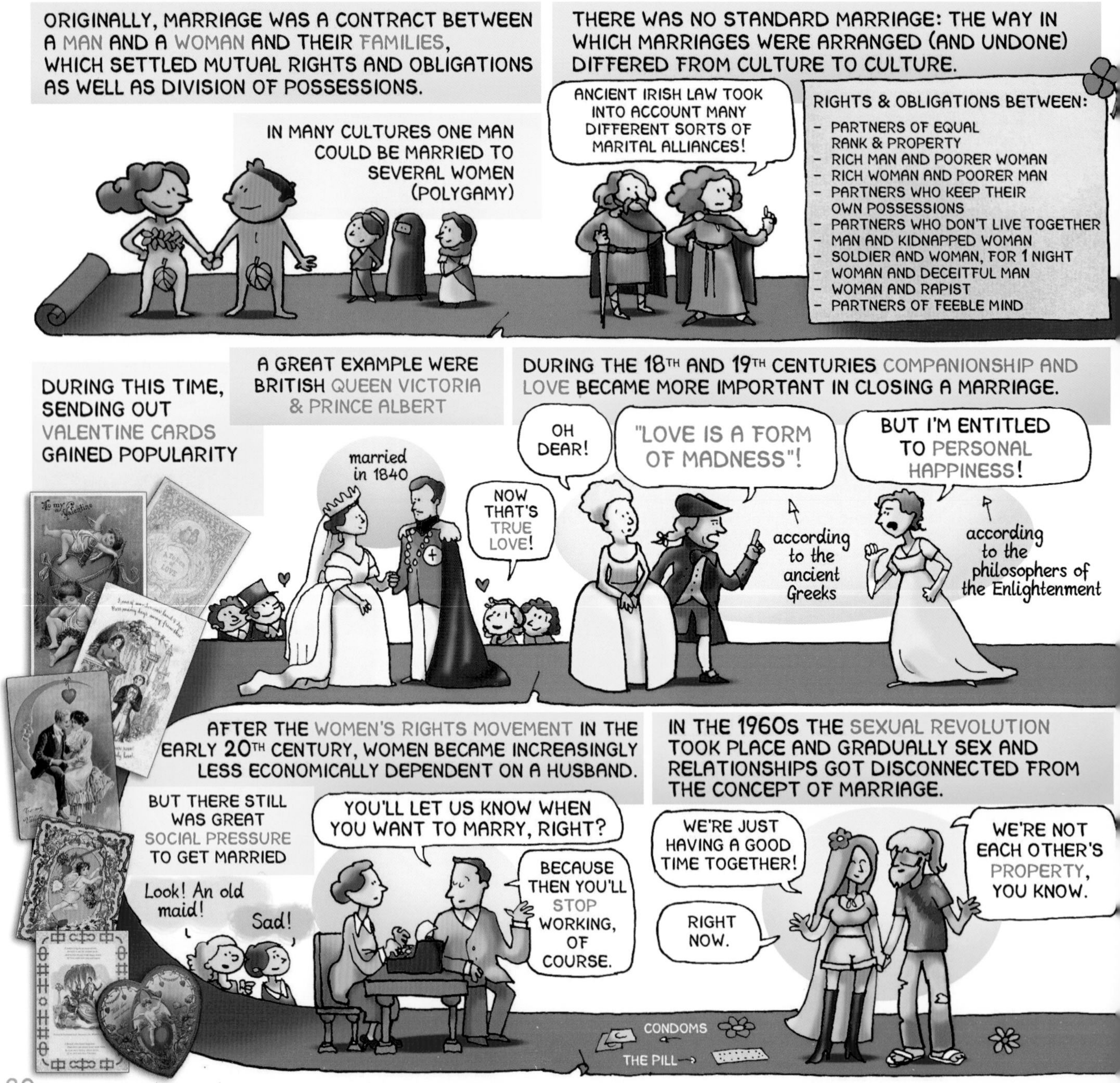
ORIGINALLY, MARRIAGE WAS A CONTRACT BETWEEN A MAN AND A WOMAN AND THEIR FAMILIES, WHICH SETTLED MUTUAL RIGHTS AND OBLIGATIONS AS WELL AS DIVISION OF POSSESSIONS.
IN MANY CULTURES ONE MAN COULD BE MARRIED TO SEVERAL WOMEN (POLYGAMY)
THERE WAS NO STANDARD MARRIAGE: THE WAY IN WHICH MARRIAGES WERE ARRANGED (AND UNDONE) DIFFERED FROM CULTURE TO CULTURE.
ANCIENT IRISH LAW TOOK INTO ACCOUNT MANY DIFFERENT SORTS OF MARITAL ALLIANCES!
RIGHTS & OBLIGATIONS BETWEEN:
- PARTNERS OF EQUAL RANK & PROPERTY
- RICH MAN AND POORER WOMAN
- RICH WOMAN AND POORER MAN
- PARTNERS WHO KEEP THEIR OWN POSSESSIONS
- PARTNERS WHO DON'T LIVE TOGETHER
- MAN AND KIDNAPPED WOMAN
- SOLDIER AND WOMAN, FOR 1 NIGHT
- WOMAN AND DECEITFUL MAN
- WOMAN AND RAPIST
- PARTNERS OF FEEBLE MIND
DURING THIS TIME, SENDING OUT VALENTINE CARDS GAINED POPULARITY
To my Valentine
A Token of LOVE
A GREAT EXAMPLE WERE BRITISH QUEEN VICTORIA & PRINCE ALBERT
married in 1840
NOW THAT'S TRUE LOVE!
DURING THE 18TH AND 19TH CENTURIES COMPANIONSHIP AND LOVE BECAME MORE IMPORTANT IN CLOSING A MARRIAGE.
OH DEAR!
"LOVE IS A FORM OF MADNESS"!
according to the ancient Greeks
BUT I'M ENTITLED TO PERSONAL HAPPINESS!
according to the philosophers of the Enlightenment
AFTER THE WOMEN'S RIGHTS MOVEMENT IN THE EARLY 20TH CENTURY, WOMEN BECAME INCREASINGLY LESS ECONOMICALLY DEPENDENT ON A HUSBAND.
BUT THERE STILL WAS GREAT SOCIAL PRESSURE TO GET MARRIED
Look! An old maid!
Sad!
YOU'LL LET US KNOW WHEN YOU WANT TO MARRY, RIGHT?
BECAUSE THEN YOU'LL STOP WORKING, OF COURSE.
IN THE 1960S THE SEXUAL REVOLUTION TOOK PLACE AND GRADUALLY SEX AND RELATIONSHIPS GOT DISCONNECTED FROM THE CONCEPT OF MARRIAGE.
WE'RE JUST HAVING A GOOD TIME TOGETHER!
RIGHT NOW.
WE'RE NOT EACH OTHER'S PROPERTY, YOU KNOW.
CONDOMS
THE PILL

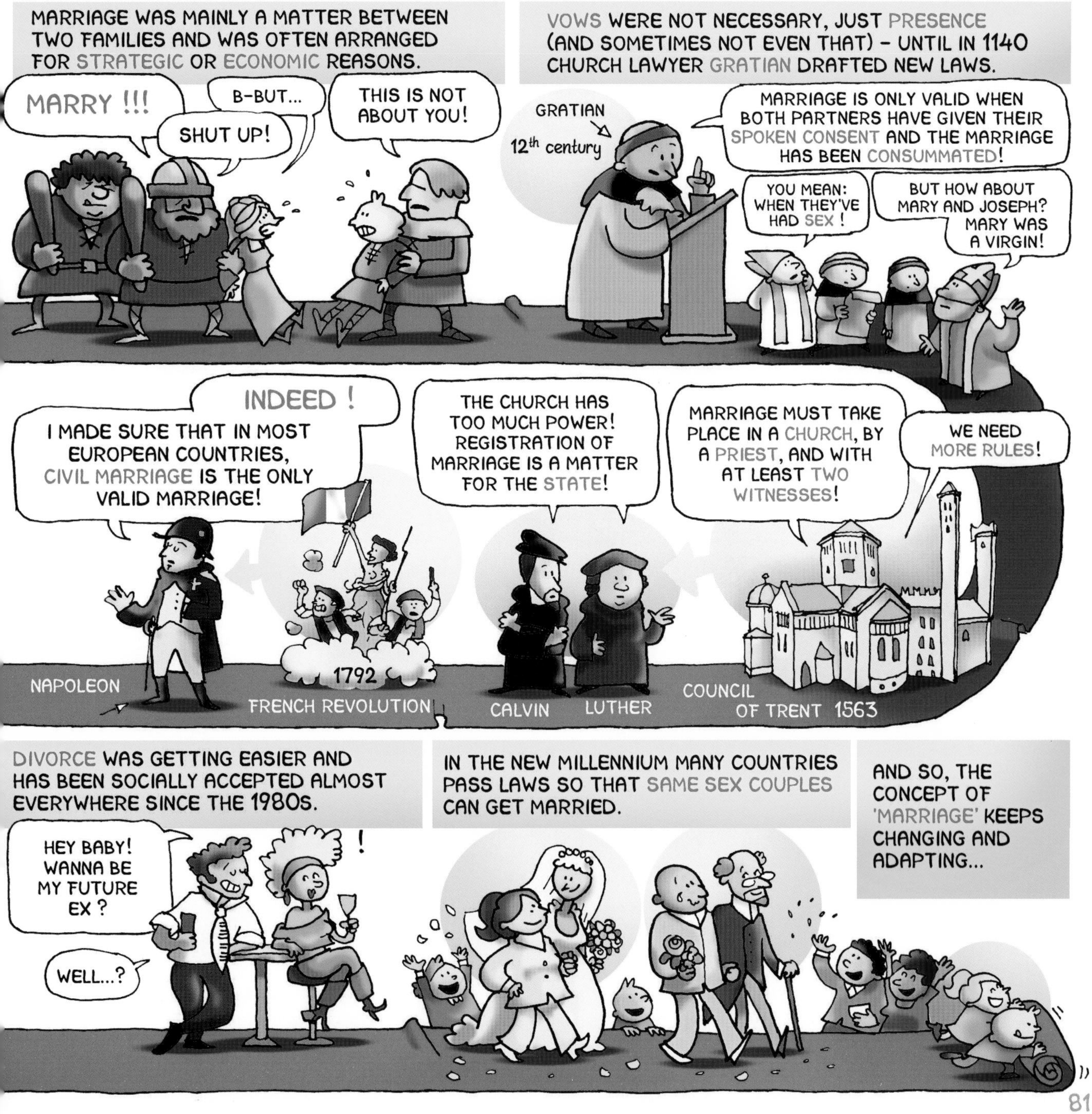
MARRIAGE WAS MAINLY A MATTER BETWEEN TWO FAMILIES AND WAS OFTEN ARRANGED FOR STRATEGIC OR ECONOMIC REASONS.
MARRY !!!
B-BUT...
SHUT UP!
THIS IS NOT ABOUT YOU!
VOWS WERE NOT NECESSARY, JUST PRESENCE (AND SOMETIMES NOT EVEN THAT) – UNTIL IN 1140 CHURCH LAWYER GRATIAN DRAFTED NEW LAWS.
GRATIAN
12th century
MARRIAGE IS ONLY VALID WHEN BOTH PARTNERS HAVE GIVEN THEIR SPOKEN CONSENT AND THE MARRIAGE HAS BEEN CONSUMMATED!
YOU MEAN: WHEN THEY'VE HAD SEX !
BUT HOW ABOUT MARY AND JOSEPH? MARY WAS A VIRGIN!
MARRIAGE MUST TAKE PLACE IN A CHURCH, BY A PRIEST, AND WITH AT LEAST TWO WITNESSES!
WE NEED MORE RULES!
COUNCIL OF TRENT 1563
THE CHURCH HAS TOO MUCH POWER! REGISTRATION OF MARRIAGE IS A MATTER FOR THE STATE!
CALVIN
LUTHER
1792
FRENCH REVOLUTION
I MADE SURE THAT IN MOST EUROPEAN COUNTRIES, CIVIL MARRIAGE IS THE ONLY VALID MARRIAGE!
INDEED !
NAPOLEON
DIVORCE WAS GETTING EASIER AND HAS BEEN SOCIALLY ACCEPTED ALMOST EVERYWHERE SINCE THE 1980S.
HEY BABY! WANNA BE MY FUTURE EX ?
!
WELL...?
IN THE NEW MILLENNIUM MANY COUNTRIES PASS LAWS SO THAT SAME SEX COUPLES CAN GET MARRIED.
AND SO, THE CONCEPT OF 'MARRIAGE' KEEPS CHANGING AND ADAPTING...

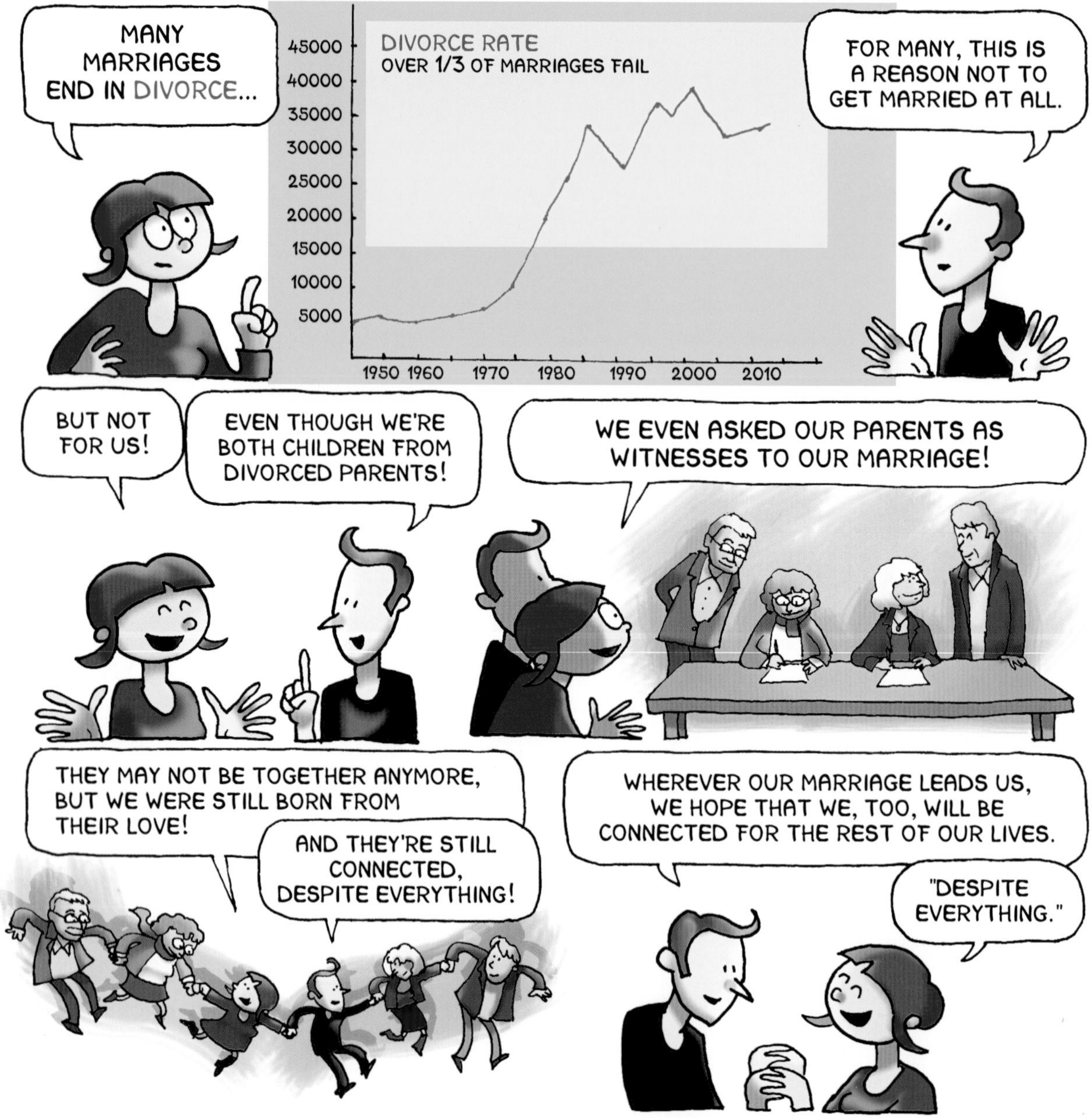
MANY MARRIAGES END IN DIVORCE...
DIVORCE RATE
OVER 1/3 OF MARRIAGES FAIL
45000
40000
35000
30000
25000
20000
15000
10000
5000
1950 1960 1970 1980 1990 2000 2010
FOR MANY, THIS IS A REASON NOT TO GET MARRIED AT ALL.
BUT NOT FOR US!
EVEN THOUGH WE'RE BOTH CHILDREN FROM DIVORCED PARENTS!
WE EVEN ASKED OUR PARENTS AS WITNESSES TO OUR MARRIAGE!
THEY MAY NOT BE TOGETHER ANYMORE, BUT WE WERE STILL BORN FROM THEIR LOVE!
AND THEY'RE STILL CONNECTED, DESPITE EVERYTHING!
WHEREVER OUR MARRIAGE LEADS US, WE HOPE THAT WE, TOO, WILL BE CONNECTED FOR THE REST OF OUR LIVES.
"DESPITE EVERYTHING."

BUT OF COURSE WE TOTALLY AIM FOR "UNTIL DEATH DO US PART" !
WE'LL DEFY THOSE STATISTICS !

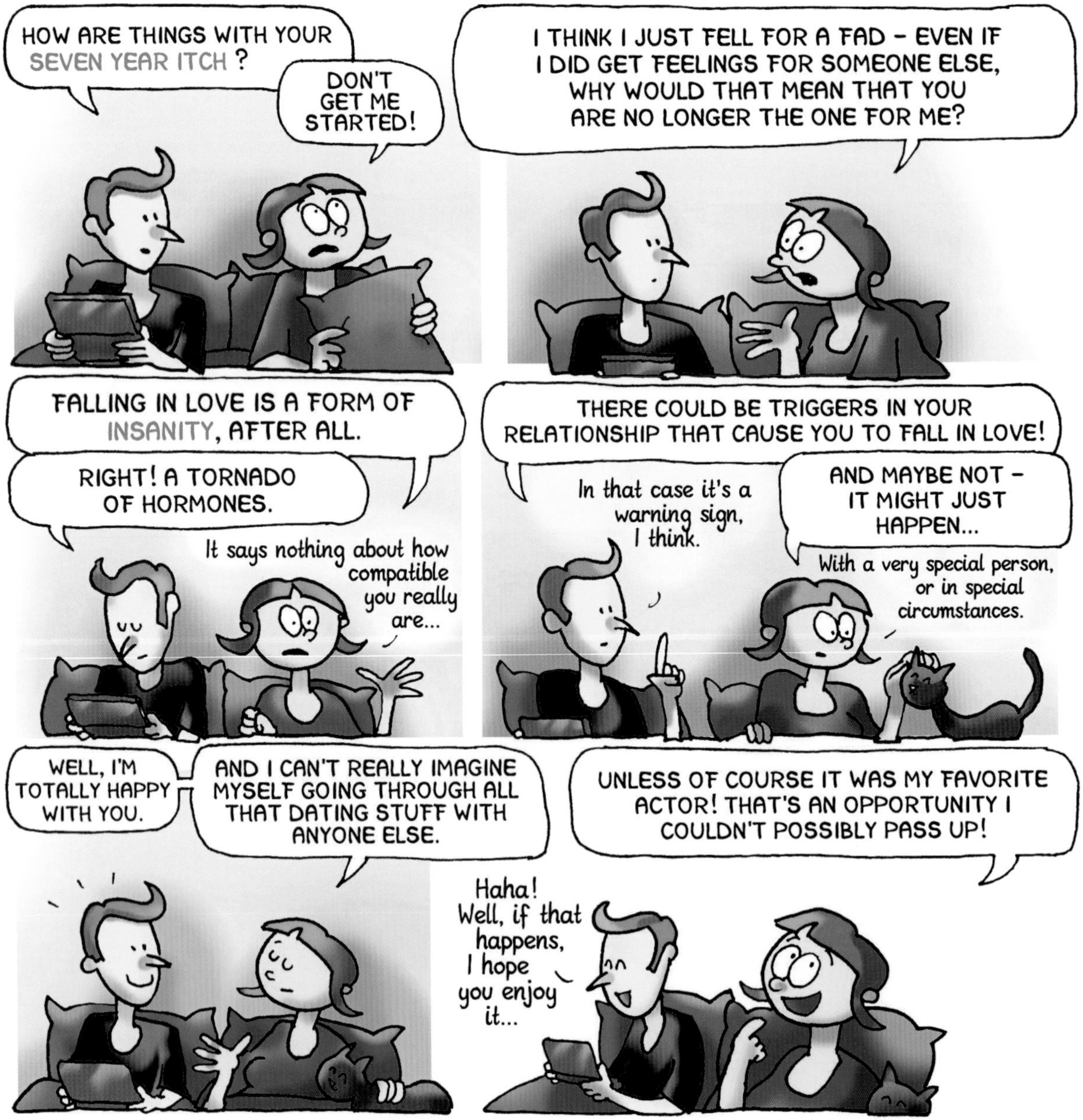
HOW ARE THINGS WITH YOUR SEVEN YEAR ITCH?
DON'T GET ME STARTED!
I THINK I JUST FELL FOR A FAD - EVEN IF I DID GET FEELINGS FOR SOMEONE ELSE, WHY WOULD THAT MEAN THAT YOU ARE NO LONGER THE ONE FOR ME?
FALLING IN LOVE IS A FORM OF INSANITY, AFTER ALL.
RIGHT! A TORNADO OF HORMONES.
It says nothing about how compatible you really are...
THERE COULD BE TRIGGERS IN YOUR RELATIONSHIP THAT CAUSE YOU TO FALL IN LOVE!
In that case it's a warning sign, I think.
AND MAYBE NOT - IT MIGHT JUST HAPPEN...
With a very special person, or in special circumstances.
WELL, I'M TOTALLY HAPPY WITH YOU.
AND I CAN'T REALLY IMAGINE MYSELF GOING THROUGH ALL THAT DATING STUFF WITH ANYONE ELSE.
UNLESS OF COURSE IT WAS MY FAVORITE ACTOR! THAT'S AN OPPORTUNITY I COULDN'T POSSIBLY PASS UP!
Haha! Well, if that happens, I hope you enjoy it...

FALLING
IN LOVE

WHAT EXACTLY HAPPENS WHEN YOU FALL IN LOVE?

1 RECOGNITION

THE MOMENT OF FALLING IN LOVE CAN FEEL LIKE A LIGHTNING STRIKE.

OR, WHEN IT'S MUTUAL, LIKE A 'SPARK' OR A 'CLICK'.

IT IS THE MOMENT YOU RECOGNIZE SOMETHING DESIRABLE IN THE OTHER PERSON...

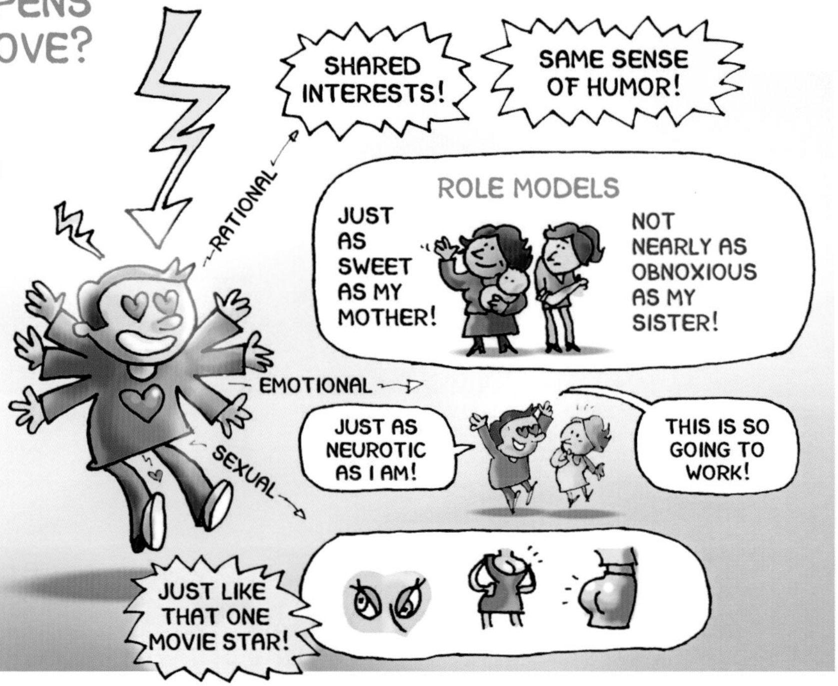
SHARED INTERESTS!
SAME SENSE OF HUMOR!
RATIONAL
ROLE MODELS
JUST AS SWEET AS MY MOTHER!
NOT NEARLY AS OBNOXIOUS AS MY SISTER!
EMOTIONAL
JUST AS NEUROTIC AS I AM!
THIS IS SO GOING TO WORK!
SEXUAL
JUST LIKE THAT ONE MOVIE STAR!

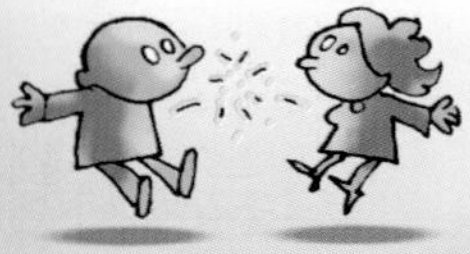

3 THE PINK CLOUD

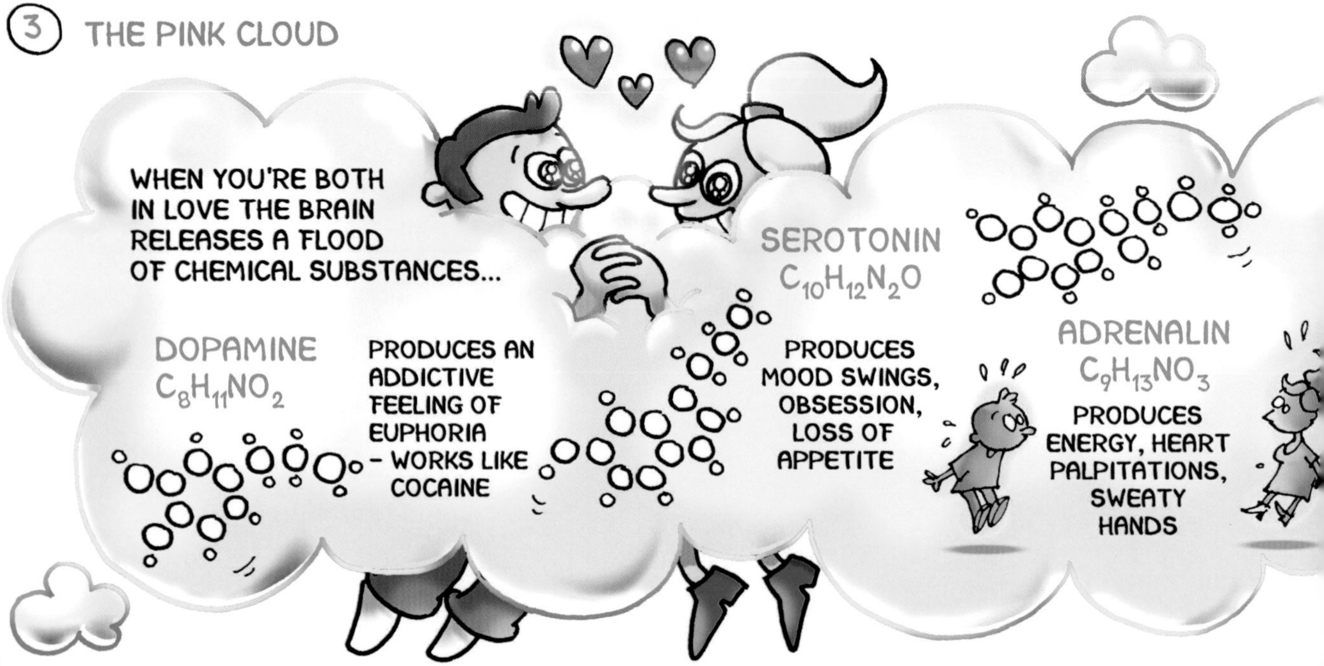
WHEN YOU'RE BOTH IN LOVE THE BRAIN RELEASES A FLOOD OF CHEMICAL SUBSTANCES...
DOPAMINE
$C_8H_{11}NO_2$
PRODUCES AN ADDICTIVE FEELING OF EUPHORIA – WORKS LIKE COCAINE
SEROTONIN
$C_{10}H_{12}N_2O$
PRODUCES MOOD SWINGS, OBSESSION, LOSS OF APPETITE
ADRENALIN
$C_9H_{13}NO_3$
PRODUCES ENERGY, HEART PALPITATIONS, SWEATY HANDS

2 DESIRE

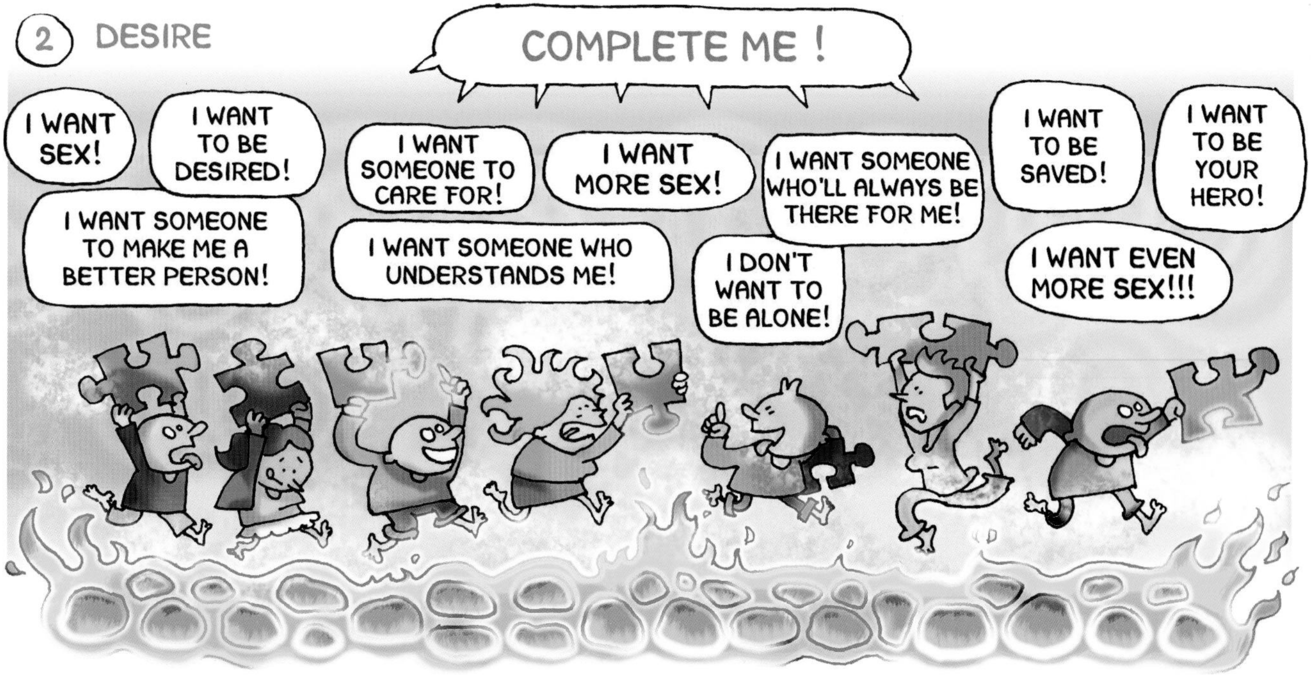
COMPLETE ME!
I WANT SEX!
I WANT TO BE DESIRED!
I WANT SOMEONE TO MAKE ME A BETTER PERSON!
I WANT SOMEONE TO CARE FOR!
I WANT SOMEONE WHO UNDERSTANDS ME!
I WANT MORE SEX!
I WANT SOMEONE WHO'LL ALWAYS BE THERE FOR ME!
I DON'T WANT TO BE ALONE!
I WANT TO BE SAVED!
I WANT TO BE YOUR HERO!
I WANT EVEN MORE SEX!!!

AFTER ABOUT THREE MONTHS, THIS CHEMICAL TURMOIL EVENS OUT A BIT...

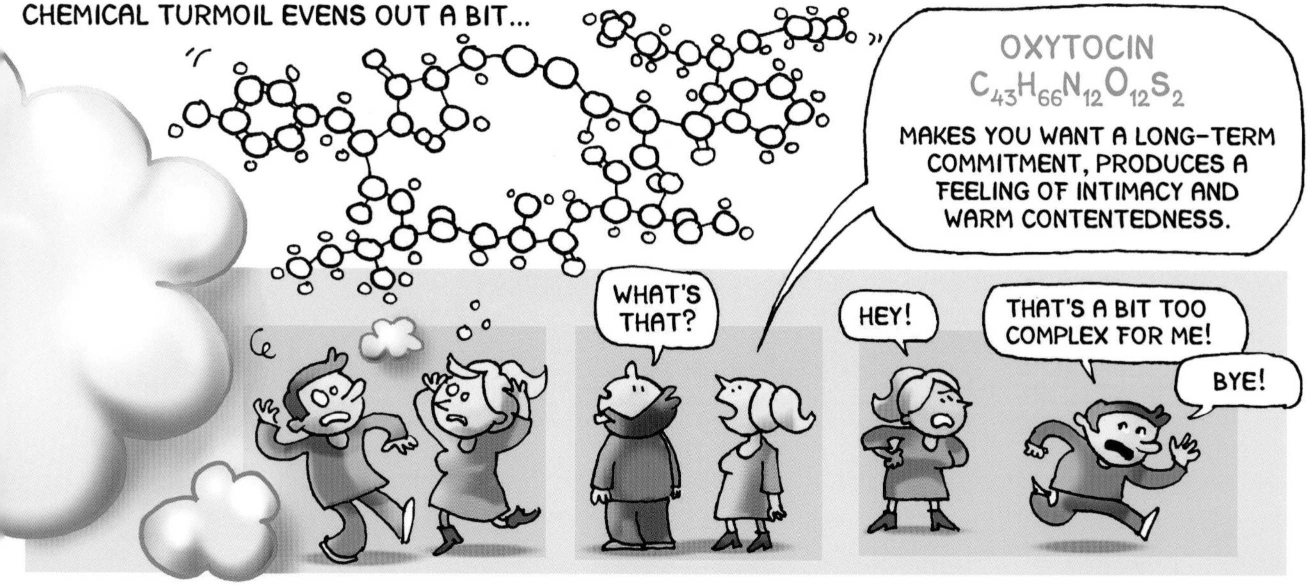
OXYTOCIN
$C_{43}H_{66}N_{12}O_{12}S_2$
MAKES YOU WANT A LONG-TERM COMMITMENT, PRODUCES A FEELING OF INTIMACY AND WARM CONTENTEDNESS.
WHAT'S THAT?
HEY!
THAT'S A BIT TOO COMPLEX FOR ME!
BYE!

YIRI & ME, AFTER THREE WEEKS IN LOVE...

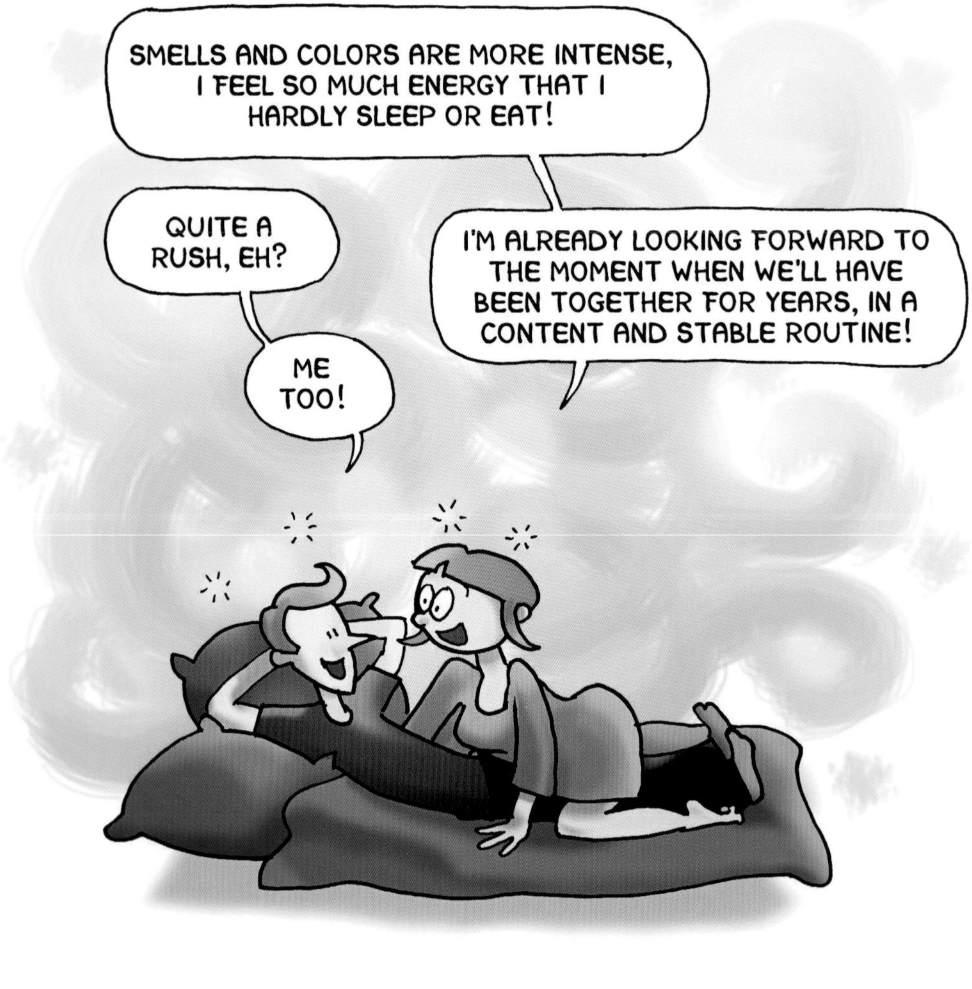
SMELLS AND COLORS ARE MORE INTENSE, I FEEL SO MUCH ENERGY THAT I HARDLY SLEEP OR EAT!
QUITE A RUSH, EH?
I'M ALREADY LOOKING FORWARD TO THE MOMENT WHEN WE'LL HAVE BEEN TOGETHER FOR YEARS, IN A CONTENT AND STABLE ROUTINE!
ME TOO!

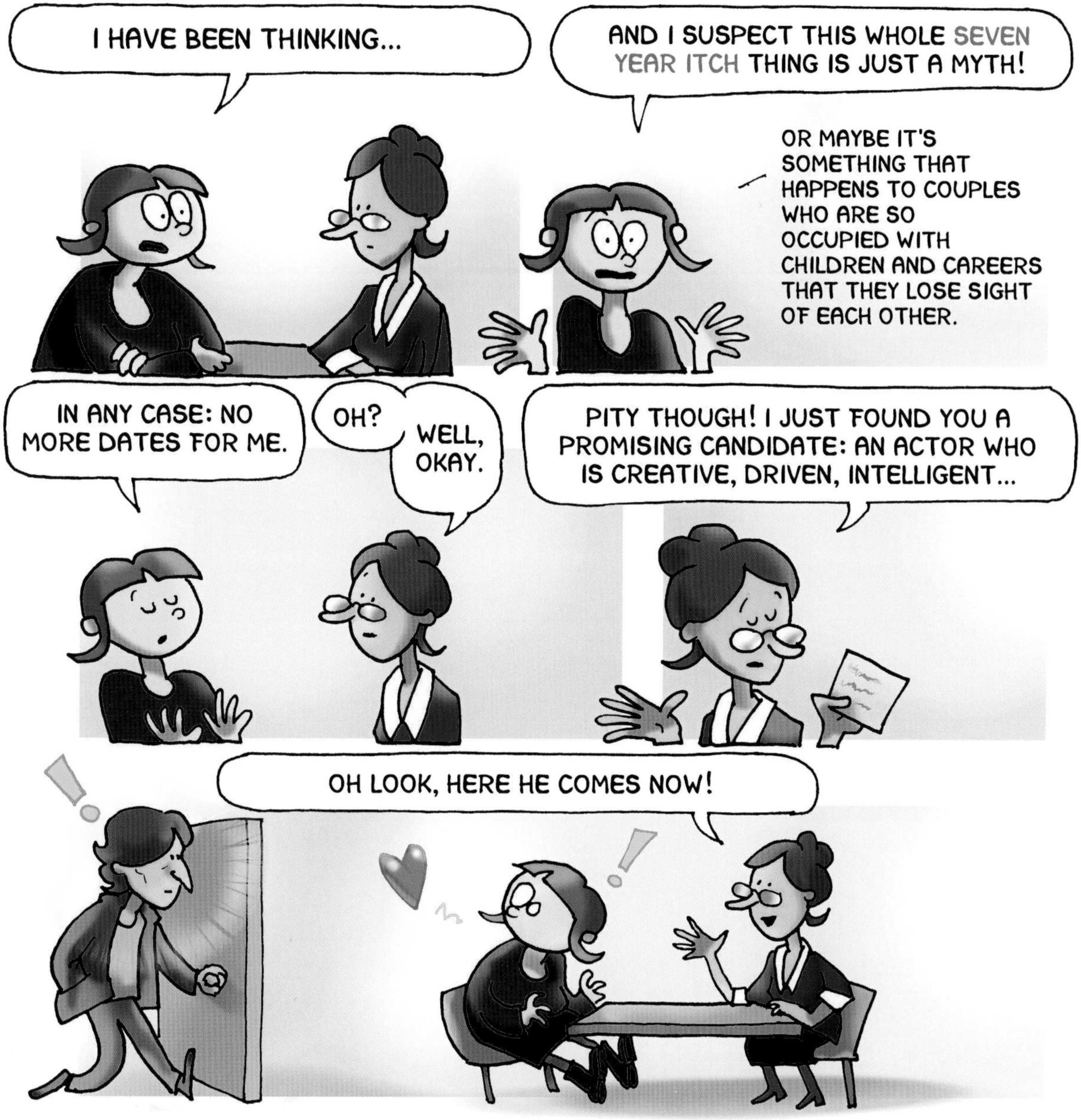

I HAVE BEEN THINKING...
AND I SUSPECT THIS WHOLE SEVEN YEAR ITCH THING IS JUST A MYTH!
OR MAYBE IT'S SOMETHING THAT HAPPENS TO COUPLES WHO ARE SO OCCUPIED WITH CHILDREN AND CAREERS THAT THEY LOSE SIGHT OF EACH OTHER.
IN ANY CASE: NO MORE DATES FOR ME.
OH?
WELL, OKAY.
PITY THOUGH! I JUST FOUND YOU A PROMISING CANDIDATE: AN ACTOR WHO IS CREATIVE, DRIVEN, INTELLIGENT...
OH LOOK, HERE HE COMES NOW!

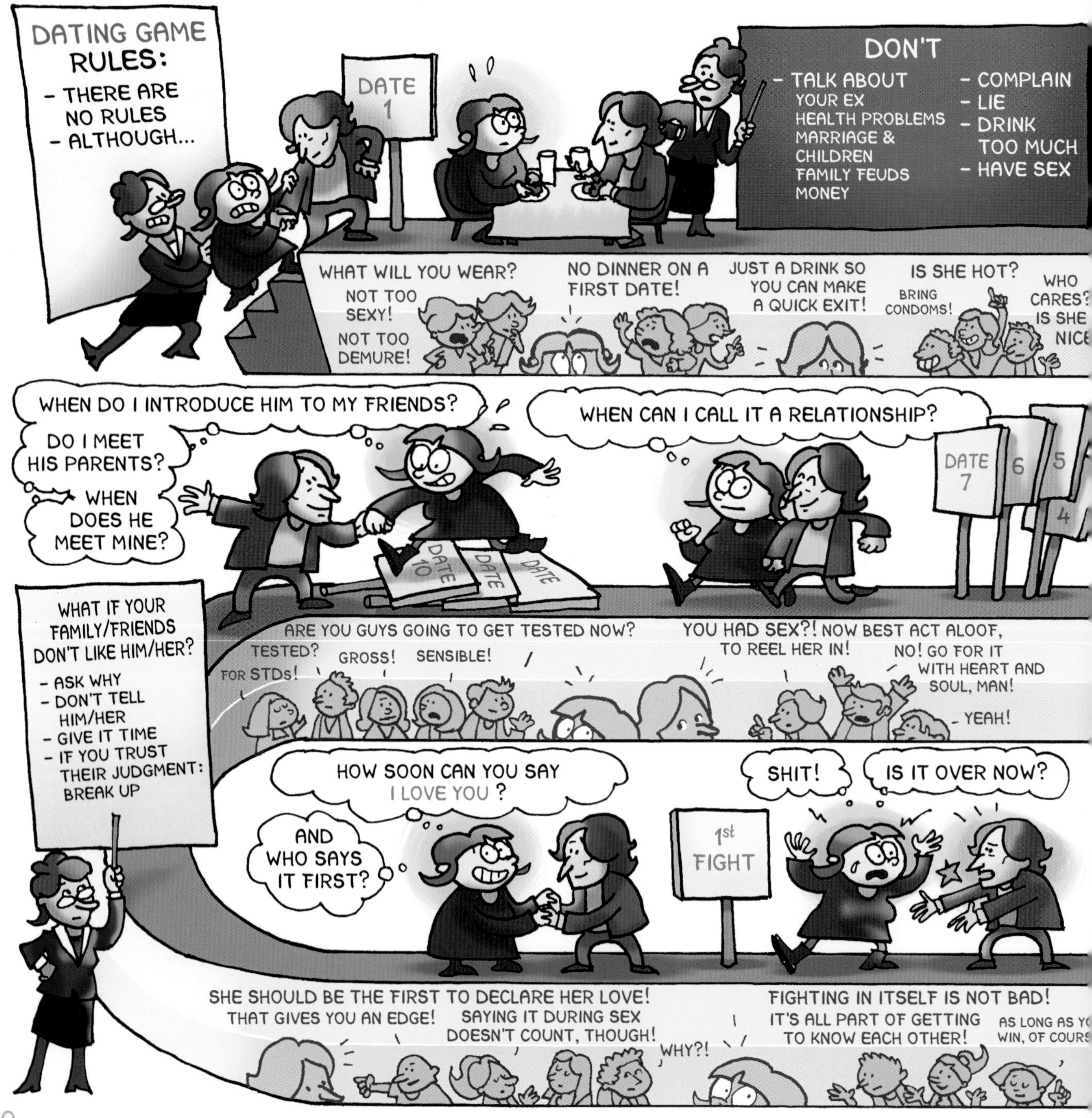

DATING GAME RULES:
- THERE ARE NO RULES
- ALTHOUGH...
DATE 1
DON'T
- TALK ABOUT YOUR EX HEALTH PROBLEMS MARRIAGE & CHILDREN FAMILY FEUDS MONEY
- COMPLAIN
- LIE
- DRINK TOO MUCH
- HAVE SEX
WHAT WILL YOU WEAR?
NOT TOO SEXY!
NOT TOO DEMURE!
NO DINNER ON A FIRST DATE!
JUST A DRINK SO YOU CAN MAKE A QUICK EXIT!
IS SHE HOT?
BRING CONDOMS!
WHO CARES? IS SHE NICE
WHEN DO I INTRODUCE HIM TO MY FRIENDS?
DO I MEET HIS PARENTS?
WHEN DOES HE MEET MINE?
DATE 10
DATE
DATE
WHEN CAN I CALL IT A RELATIONSHIP?
DATE 7
6
5
4
WHAT IF YOUR FAMILY/FRIENDS DON'T LIKE HIM/HER?
- ASK WHY
- DON'T TELL HIM/HER
- GIVE IT TIME
- IF YOU TRUST THEIR JUDGMENT: BREAK UP
ARE YOU GUYS GOING TO GET TESTED NOW?
TESTED?
FOR STDs!
GROSS!
SENSIBLE!
YOU HAD SEX?! NOW BEST ACT ALOOF, TO REEL HER IN!
NO! GO FOR IT WITH HEART AND SOUL, MAN!
YEAH!
HOW SOON CAN YOU SAY I LOVE YOU?
AND WHO SAYS IT FIRST?
1st FIGHT
SHIT!
IS IT OVER NOW?
SHE SHOULD BE THE FIRST TO DECLARE HER LOVE!
THAT GIVES YOU AN EDGE!
SAYING IT DURING SEX DOESN'T COUNT, THOUGH!
WHY?!
FIGHTING IN ITSELF IS NOT BAD!
IT'S ALL PART OF GETTING TO KNOW EACH OTHER!

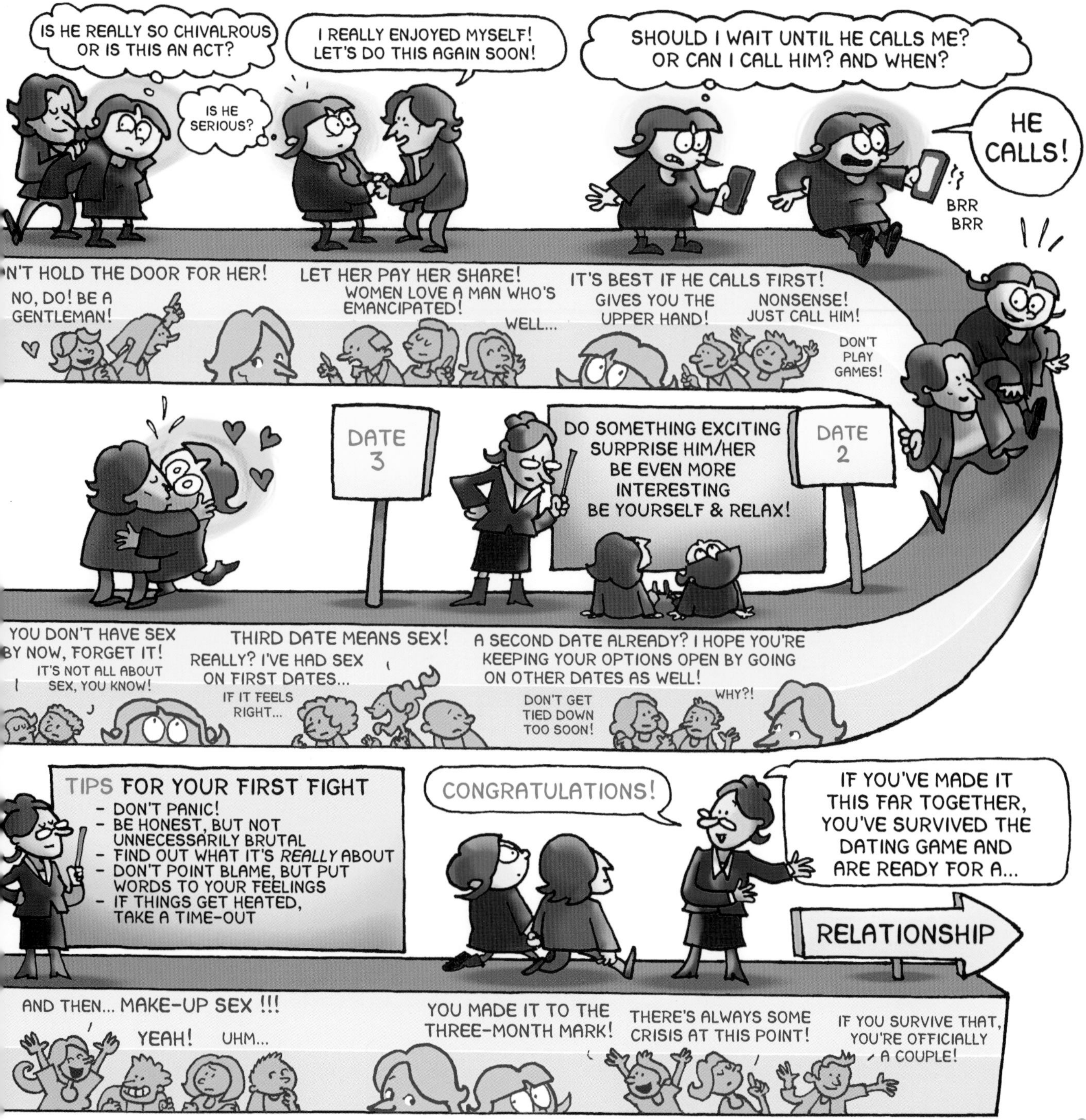
IS HE REALLY SO CHIVALROUS OR IS THIS AN ACT?
IS HE SERIOUS?
I REALLY ENJOYED MYSELF! LET'S DO THIS AGAIN SOON!
SHOULD I WAIT UNTIL HE CALLS ME? OR CAN I CALL HIM? AND WHEN?
HE CALLS!
BRR BRR
N'T HOLD THE DOOR FOR HER!
NO, DO! BE A GENTLEMAN!
LET HER PAY HER SHARE!
WOMEN LOVE A MAN WHO'S EMANCIPATED!
WELL...
IT'S BEST IF HE CALLS FIRST!
GIVES YOU THE UPPER HAND!
NONSENSE! JUST CALL HIM!
DON'T PLAY GAMES!
DATE 3
DO SOMETHING EXCITING
SURPRISE HIM/HER
BE EVEN MORE INTERESTING
BE YOURSELF & RELAX!
DATE 2
YOU DON'T HAVE SEX BY NOW, FORGET IT!
IT'S NOT ALL ABOUT SEX, YOU KNOW!
THIRD DATE MEANS SEX!
REALLY? I'VE HAD SEX ON FIRST DATES...
IF IT FEELS RIGHT...
A SECOND DATE ALREADY? I HOPE YOU'RE KEEPING YOUR OPTIONS OPEN BY GOING ON OTHER DATES AS WELL!
DON'T GET TIED DOWN TOO SOON!
WHY?!
TIPS FOR YOUR FIRST FIGHT
- DON'T PANIC!
- BE HONEST, BUT NOT UNNECESSARILY BRUTAL
- FIND OUT WHAT IT'S REALLY ABOUT
- DON'T POINT BLAME, BUT PUT WORDS TO YOUR FEELINGS
- IF THINGS GET HEATED, TAKE A TIME-OUT
CONGRATULATIONS!
IF YOU'VE MADE IT THIS FAR TOGETHER, YOU'VE SURVIVED THE DATING GAME AND ARE READY FOR A...
RELATIONSHIP
AND THEN... MAKE-UP SEX !!!
YEAH!
UHM...
YOU MADE IT TO THE THREE-MONTH MARK!
THERE'S ALWAYS SOME CRISIS AT THIS POINT!
IF YOU SURVIVE THAT, YOU'RE OFFICIALLY A COUPLE!

THE
DARK SIDE
OF LOVE

THE THINGS WE DO FOR LOVE...

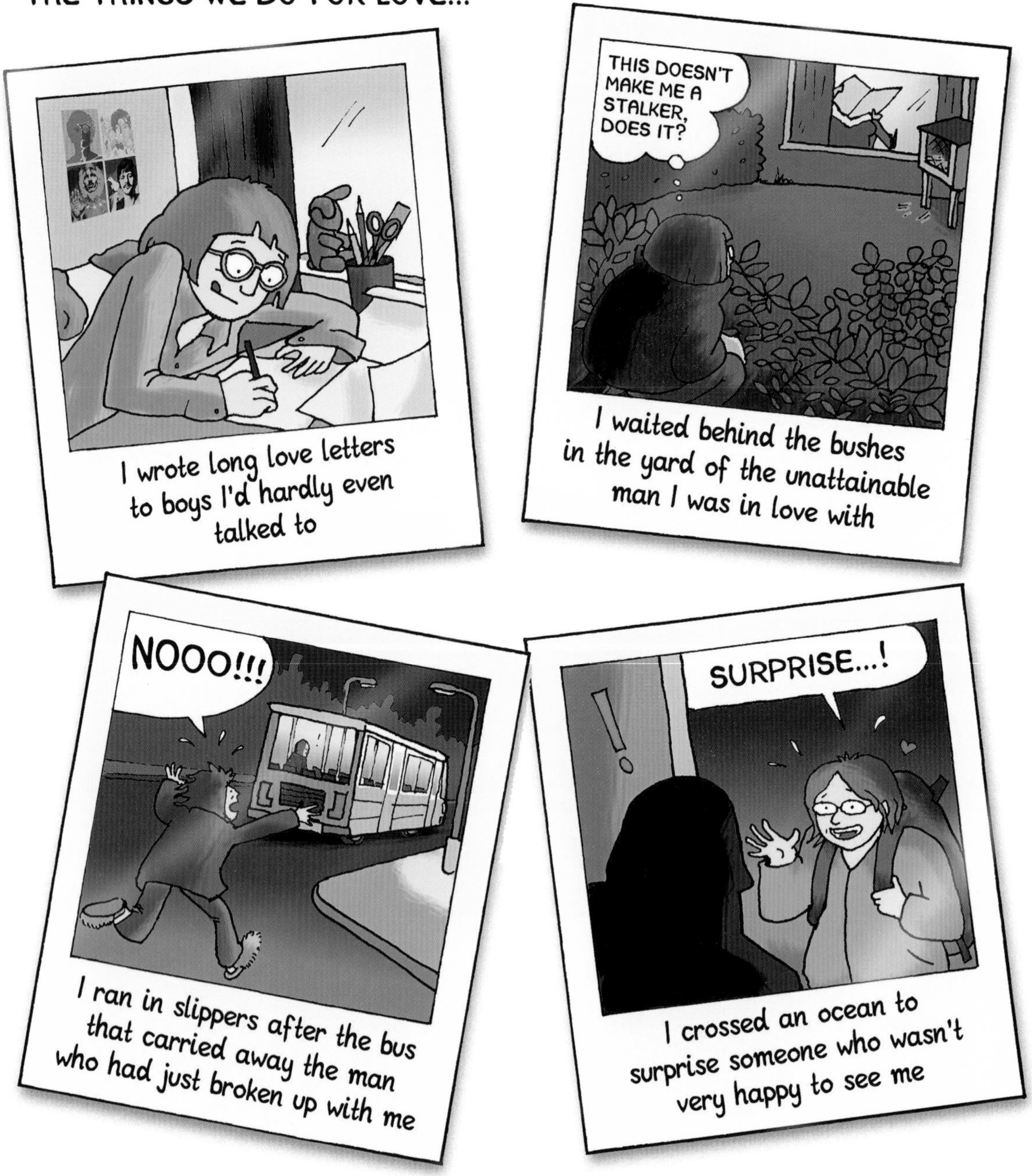
I wrote long love letters to boys I'd hardly even talked to
THIS DOESN'T MAKE ME A STALKER, DOES IT?
I waited behind the bushes in the yard of the unattainable man I was in love with
NOOO!!!
I ran in slippers after the bus that carried away the man who had just broken up with me
SURPRISE...!
I crossed an ocean to surprise someone who wasn't very happy to see me

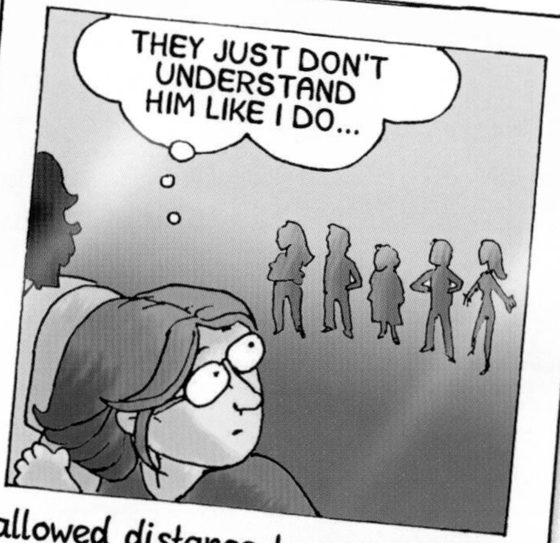
THEY JUST DON'T UNDERSTAND HIM LIKE I DO...

I allowed distance to grow between me and family/friends because my boyfriend didn't like them

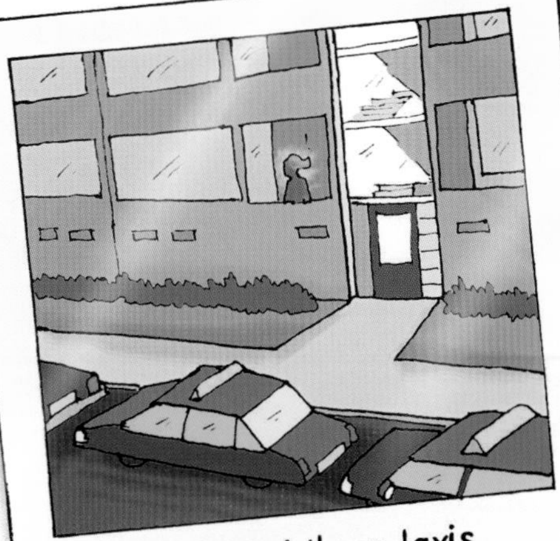

I ordered three taxis to the address of another woman my boyfriend was seeing

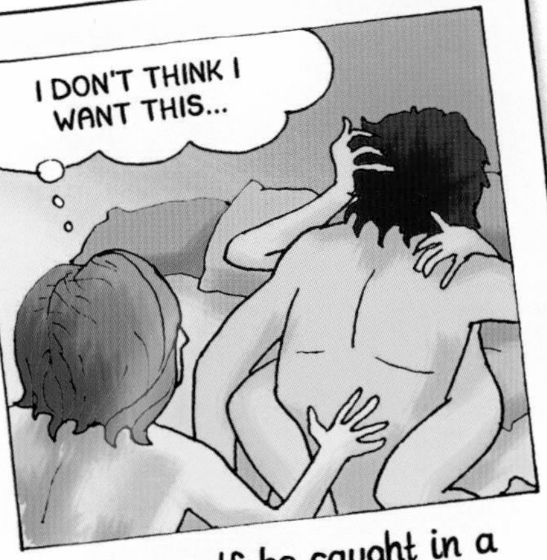
I DON'T THINK I WANT THIS...

I let myself be caught in a threesome because my boyfriend 'refused to chose'

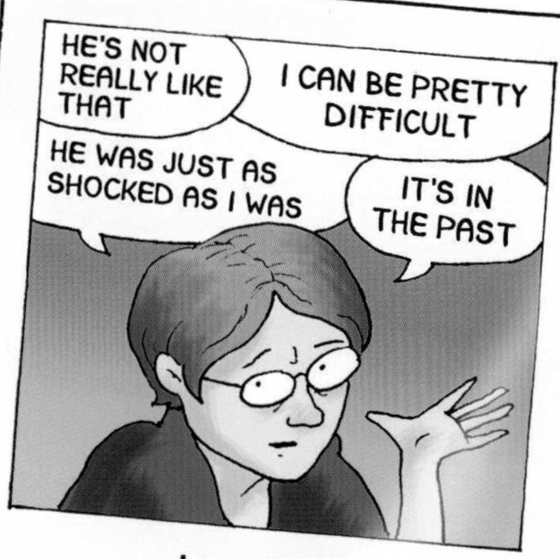
HE'S NOT REALLY LIKE THAT
I CAN BE PRETTY DIFFICULT
HE WAS JUST AS SHOCKED AS I WAS
IT'S IN THE PAST

I condoned violent behavior

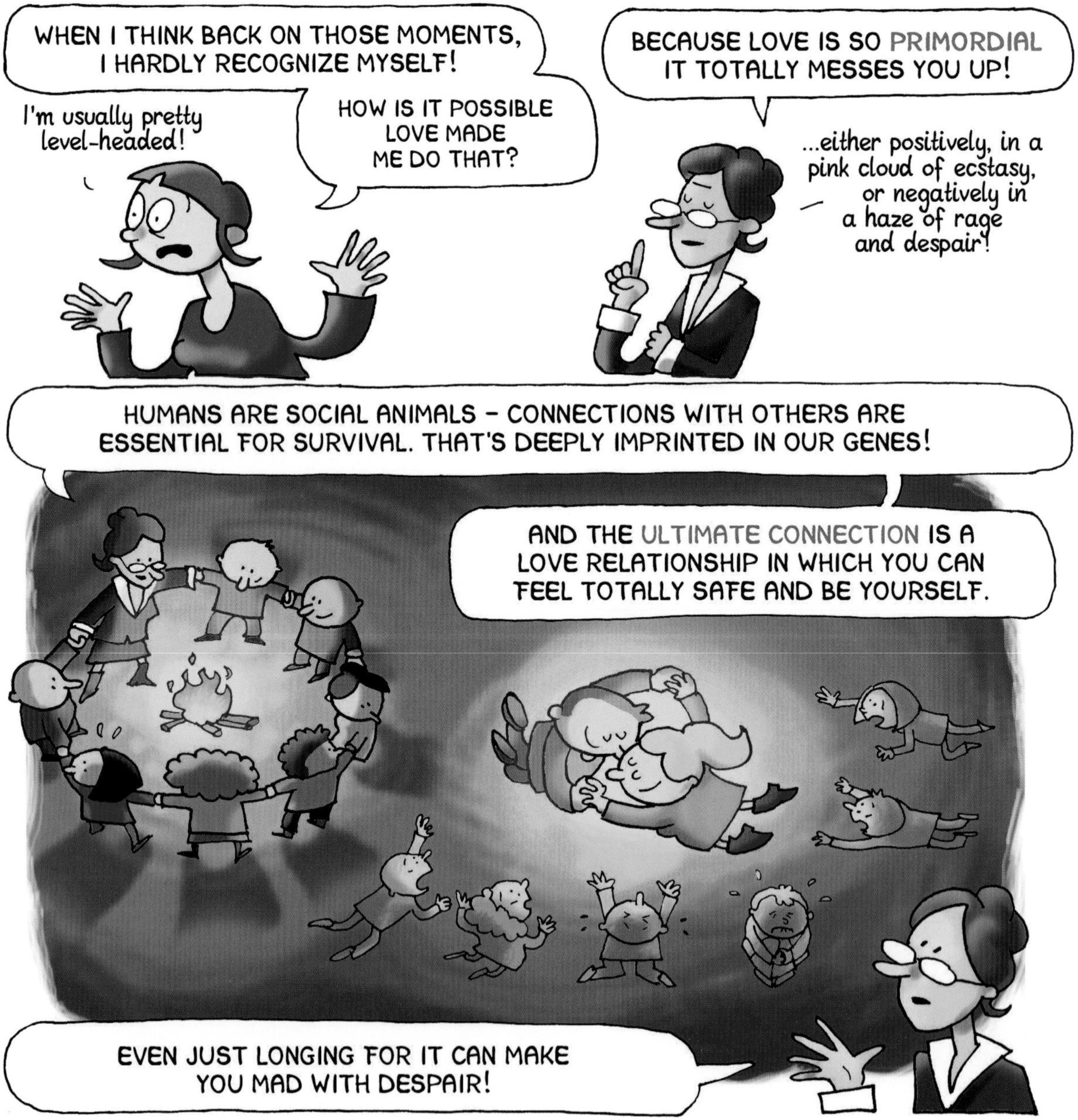
WHEN I THINK BACK ON THOSE MOMENTS, I HARDLY RECOGNIZE MYSELF!
I'm usually pretty level-headed!
HOW IS IT POSSIBLE LOVE MADE ME DO THAT?
BECAUSE LOVE IS SO PRIMORDIAL IT TOTALLY MESSES YOU UP!
...either positively, in a pink cloud of ecstasy, or negatively in a haze of rage and despair!
HUMANS ARE SOCIAL ANIMALS – CONNECTIONS WITH OTHERS ARE ESSENTIAL FOR SURVIVAL. THAT'S DEEPLY IMPRINTED IN OUR GENES!
AND THE ULTIMATE CONNECTION IS A LOVE RELATIONSHIP IN WHICH YOU CAN FEEL TOTALLY SAFE AND BE YOURSELF.
EVEN JUST LONGING FOR IT CAN MAKE YOU MAD WITH DESPAIR!

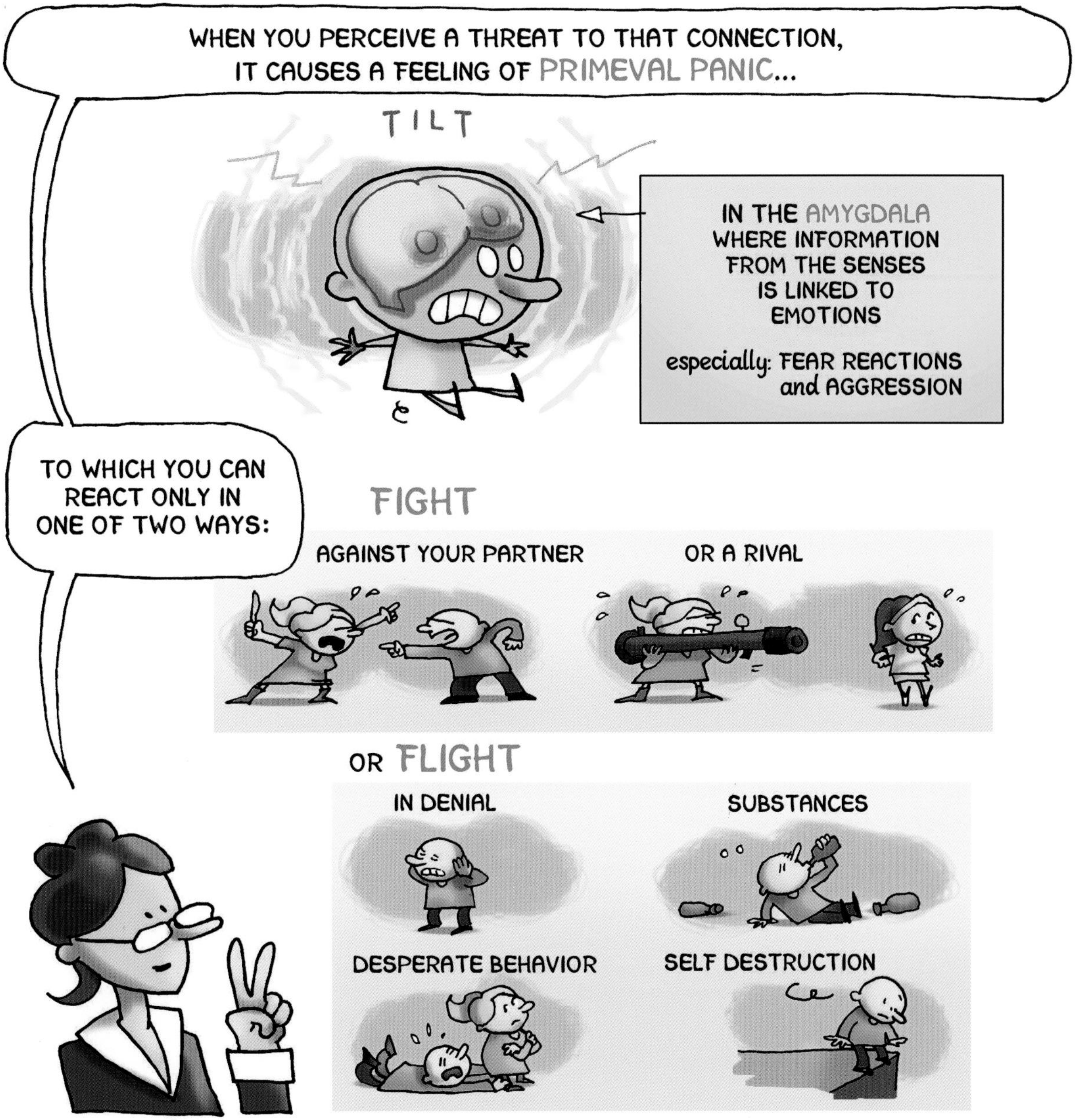
WHEN YOU PERCEIVE A THREAT TO THAT CONNECTION, IT CAUSES A FEELING OF PRIMEVAL PANIC...
TILT
IN THE AMYGDALA WHERE INFORMATION FROM THE SENSES IS LINKED TO EMOTIONS
especially: FEAR REACTIONS and AGGRESSION
TO WHICH YOU CAN REACT ONLY IN ONE OF TWO WAYS:
FIGHT
AGAINST YOUR PARTNER
OR A RIVAL
OR FLIGHT
IN DENIAL
SUBSTANCES
DESPERATE BEHAVIOR
SELF DESTRUCTION

TEN TIPS FOR A BROKEN HEART

YOUR LOVER IS GONE AND IT FEELS SOMETHING LIKE THIS:

HOW CAN YOU GET PAST THIS?

NEVER!!!

YES, YOU CAN! AND IT ALL STARTS WITH THESE TIPS:

1 CRY A LOT

- REDUCES STRESS
- PRODUCES PAINKILLING HORMONES
- RELAXES THE BODY

2 SLEEP A LOT

LOSS OF LOVE IS A VERY PHYSICAL BLOW. YOUR BODY NEEDS TIME TO HEAL.

3 KEEP EATING

YOU'RE NOT HUNGRY NOW, BUT MAKE SURE YOU GET AT LEAST SOMETHING INSIDE YOU.

EASY FOODSTUFFS:
ICE CREAM
PORRIDGE
SOUP
BANANA
YUM
SOUP
CHOCOLATE

4 WATCH MOVIES & LISTEN TO MUSIC

PET AN ANIMAL 5

6 TAKE A LONG BATH

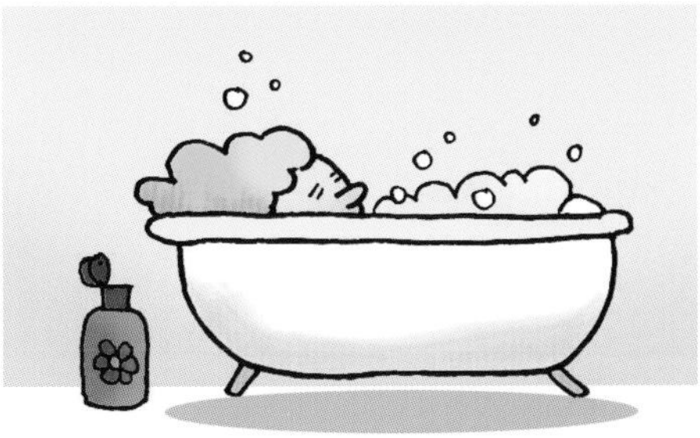

7 GO OUTSIDE

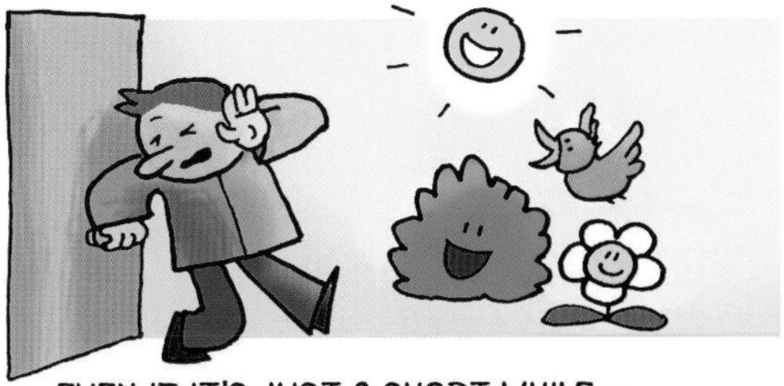

EVEN IF IT'S JUST A SHORT WHILE –
FRESH AIR AND EXERCISE WILL DO YOU GOOD.

8 GO TO THE HAIRDRESSER

IT'S NICE TO BE PAMPERED,
AND GOOD FOR YOUR SELF-ESTEEM.

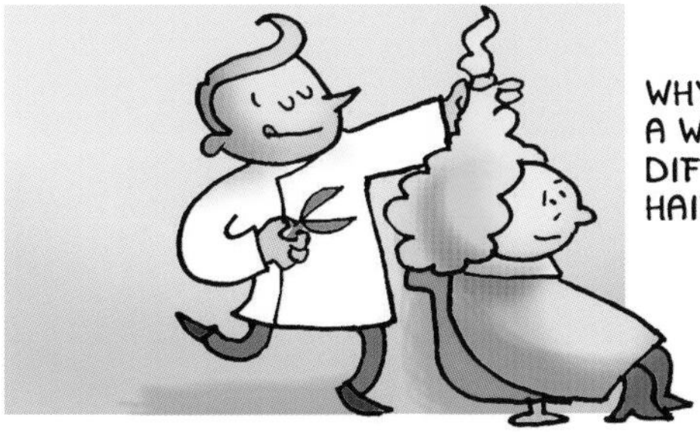

WHY NOT TRY
A WHOLE
DIFFERENT
HAIRDO?

9 HANG OUT WITH FRIENDS

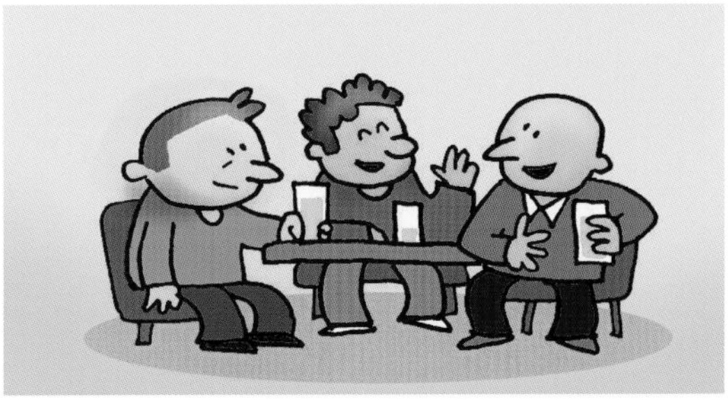

10 GET CREATIVE

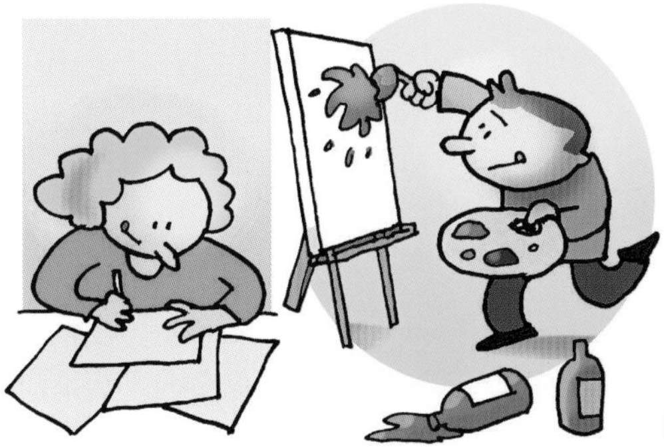

AND THEN, ONE DAY, YOU'LL FEEL A LITTLE BETTER...

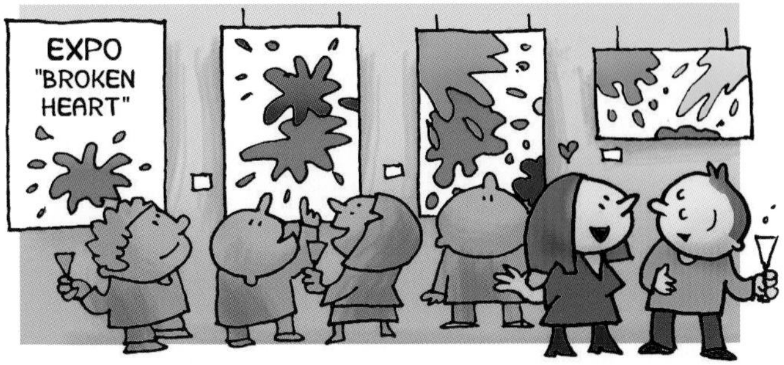
EXPO
"BROKEN
HEART"

AND THAT WILL BE THE START OF YOUR COMEBACK.

LOVE ADDICTION

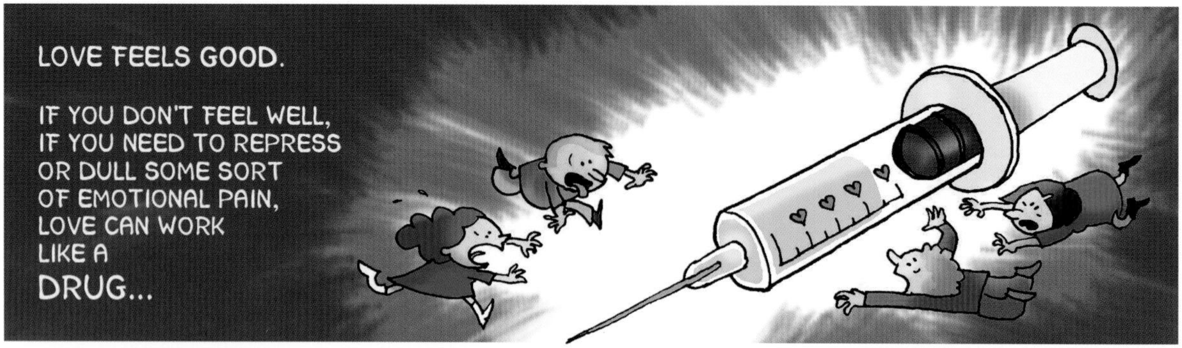
LOVE FEELS GOOD.
IF YOU DON'T FEEL WELL, IF YOU NEED TO REPRESS OR DULL SOME SORT OF EMOTIONAL PAIN, LOVE CAN WORK LIKE A DRUG...

LOVE CAN BE USED TO EVADE NEGATIVE FEELINGS...

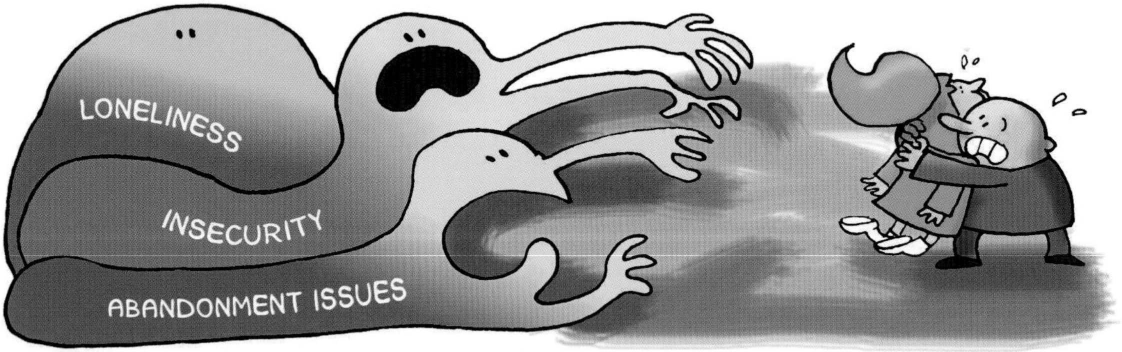
LONELINESS
INSECURITY
ABANDONMENT ISSUES

...EVEN WHEN IT CAN PRODUCE MORE NEGATIVE FEELINGS ITSELF, JUST AT THE THOUGHT OF LOSING THE SOURCE OF LOVE.

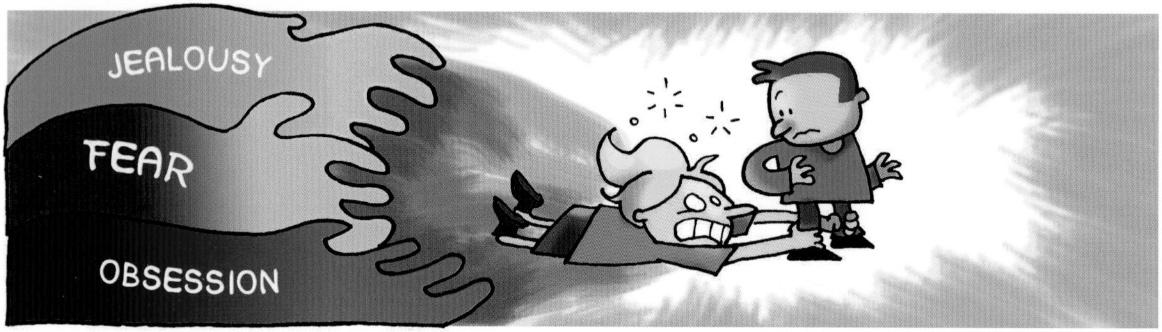
JEALOUSY
FEAR
OBSESSION

YOU NEED INCREASINGLY MORE TO GET THE SAME EFFECT...

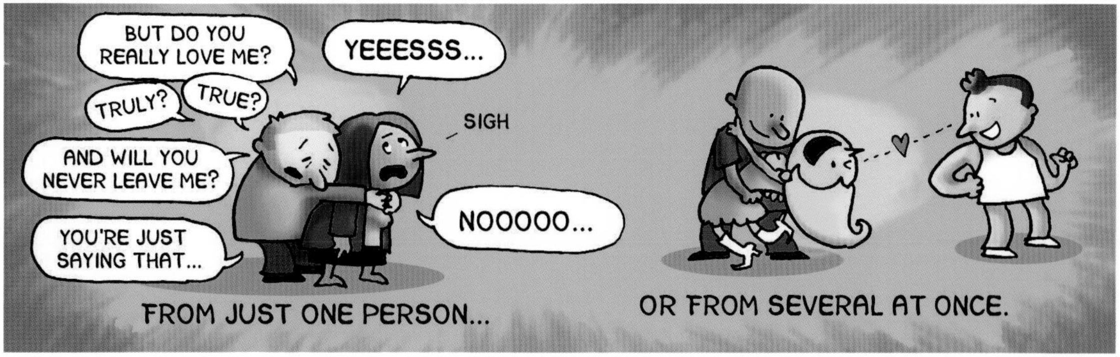
BUT DO YOU REALLY LOVE ME?
YEEESSS...
TRULY?
TRUE?
SIGH
AND WILL YOU NEVER LEAVE ME?
NOOOOO...
YOU'RE JUST SAYING THAT...
FROM JUST ONE PERSON...
OR FROM SEVERAL AT ONCE.

YOU NEGLECT IMPORTANT THINGS...

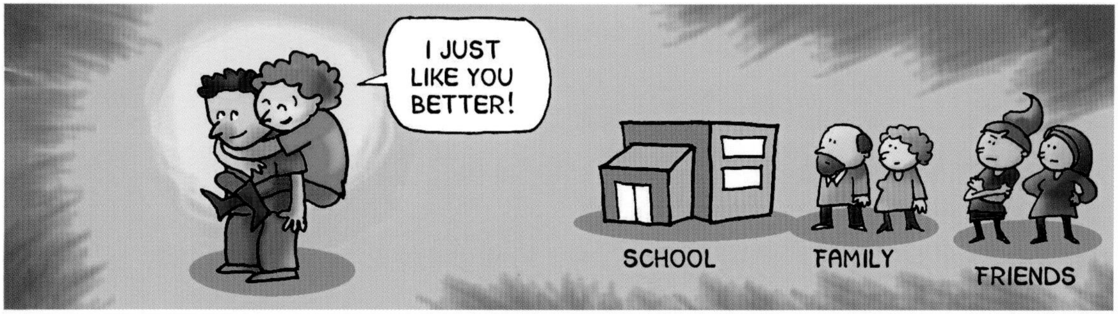
I JUST LIKE YOU BETTER!
SCHOOL
FAMILY
FRIENDS

IN THE END YOU PUT UP WITH A LOT IN EXCHANGE FOR VERY LITTLE.

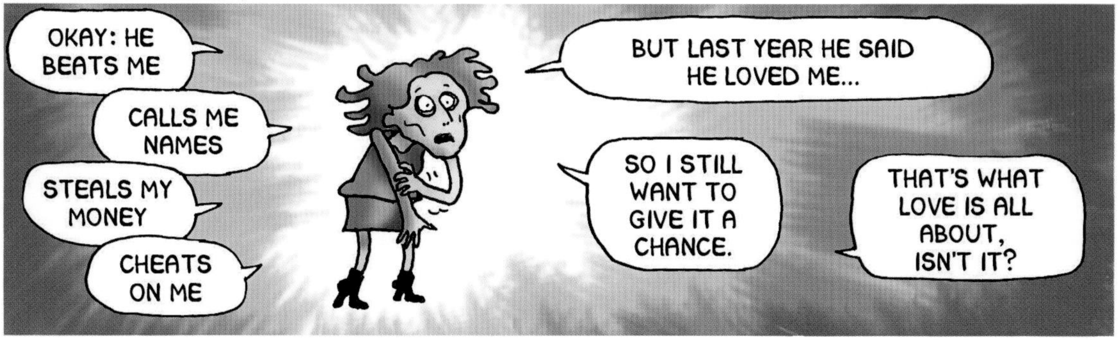
OKAY: HE BEATS ME
CALLS ME NAMES
STEALS MY MONEY
CHEATS ON ME
BUT LAST YEAR HE SAID HE LOVED ME...
SO I STILL WANT TO GIVE IT A CHANCE.
THAT'S WHAT LOVE IS ALL ABOUT, ISN'T IT?

PITFALLS

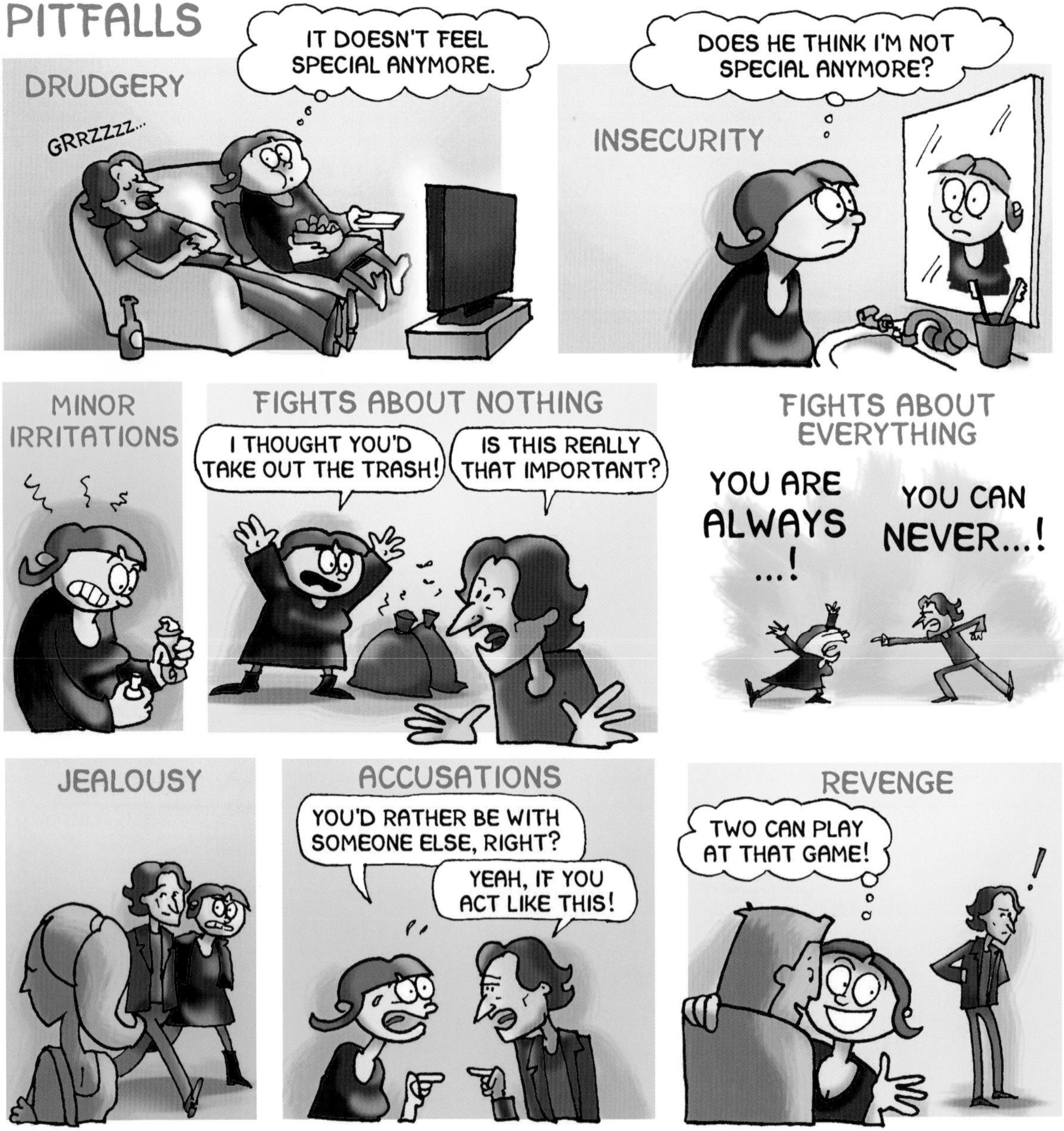

DRUDGERY
GRRZZZZ...
IT DOESN'T FEEL SPECIAL ANYMORE.
INSECURITY
DOES HE THINK I'M NOT SPECIAL ANYMORE?
MINOR IRRITATIONS
FIGHTS ABOUT NOTHING
I THOUGHT YOU'D TAKE OUT THE TRASH!
IS THIS REALLY THAT IMPORTANT?
FIGHTS ABOUT EVERYTHING
YOU ARE ALWAYS ...!
YOU CAN NEVER...!
JEALOUSY
ACCUSATIONS
YOU'D RATHER BE WITH SOMEONE ELSE, RIGHT?
YEAH, IF YOU ACT LIKE THIS!
REVENGE
TWO CAN PLAY AT THAT GAME!
!

VICIOUS CIRCLE

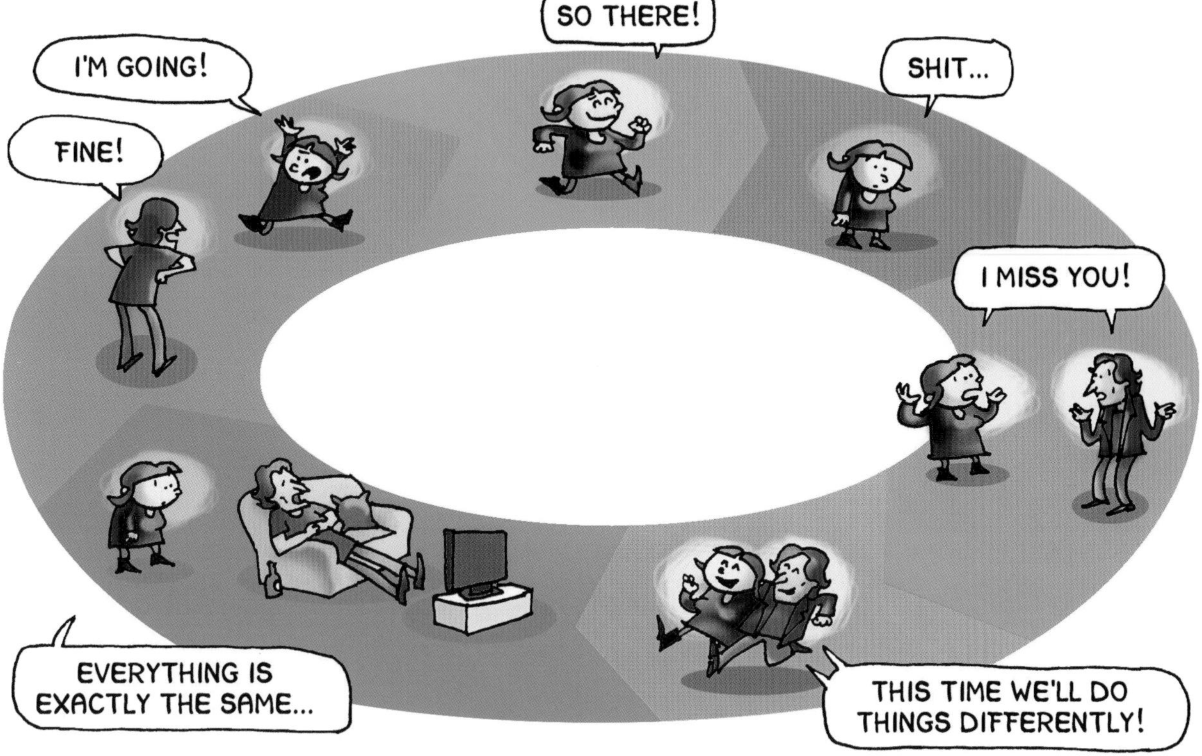

FINE!
I'M GOING!
SO THERE!
SHIT...
I MISS YOU!
THIS TIME WE'LL DO THINGS DIFFERENTLY!
EVERYTHING IS EXACTLY THE SAME...

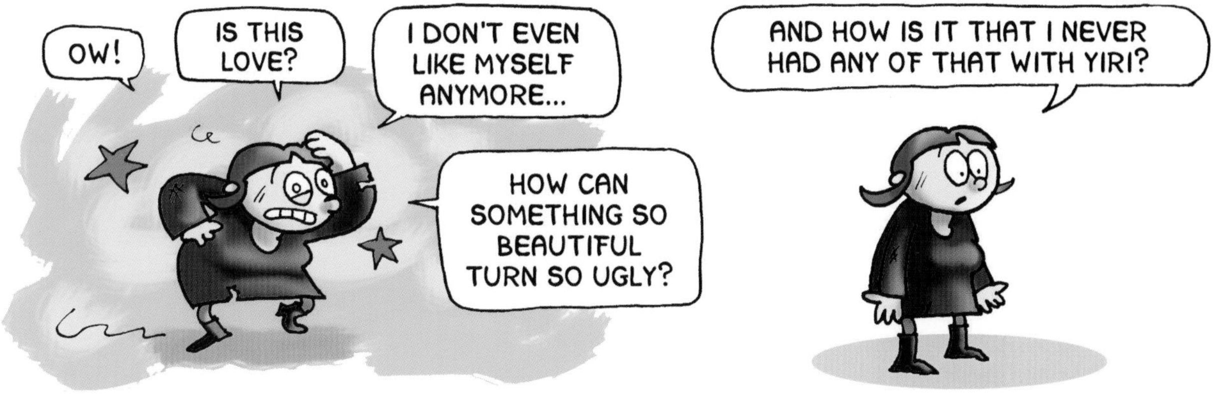

OW!
IS THIS LOVE?
I DON'T EVEN LIKE MYSELF ANYMORE...
HOW CAN SOMETHING SO BEAUTIFUL TURN SO UGLY?
AND HOW IS IT THAT I NEVER HAD ANY OF THAT WITH YIRI?

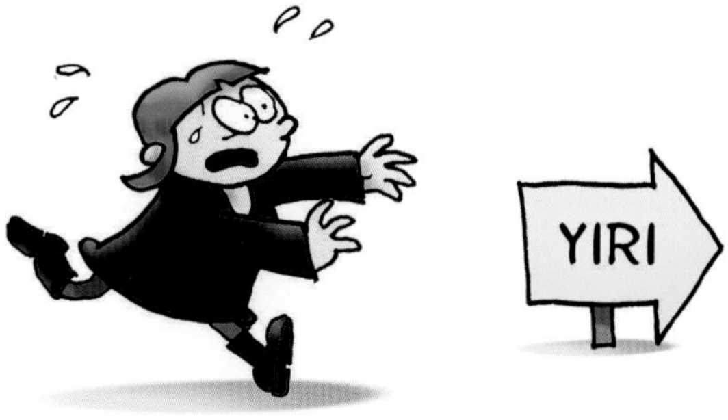
YIRI

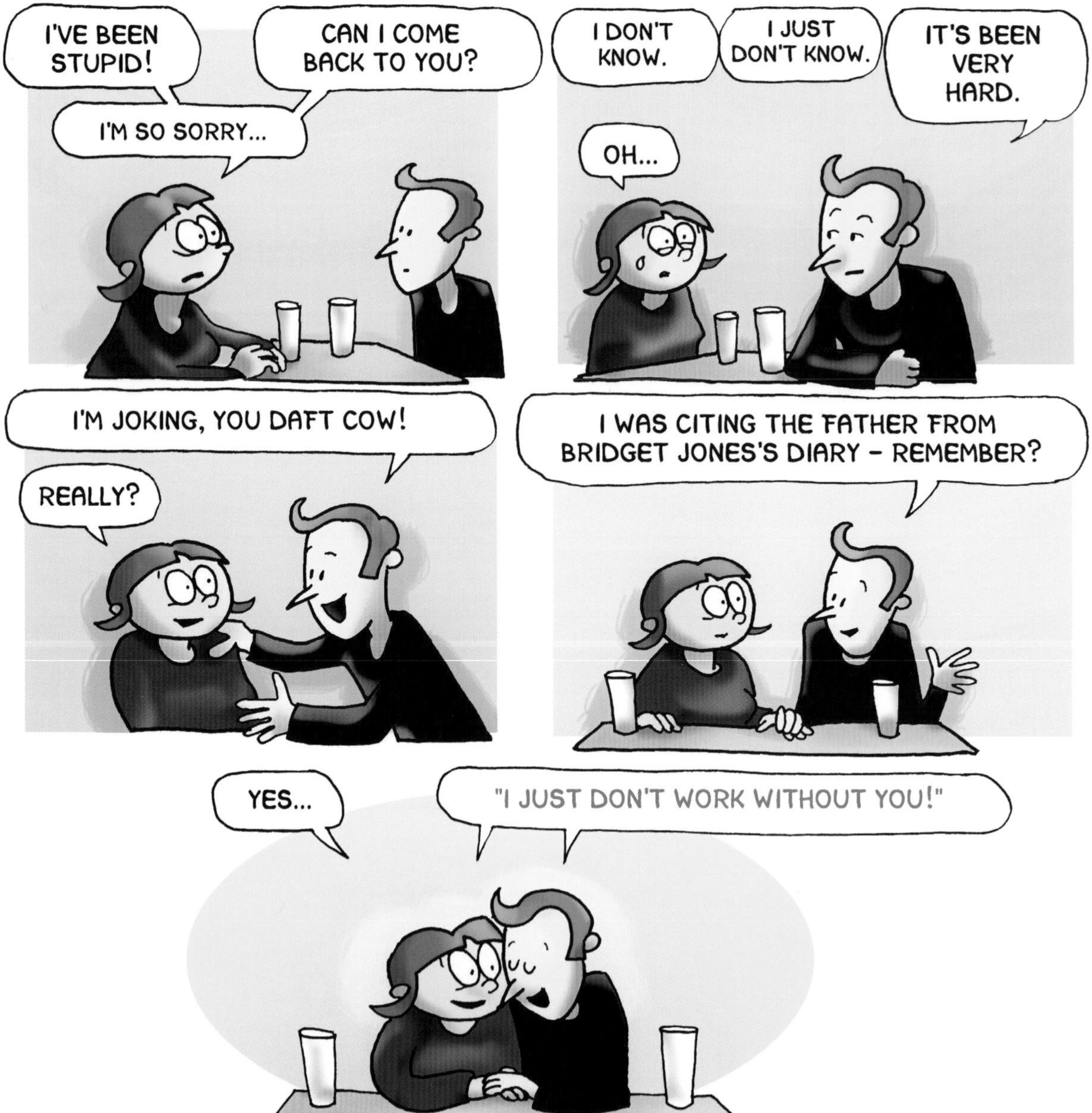
I'VE BEEN STUPID!
I'M SO SORRY...
CAN I COME BACK TO YOU?
I DON'T KNOW.
I JUST DON'T KNOW.
IT'S BEEN VERY HARD.
OH...
I'M JOKING, YOU DAFT COW!
REALLY?
I WAS CITING THE FATHER FROM BRIDGET JONES'S DIARY - REMEMBER?
YES...
"I JUST DON'T WORK WITHOUT YOU!"

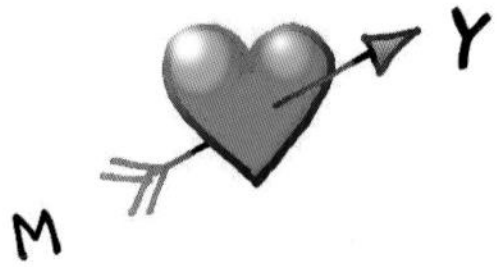
M
Y

EPILOGUE

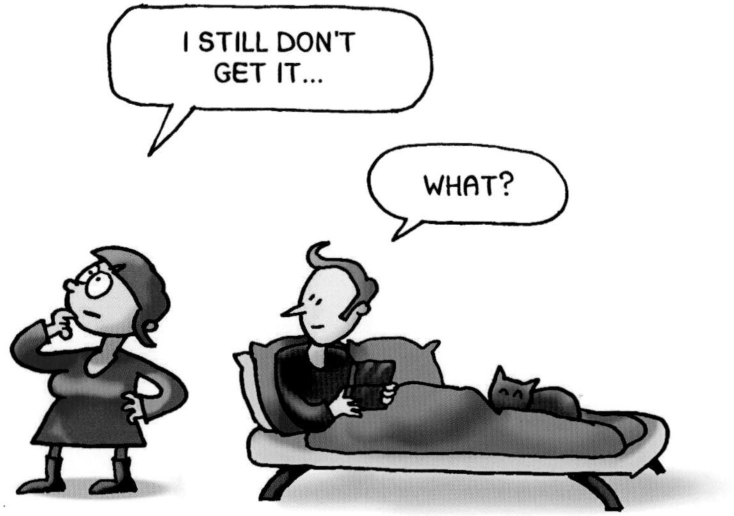
I STILL DON'T GET IT...
WHAT?

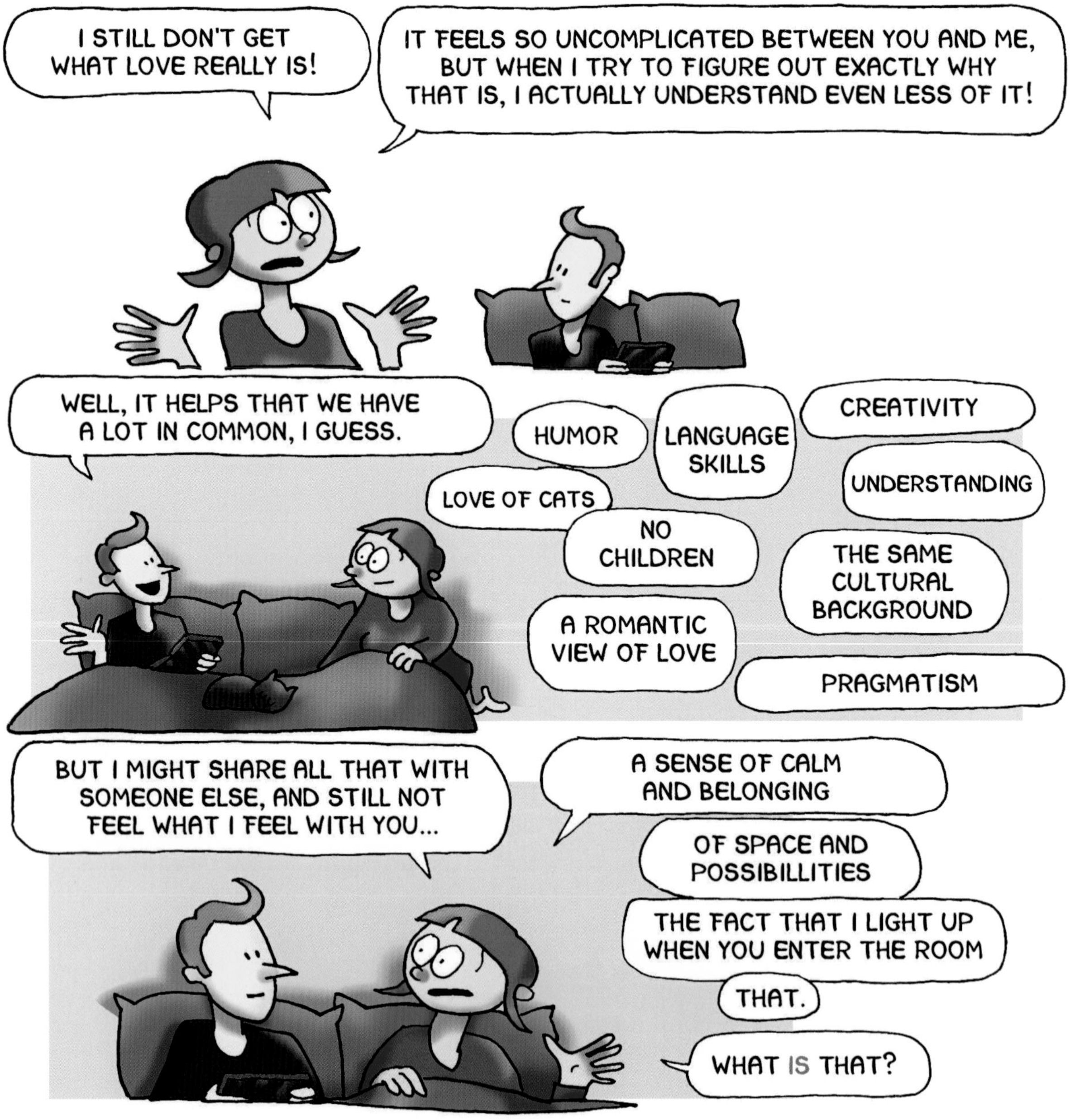
I STILL DON'T GET WHAT LOVE REALLY IS!
IT FEELS SO UNCOMPLICATED BETWEEN YOU AND ME, BUT WHEN I TRY TO FIGURE OUT EXACTLY WHY THAT IS, I ACTUALLY UNDERSTAND EVEN LESS OF IT!
WELL, IT HELPS THAT WE HAVE A LOT IN COMMON, I GUESS.
HUMOR
LANGUAGE SKILLS
CREATIVITY
UNDERSTANDING
LOVE OF CATS
NO CHILDREN
THE SAME CULTURAL BACKGROUND
A ROMANTIC VIEW OF LOVE
PRAGMATISM
BUT I MIGHT SHARE ALL THAT WITH SOMEONE ELSE, AND STILL NOT FEEL WHAT I FEEL WITH YOU...
A SENSE OF CALM AND BELONGING
OF SPACE AND POSSIBILLITIES
THE FACT THAT I LIGHT UP WHEN YOU ENTER THE ROOM
THAT.
WHAT IS THAT?

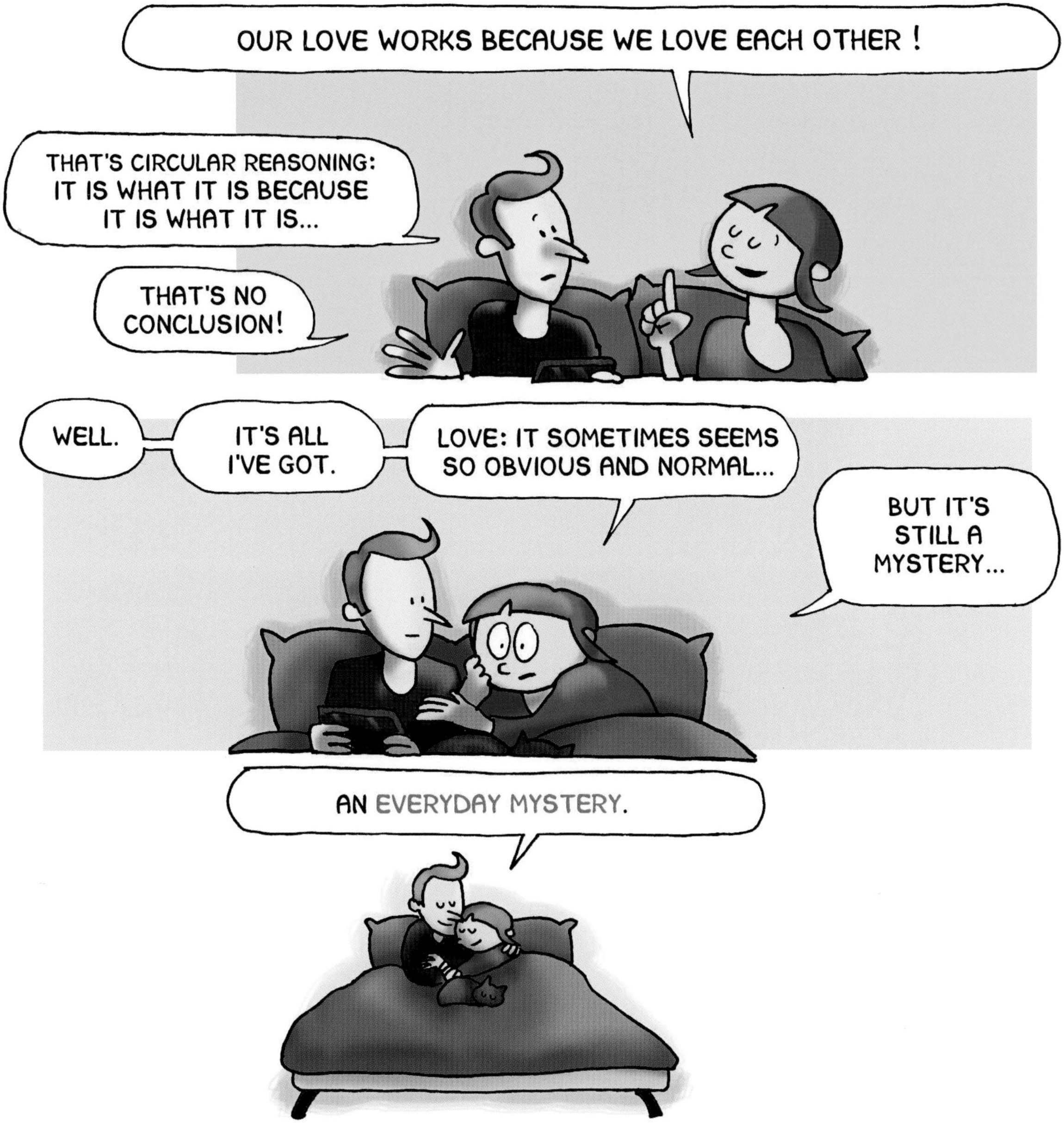
OUR LOVE WORKS BECAUSE WE LOVE EACH OTHER !
THAT'S CIRCULAR REASONING: IT IS WHAT IT IS BECAUSE IT IS WHAT IT IS...
THAT'S NO CONCLUSION!
WELL.
IT'S ALL I'VE GOT.
LOVE: IT SOMETIMES SEEMS SO OBVIOUS AND NORMAL...
BUT IT'S STILL A MYSTERY...
AN EVERYDAY MYSTERY.

EXTRAS

A FILM THAT FEATURES ALL SEVEN KINDS OF LOVE, IS

LOVE ACTUALLY (2003)

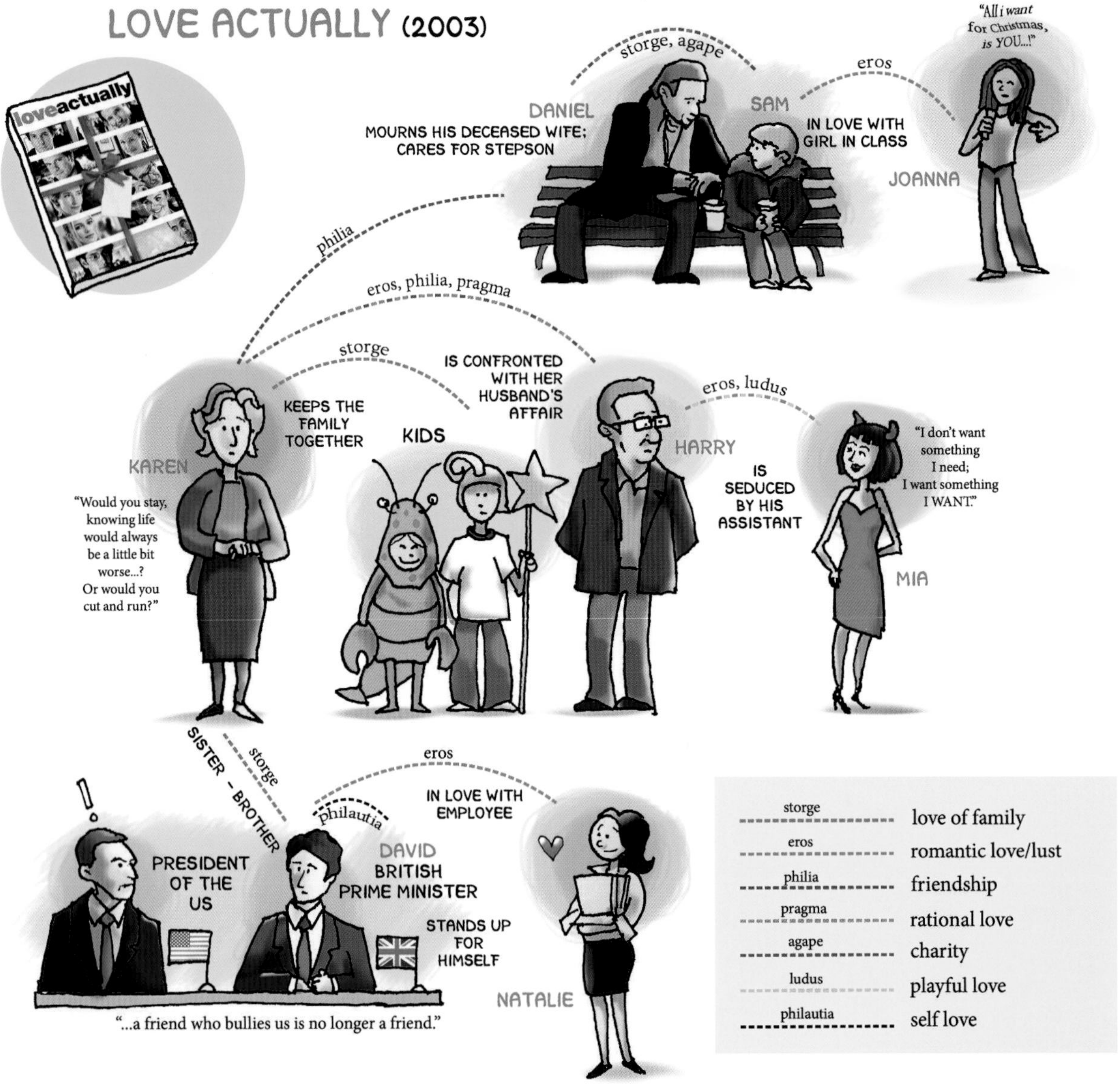

loveactually
"All i want for Christmas, is YOU...!"
storge, agape
eros
DANIEL
MOURNS HIS DECEASED WIFE; CARES FOR STEPSON
SAM
IN LOVE WITH GIRL IN CLASS
JOANNA
philia
eros, philia, pragma
storge
KEEPS THE FAMILY TOGETHER
KIDS
IS CONFRONTED WITH HER HUSBAND'S AFFAIR
eros, ludus
KAREN
"Would you stay, knowing life would always be a little bit worse...? Or would you cut and run?"
HARRY
IS SEDUCED BY HIS ASSISTANT
"I don't want something I need; I want something I WANT."
MIA
SISTER – BROTHER
storge
eros
philautia
IN LOVE WITH EMPLOYEE
PRESIDENT OF THE US
DAVID
BRITISH PRIME MINISTER
STANDS UP FOR HIMSELF
NATALIE
"...a friend who bullies us is no longer a friend."
storge love of family
eros romantic love/lust
philia friendship
pragma rational love
agape charity
ludus playful love
philautia self love

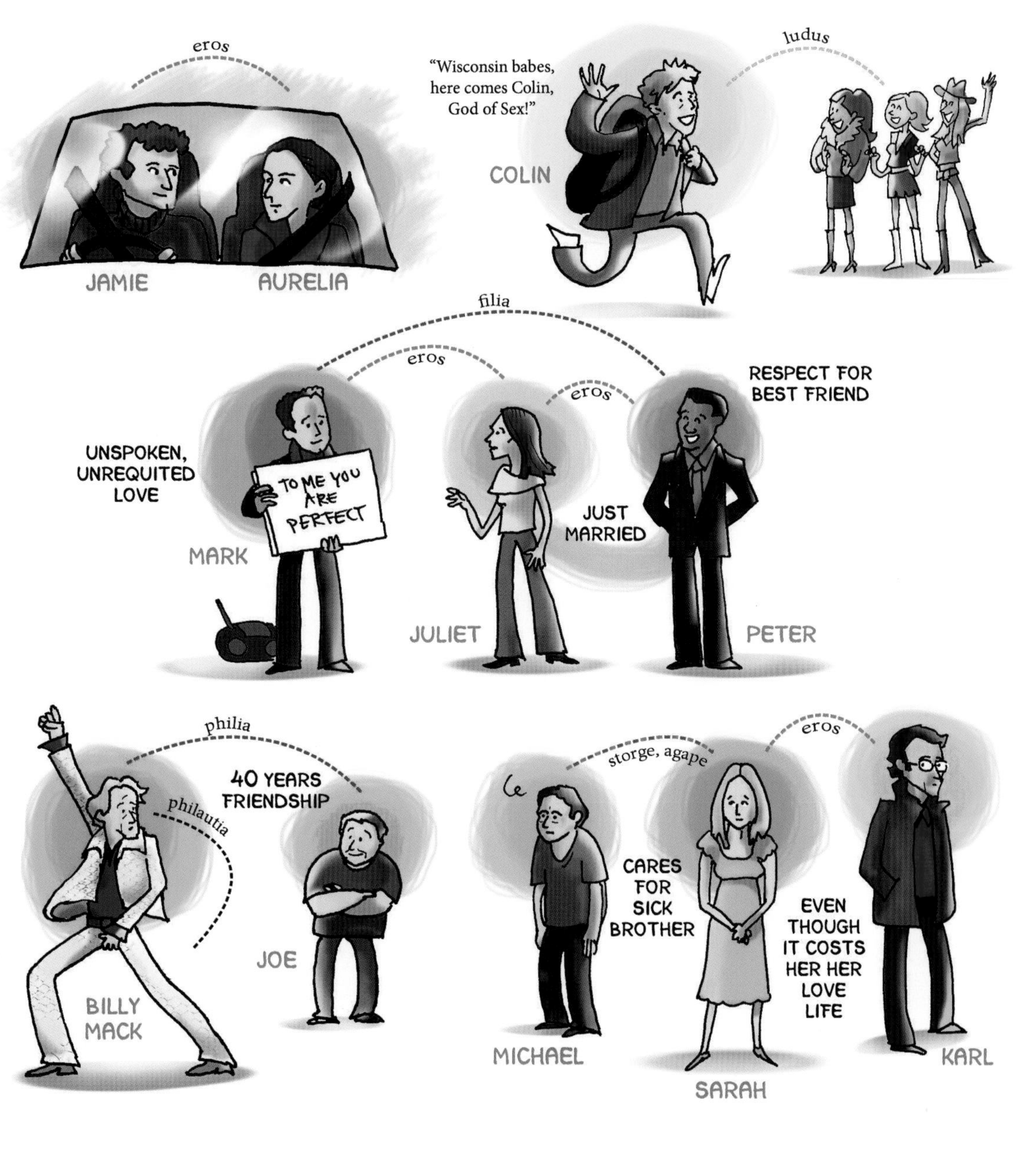
eros
JAMIE
AURELIA
"Wisconsin babes, here comes Colin, God of Sex!"
ludus
COLIN
filia
eros
eros
RESPECT FOR BEST FRIEND
UNSPOKEN, UNREQUITED LOVE
TO ME YOU ARE PERFECT
MARK
JUST MARRIED
JULIET
PETER
philia
40 YEARS FRIENDSHIP
philautia
JOE
BILLY MACK
storge, agape
eros
CARES FOR SICK BROTHER
EVEN THOUGH IT COSTS HER HER LOVE LIFE
MICHAEL
SARAH
KARL

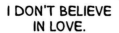

CAMPFIRE SCENE

I DON'T BELIEVE IN LOVE.

EVERYONE WANTS SELF-AFFIRMATION, ATTENTION, SEX... WHEN SOMEONE GIVES IT, IT FEELS GOOD AND PEOPLE CALL IT LOVE. BUT IT'S REALLY JUST SATISFACTION OF NEEDS.

IF YOU FEED AN ANIMAL, IT WILL COME TO YOU...

BUT IF YOU DON'T HAVE ANYTHING TO OFFER, IT WILL BE GONE IN A BLINK. IT'S THE SAME WITH PEOPLE: IT'S ALL ABOUT NEEDS...

HE SAYS IT SO WELL!

HE'S SO COOL!

SIGH!

LOVE.

HUH.

THEY WON'T CATCH ME!

I WISH HE'D FALL FOR ME, THEN I COULD SHOW HIM WHAT REAL LOVE IS!

116

JEALOUSY

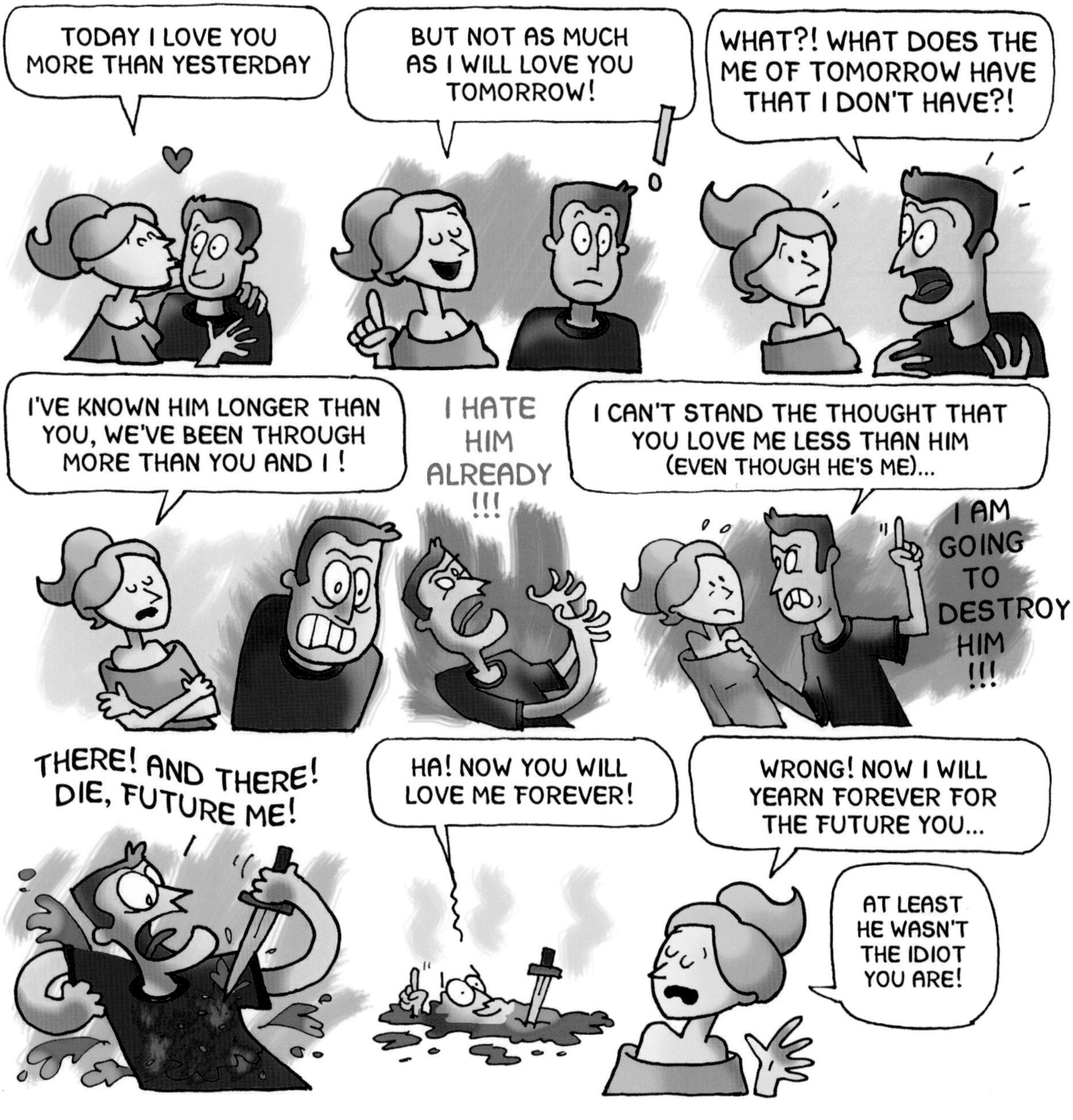
TODAY I LOVE YOU MORE THAN YESTERDAY
BUT NOT AS MUCH AS I WILL LOVE YOU TOMORROW!
WHAT?! WHAT DOES THE ME OF TOMORROW HAVE THAT I DON'T HAVE?!
I'VE KNOWN HIM LONGER THAN YOU, WE'VE BEEN THROUGH MORE THAN YOU AND I !
I HATE HIM ALREADY !!!
I CAN'T STAND THE THOUGHT THAT YOU LOVE ME LESS THAN HIM (EVEN THOUGH HE'S ME)...
I AM GOING TO DESTROY HIM !!!
THERE! AND THERE! DIE, FUTURE ME!
HA! NOW YOU WILL LOVE ME FOREVER!
WRONG! NOW I WILL YEARN FOREVER FOR THE FUTURE YOU...
AT LEAST HE WASN'T THE IDIOT YOU ARE!

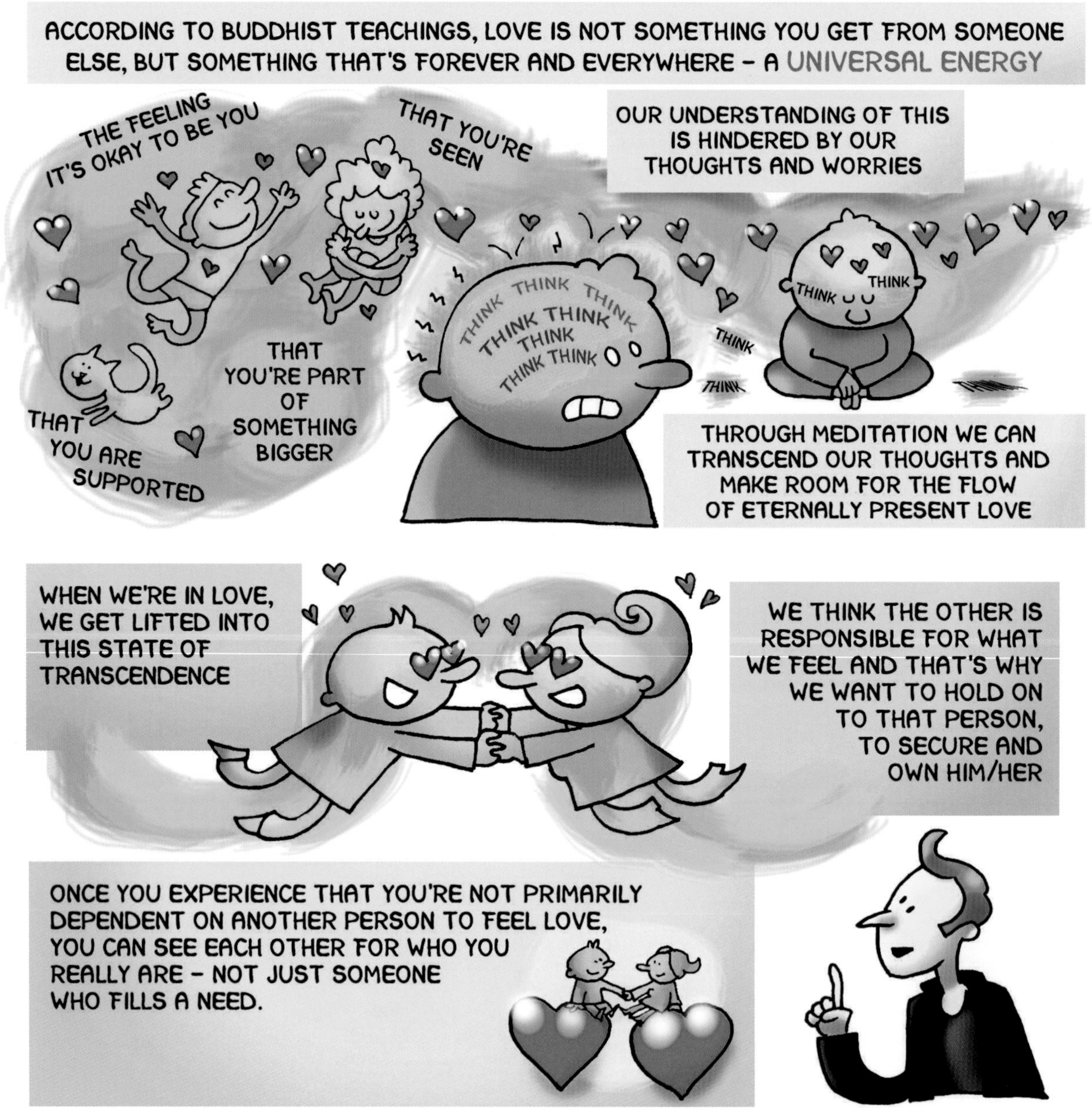
ACCORDING TO BUDDHIST TEACHINGS, LOVE IS NOT SOMETHING YOU GET FROM SOMEONE ELSE, BUT SOMETHING THAT'S FOREVER AND EVERYWHERE – A UNIVERSAL ENERGY
THE FEELING IT'S OKAY TO BE YOU
THAT YOU'RE SEEN
THAT YOU'RE PART OF SOMETHING BIGGER
THAT YOU ARE SUPPORTED
OUR UNDERSTANDING OF THIS IS HINDERED BY OUR THOUGHTS AND WORRIES
THINK THINK THINK THINK THINK THINK THINK THINK
THINK
THINK
THINK
THINK
THROUGH MEDITATION WE CAN TRANSCEND OUR THOUGHTS AND MAKE ROOM FOR THE FLOW OF ETERNALLY PRESENT LOVE
WHEN WE'RE IN LOVE, WE GET LIFTED INTO THIS STATE OF TRANSCENDENCE
WE THINK THE OTHER IS RESPONSIBLE FOR WHAT WE FEEL AND THAT'S WHY WE WANT TO HOLD ON TO THAT PERSON, TO SECURE AND OWN HIM/HER
ONCE YOU EXPERIENCE THAT YOU'RE NOT PRIMARILY DEPENDENT ON ANOTHER PERSON TO FEEL LOVE, YOU CAN SEE EACH OTHER FOR WHO YOU REALLY ARE – NOT JUST SOMEONE WHO FILLS A NEED.

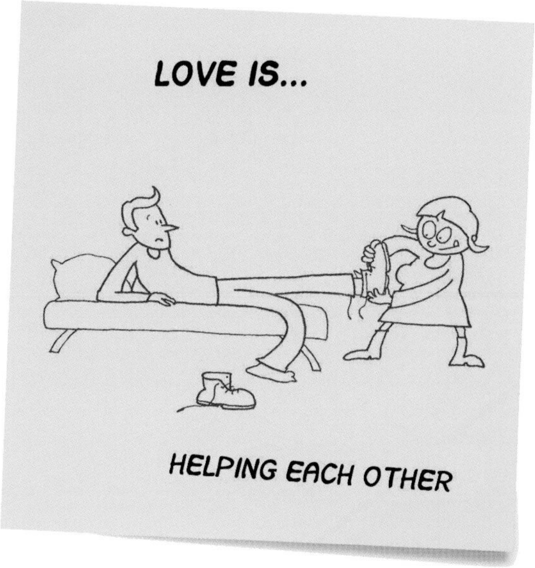
LOVE IS...
HELPING EACH OTHER

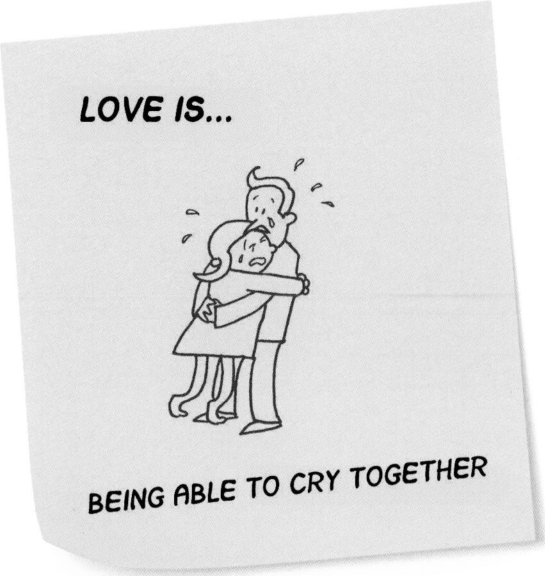
LOVE IS...
BEING ABLE TO CRY TOGETHER

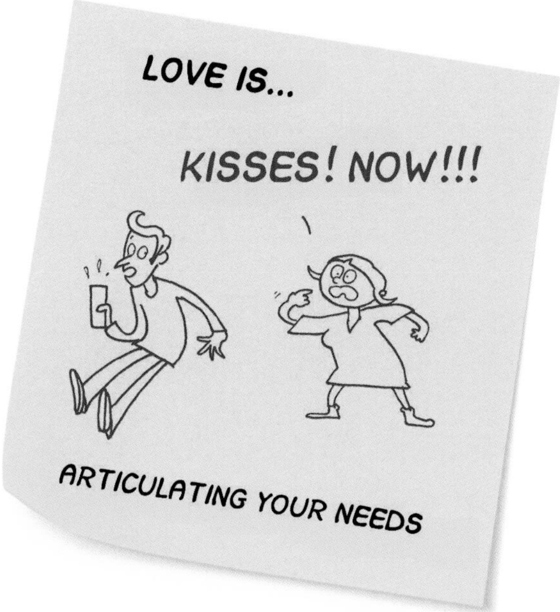
LOVE IS...
KISSES! NOW!!!
ARTICULATING YOUR NEEDS

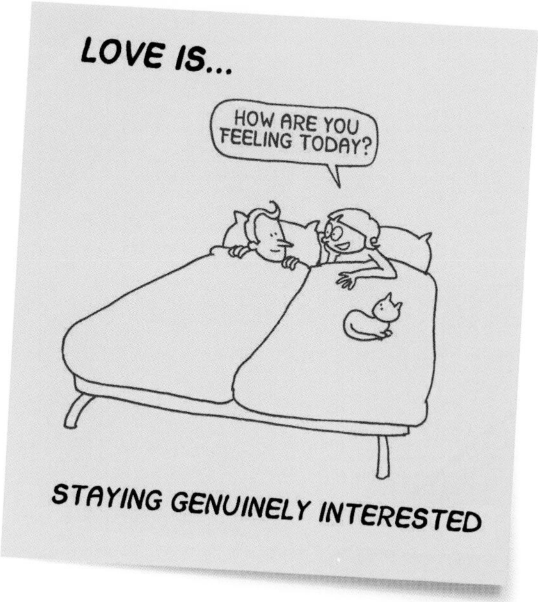
LOVE IS...
HOW ARE YOU FEELING TODAY?
STAYING GENUINELY INTERESTED

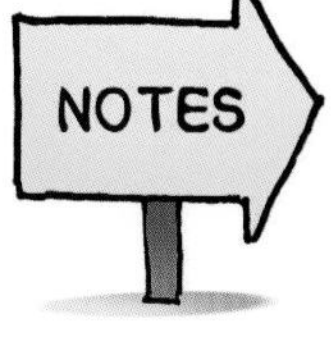
NOTES

NOTES

12:
The Erotes were winged gods who accompanied Aphrodite. Their number varies — I chose the four most important, but there are at least seven:

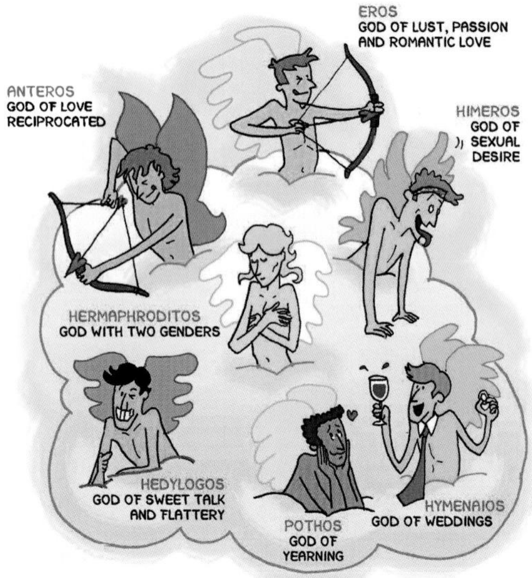
EROS
GOD OF LUST, PASSION AND ROMANTIC LOVE
ANTEROS
GOD OF LOVE RECIPROCATED
HIMEROS
GOD OF SEXUAL DESIRE
HERMAPHRODITOS
GOD WITH TWO GENDERS
HEDYLOGOS
GOD OF SWEET TALK AND FLATTERY
POTHOS
GOD OF YEARNING
HYMENAIOS
GOD OF WEDDINGS

16:
The list with pros and cons by **Charles Darwin** is authentic. This is what the original page from his notebook looks like:

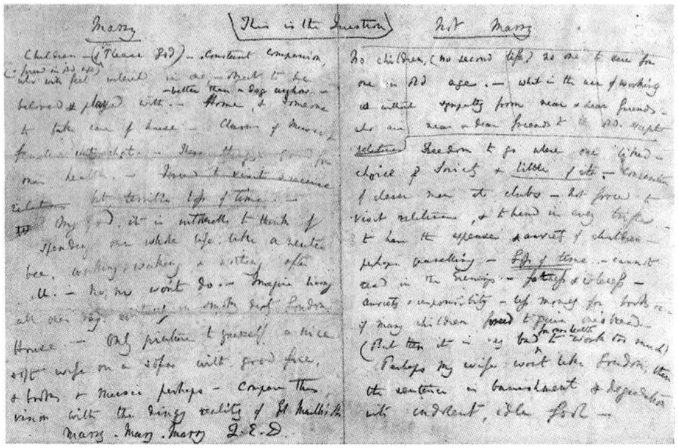
Marry
This is the Question
Not Marry

24:
The term **Seven Year Itch** originally referred to the symptoms of certain veneral diseases, whose intensity seemed to diminish after about seven years.

In 1952 it was used for the first time in a play by George Axelrod to denote the urge to look elsewhere after seven years of marriage. It was made into a movie in 1955, starring Marilyn Monroe.

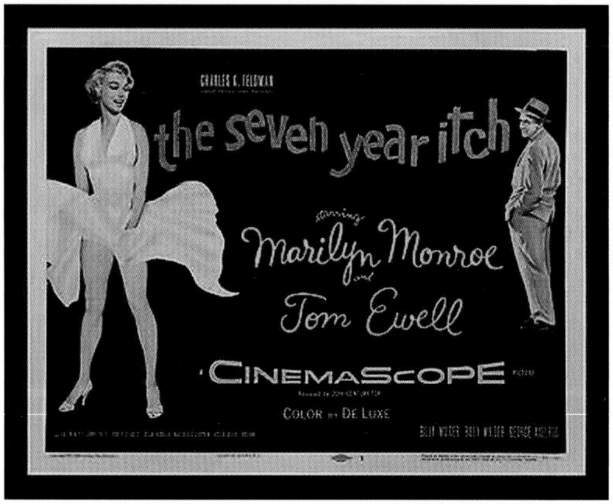
CHARLES K. FELDMAN
the seven year itch
starring
Marilyn Monroe
and
Tom Ewell
CINEMASCOPE
COLOR by DE LUXE

24, 89-92, 102-104:

My favorite actor is **Robert Carlyle** and no, I did not have an affair with him.

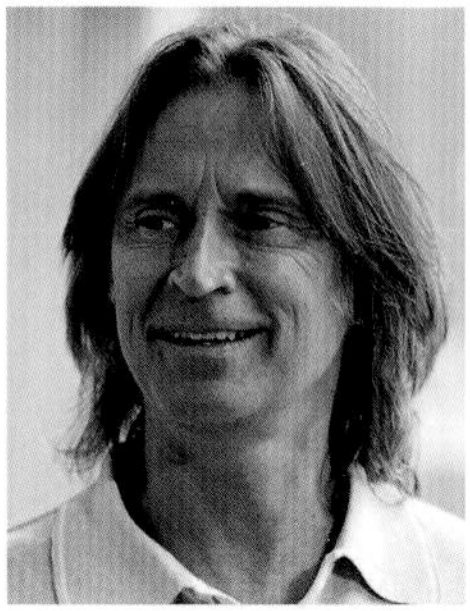

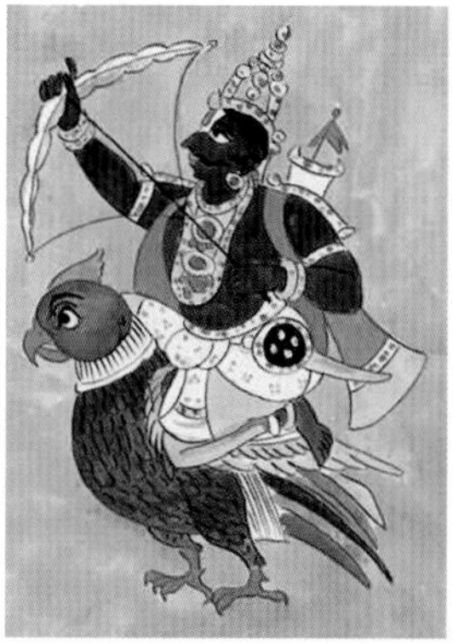

35:

The hindu god **Kama** and the Greek/Roman Eros/Cupid have the same, centuries-old roots.
They are all depicted with bow and arrows and wings
(in Kama's case:
the wings of his canary).

All three of them are gods of love — including the dark and dangerous aspects of being in love.
A 17th century commentator described the effects of Kama's arrows as follows:

> *"First comes attraction expressed through the eyes, then intense attachment in the mind, then determination, loss of sleep, becoming emaciated, uninterested in external things, shamelessness, madness, becoming stunned, and death."*

36-37:
The **Kama Sutra** is a diverse collection of texts about sexuality, marriage and proper behavior in society. Only about 20% actually deals with sexual positions.

40:
The translation of **Song of Songs** I'm using here is from myself and rather liberal.

50:
These tips about **the one** are from Canadian author Karen M. Black. See www.the-soulmate-site.com.

69-71:
This **true story** is from American author Richard Paul Evans.

75:
Our **'wedding locations'** depicted here are: Westminster Abbey, the peer at IJmuiden, a canal in Amsterdam, Manhattan, the isle of Vlieland, Niagara Falls, the Waddenzee, the Treacle Well in Binsey, amusement park the Efteling.

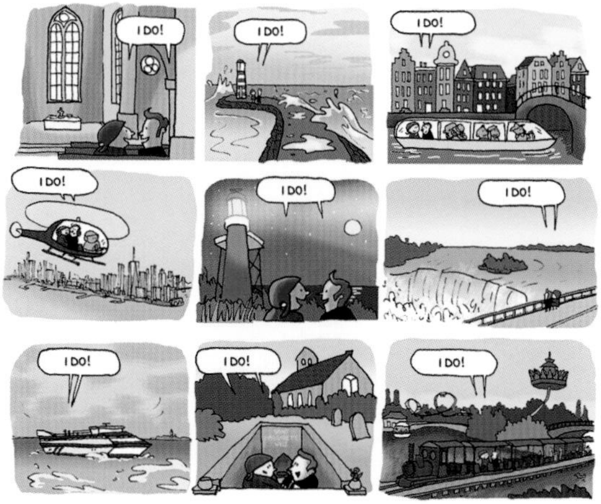
I DO!
I DO!
I DO!
I DO!
I DO!
I DO!
I DO!
I DO!
I DO!

80:
Valentine's Day is named after Saint Valentine, a third century Christian martyr. In 496 AD, February 14th was designated as his day, probably to Christianize the Roman feast of Lupercalia: on this occasion names of unwed women were gathered into a bowl and an unwed man would draw a name at random — for the duration of the festivities, this man and woman would be partners.

In the fourteenth century, the day of Saint Valentine was linked to courtly, platonic love. During the centuries that followed, the occasion evolved into one where people declared their love by sending handwritten notes.
By the end of the nineteenth century, Valentine's Day was widely commercialized and the printing and sending of special Valentine's cards became a common practice.

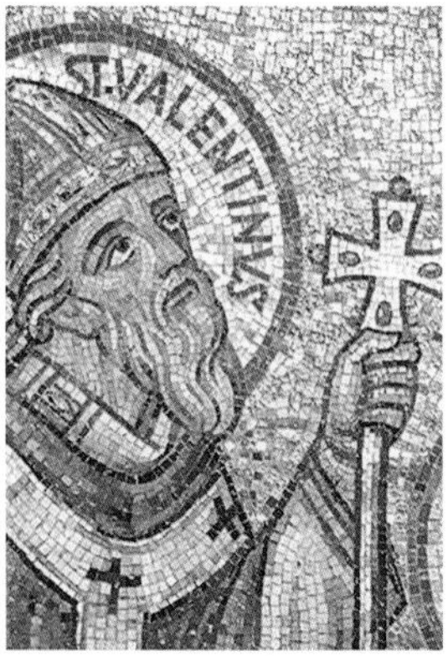
ST.VALENTINVS

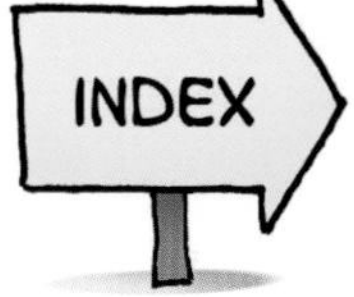
INDEX

INDEX

abandonment issues, 100
addiction, 86, 97, 100-101
adrenalin, 86
Agapè, 11, 114-115
Albert, Prince, 80
amygdala, 97
ancient Greece, 80
Anteros, 12, 122
antiquity, 10-17
Aphrodite, 12
Aristophanes, 46-47
Aristotle, 13, 17
artha, 36
attraction, 58, 63

baseball, 32
Bible, 11, 40-42
Buddhism, 118
Bridget Jones's Diary, 63, 106

Calvin, 81
chakras, 39
charity, 11, 114-115
chemistry, 8, 86-87
children, 48, 63, 66-68, 79, 90
confidence, 17, 49
Corinthians, 11
Cupid, 12, 122

Darwin, Charles, 16, 122
dating, 50-52, 90-91
dating site, 20
dependence, 53,
desire, 63, 87
despair, 96-96
dharma, 36
divorce, 14, 74, 81, 82

dopamine, 86
Dr. Phil, 34
duality, 41

emancipation, 91
Enlightenment, 80
Erotes, 12, 122
ex, 53, 81, 90

fairy tales, 46, 62
falling in love, 84-88
family, 14, 48, 67, 79, 81, 90, 101
family love, 14, 114-115
femme fatale, 59
fight, 90-91, 97, 102
first love, 48
French Revolution, 81
friendship, 13, 79, 114-115

gods of Olympus, 46-47
Gratian, 81

heartbreak, 98-99
Hedylogos, 12, 122
Himeros, 12, 122
homosexual, 81
hormones, 30, 84, 98

Ikea test, 65
imaginary boyfriend, 26-28

jealousy, 100, 102, 117
Jesus, 17, 41

Kama, 35, 36, 122
Kama Sutra, 35-37, 123
kundalini, 39

living together, 63, 64, 65
Love Actually, 63, 114-115
looks, 24, 25, 33, 79
Ludus, 15, 114-115
lust, 41-42, 63, 114
Luther, 81

marriage, 14, 16, 73-82, 90
meditation, 38-39, 118

Napoleon, 81
Narcissus, 17
Nemesis, 17

obsession, 49, 86, 100
one, the, 44-49, 53, 84, 123
orgasm, 38
oxytocin, 87

Paul, 11
Philautia, 17, 114-115
Philia, 13, 14, 114-115
pink cloud, 86-87
Plato, 46
polygamy, 80
Pothos, 12
Pragma, 16, 114-115

romance novels, 58-61
romance, 58-63, 90, 114-115
routine, 88

satisfaction of needs, 116
self love, 17, 114-115
serotonin, 86
Seven Year Itch, 22, 24, 84, 89, 122
sex, 15, 29-43, 48, 79-81, 87, 90-91
sexual revolution, 80
Socrates, 17

tantric sex, 38-39
Trent, Council of, 81

Valentine, 80, 123-124
Vatsyayana, 36
Victoria, Queen, 80
vows, 54, 74-75, 81
visualisation, 25

wedding, 11, 77
Wedgwood, Emma, 16
women's rights, 80

Yue Lao, 45

Also available by the author:

SCIENCE
a Discovery in Comics
Margreet de Heer

Science: a Discovery in Comics

“A great many topics are treated, thanks to the economy of de Heer’s visual presentation, and they’re all handled very well, thanks to the energy of her drawing style.”
-Booklist

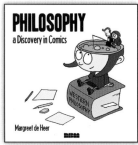

PHILOSOPHY
a Discovery in Comics
WESTERN PHILOSOPHY
Margreet de Heer

Philosophy: a Discovery in Comics

“Colorful, clever, and bouncy cartoons provide an educated philosophy scholar-cartoonist with the method for engaging and informing casual readers about the why and how of Western philosophy’s foundations and development.”
-School Library Journal

RELIGION
a Discovery in Comics
Margreet de Heer
nbm

Religion: a Discovery in Comics

“Outstanding Dutch comics artist de Heer follows her previous books in the Discovery series on philosophy and science with his lively, intelligent survey of he world’s major religions.”
-Publisher’s Weekly

See more including reviews, Margreet’s blog posts, and order from:
NBMPUB.COM

We have over 200 graphic novels available
Catalog upon request
NBM
160 Broadway, Ste. 700, East Wing
New York, NY 10038